The Last Laugh

Also from Crowbar Press

Inside Out
by Ole Anderson with Scott Teal
0-9745545-0-2

Wrestlers Are Like Seagulls
by James J. Dillon with Scott Teal and Philip Varriale
0-9745545-2-9

Assassin: The Man Behind the Mask
by Joe Hamilton with Scott Teal
0-9745545-3-7

"Is That Wrestling Fake?"
by Ivan Koloff with Scott Teal
978-0-9745545-4-9

Bruiser Brody
by Emerson Murray
978-0-9745545-5-6

Wrestling with the Truth
by Bruno Lauer
0-9745545-7-0

The Solie Chronicles
by Bob Allyn with Pamela S Allyn and Scott Teal
978-0-9745545-8-7

Wrestling in the Canadian West
by Vance Nevada
978-0-9745545-9-4

Long Days and Short Pays
by Hal West
978-0-9844090-0-6

Drawing Heat
by Jim Freedman
978-0-9844090-1-3

ATLAS: Too Much, Too Soon
by Tony Atlas with Scott Teal
978-0-9844090-2-0

Hooker
by Lou Thesz with Kit Bauman
978-0-9844090-4-4

The Last Laugh

by

Bill DeMott

with

Scott Teal

CROWBAR PRESS
Gallatin, Tennessee

The Last Laugh

Published by Crowbar Press
106 Tattnal Court
Gallatin, Tennessee 37066.

http://www.crowbarpress.com

Book layout and cover design by Scott Teal
Cover photo by Richard Nieves

Library of Congress Cataloging-in-Publication Data

De Mott, Bill
The Last Laugh / by Bill De Mott with Scott Teal — 1st ed.

1. De Mott, Bill. 2. Sports—United States—Biography. 3. Wrestling—United States—Biography. I. Teal, Scott. II. Title.

Printed in the United States of America
ISBN 978-0-9844090-3-7

First Edition / June 2011

TABLE OF CONTENTS

Foreword 6
Acknowledgements 8
1. Cow Tipping 13
2. Learning to Crawl 22
3. Key to the City 30
4. Dog Meat 38
5. Urinal Balls 48
6. Batteries and Pesos 57
7. The Man of Question 63
8. The Chubba Bubbas 74
9. The Chemist 90
10. Misfits in Action 104
11. The Invasion 112
12. On the Sidelines (again) 125
13. Tough Enough 134
14. Lacey 141
15. The Doody Man 161
16. Jackass of All Trades 174
17. The Heat Guy 184
18. Crybabies and Complainers 194
19. The Go-To Guys (and Girls) 199
20. Falling Up the Wall 206
21. Deep South Divas 214
22. Attack of the Killer Squats 217
23. A Real Job 223
24. Billy De Mott, Celebrity 229
25. The "Real" First Family 231
Addendum: Another Last Laugh 237
Index 240

Foreword

by Les Thatcher

Les Thatcher, 1978

Les Thatcher, 2005

I first met Bill when the WWE was sending prospective talent to train with me at Heartland Wrestling Association. On occasion, when contracted talent was sitting on the sidelines with nothing to do, the WWE sent them to me to help train the kids.

At the time, all I knew about Bill was what I had seen on television. The thing that impressed me the most was that he gave more than what was expected. My personal students, who paid for their training, worked out in the evening while the WWE developmental crew trained in the afternoon. Bill's only obligation was to the WWE crew. He could have gone through the motions and collected his paycheck at the end of the day, but he often returned in the evenings to work with my kids. Not only did he spend time with them in the ring, but he talked to them and gave them personal attention. I can remember many times when he would get so involved that I would just step back and let him go. He had a passion for training, which is so important, and he pushed those kids to be the best they could be. Bill would also arrive early for the afternoon developmental sessions at times to help those athletes with little things such as footwork, timing, and so on.

Trainers often get a bum rap from students, who complain and whine about being mistreated. In the wrestling industry, the further up you move, the more that is expected and the more intense the pressure. If you can't handle it in training, you will never handle it at the higher level. In that regard, Bill and I were on the same page. Nobody likes to be told we aren't fast enough, quick enough, or sharp enough. Many of the guys in developmental think they're important because they have a contract, and come to camp with an attitude and the office on speed dial to complain when they were pushed.

If you talk to any Marine coming out of Boot Camp, he'll tell you he hated his drill instructor, but in time, he came to realize that his DI was trying to make him a better soldier so that he would be able to, possibly, save his own or his buddies' lives. As trainers, we push our students to see how they handle his or herself, to a point where they want to punch or shoot us, but once they mature and begin to understand our business, they appreciate what we've done for them. I'm sure there were times when Bill (or I) came across as a heartless bastard, but when push came to shove, he opened his heart to those kids, and again, we were alike in our mindsets.

I've read reports on the Internet and in newsletters about the developmental territories being a waste of time. Yes, it's a numbers game, but it's not always who we turn out, but who the people in charge want to use. We might have done a good job getting someone ready for the talent roster, but Creative didn't see what they were looking for, so they weren't able to use them to their full potential.

Training people on the Tough Enough show is even tougher because the instructors have a very short timeframe in which to get the kids ready. I don't know anyone who could do any better job then Bill when it comes to speed-training someone, especially when many of the people he has to work with have little or no experience.

As a wrestler, Bill also excels, and always gives one hundred percent. At the Brian Pillman Memorial Show I promoted in 2001, Bill wrestled Mark Henry. You might have expected a standard big men's match from those two 300-pounders on a charity event. However, they stepped up and had what might have been the best match of their careers. They are two huge guys, but both went out and ran spots like guys who were 50 pounds lighter.

Bill has great personality and a love and passion for the wrestling business. More importantly, he has respect for the business ... a respect he instills in the people he trains. If I ever open another training center, I would not hesitate to invite the big guy to be a part of my staff.

This book is a testament to a man who is a very talented trainer of pro wrestlers and for whom I have a great deal of respect.

Acknowledgements

by Bill De Mott

Johnny Rodz and Kevin Sullivan. You two taught me more about the wrestling business than anyone else. Your lessons, discussions, rants, and raves helped bring me to where I am today. I pass along your knowledge by using your methods when I teach my students. I'll always be thankful for your willingness to take a chance on me. Thanks for being who you are and helping make me what I am, both inside and outside the squared circle.

I owe thanks to many other people, but the listing alone would fill another book entirely. I do want to thank Victor Quinones for taking a chance on a guy he never met and for giving me my first big shot at the business. My hat is also off to Eric Bischoff and the immortal Hulk Hogan for taking the time to meet with me in Macon, Georgia, and giving me an opportunity to wrestle for WCW. Finally, I will be forever grateful to the McMahon family and the WWE for allowing me to join their elite group of athletes and entertainers.

This book began as a "project" to help me recall my day-to-day life while dealing with some medical issues, but it wound up as a form of therapy. My journal became a place for me to vent and discuss "myself" with "myself." I never had any intention of turning it into a book, but later, when I began reading through my notes, it seemed like a good way to bring closure to certain things in my life. So, it became a "book."

To me, the toughest part of the process was the final reading after Scott finished with the edit. I honestly didn't think I had been through as much, or done as many 'things," as I did until I actually saw my life in print. The process of writing this book, however, was easy compared to what I'll have to deal with when I face my family and friends and have to own up to my faults. I think it will be hard to answer questions they will have about things that were, until now, known only to me.

On the other hand ... man, do I feel better now that things are out in the open.

There are some things people still won't know. Whether or not I share those stories in another book is something I haven't decided, but for now, I'm glad Scott Teal and I have reached the finish line with this project.

When I first began looking for a co-writer, I knew I needed someone who had no interest in me as a person. I wanted someone who had an interest in the project for what it was. I had heard Scott's name from other people he has been involved with and books he has written, so I thought, *"Who better?"* When I reached out to him, I was met with hesitation. In fact, he first told me he had little or no interest in anything having to do with wrestling after the year 1982. When he said that, I knew he was exactly the person I was looking for, because Scott didn't know much about Bill De Mott or his faults. Based on our initial conversation, I also knew he would dissect my writing and give me his unbiased opinion.

It has been almost fifteen months since we talked for the first time ... and I still think he has no idea of who I am. He does, however, have a better idea of who I was!

Scott has been the captain of this ship and his efforts have made my life worth reading. He's a wrestling encyclopedia and he spent a lot of time researching and telling me things about my life that even I didn't remember. If there was something he didn't know, he knew someone who did. He corrected me on events in my life and put a timeline to things I had out of kilter. Scott sent me pages and pages of questions, and when I answer those questions, he demanded answers to my answers, and then sent more questions. He would "call me out" on things I had written, making sure everything (to the best of our knowledge) was correct and factual. I'm not a wordsmith, and at times, my writing and language can be very vulgar, but Scott did his best to help me preserve the babyface image I've maintained all these years (that's sarcasm).

If I never said this before, Scott, I can never thank you for helping me finish what I started. I appreciate you not only as an editor, but for the person you are. Looking back over the past 23 years, you might have been my toughest opponent, but I'd be willing to mix it up with you anytime. I'm proud of this project, but I'm prouder that you and I have formed a bond. Thank you, my friend.

I also have to thank three people for their contributions to the proofreading and fact-finding: Koji Miyamoto, J Michael Kenyon, and William Burnett.

I had a long and tremendous career. At one point in time, I was lumped in with a group of wrestlers known as the "First Family." However, there is only one "true" first family for me. Those people are the ones who urge me to do and be my best. While I am sure they will be disappointed when they read some of the things about me in this book, I want them to know it was never my intention to hurt them. Even the best and (seemingly) most successful people in the world have skeletons in their closets. I've just decided to share mine. Whether or not my family realizes it, the telling of my story has been therapeutic and has helped me move on.

One of the things I've learned through the years is that there is nothing more important than family and taking care of the ones you love." First and foremost, there is no one more responsible than the man who loved me and cared for me — my Pop. Pop did everything in his power to make me a man and to raise me as his own. I love him more than he could have ever known and I miss him. He was the glue that held our family together, and despite all the crazy things he saw me do, I hope he looks down with pride at how I've turned out. I never wanted to disappoint him. In fact, he was the man I strived to be. Without his guidance, care, and straight-forward dealing with everything, I would probably still be in Paramus, New Jersey. I love you, Pop, and I am sorry for the things I did that troubled you.

My beautiful and loving wife, Lacey. More than likely, without Lacey, I wouldn't be around to tell these stories. One of the most important stories in this book is how she saved me from myself. She pulled me off what might have been a destructive path and changed my life. She is responsible for me being the man, father, and husband I am today. There are no words strong enough to describe how much I adore and admire her as a person, as a woman, and as my wife. She lived a thousand lives with me and never turned away. Her involvement in my life is an example of the old saying, "Behind every man is a great woman." While I am just "okay," she is truly "great."

Casey, Keri, and Butchie — what you read on these pages and what you thought you knew about your dad might be two very different things, but it's a fact that you inspired me to better myself. I'm blessed to have you as a part of my life. If there ever was a picture-perfect family, it's the De Mott family. We went through a lot over the years, but we weathered the storms and came out (relatively) unscathed. My goal in life now is to do whatever I can to equip the three of you change the world. When it's my time to "go," I know the De Mott name will be carried on proudly.

I would be remiss if I didn't give thanks and glory to God. I don't say that flippantly as they do at awards shows. I have learned that I have been saved and I believe in Jesus Christ's power to change even the unworthy. Some of the words I use, or the manner in which I write my stories, might lead one to believe my salvation isn't real, but I can assure you, it is. I tell my stories in a way that will get my point across succinctly, and that occasionally call for blunt or crude language. I hope some young kid will read between the lines and realize that if he or she is blessed with talent, heart, and desire for the wrestling business, they don't have to self-destruct to make an impact. The Lord saves all, but few recognize when the window is open for redemption. This book is the first step I take to redeem myself. For that, I give all the glory and praise to my Lord, my Savior, and my friend.

Alice happens to be my mom, but more importantly, she has been there for me through good times and bad. I think every parent (note that I write that in the singular) wants to think they have done everything they could for their kids, and that they gave them the tools necessary to live a good life. Well, Alice did everything she could to give us (Darryl, Debbie and me) what we "needed," but not always what we "wanted." It was no "Leave it to Beaver" childhood.

The things that lady has been through is the stuff of books and movies. She has been walked on, pissed on, and mistreated for most of her life — especially by her family. We all put her through hell. Everybody took for granted that Alice was there and could handle whatever situation arose, but I know the toll it took on her. The things said and done to her would have broken any two people to the point where they wanted to sit alone in a dark room forever. She went through bouts of depression and anger that made her physically sick. At other times, she would just sit and cry. Later in life, she had several heart attacks, one right after the other.

And yet, she never turned her back on us.

More importantly, she kept us alive. I don't say that to make this story more dramatic. I mean it literally when I say, "She kept us alive."

No matter what I did, I have always been able to relate and talk to my mom. The bond I had with my mom was the one constant in my life. As a kid, I was a prick, and I morphed into an asshole when I got older, but I never was towards her. No, we didn't always get along, and we often disagreed on things, but she taught me to be a man, to be responsible, and showed me how to open up, love, and take care of people. The worst thing about it is that I failed her so many times.

As I put my life on paper, I thought about the things about my life I wanted to share. There wasn't anything I wasn't willing to talk about, but I decided my "Alice stories" would stay with me. I would like to write about the time I stayed up all night with my mom and painted the staircase and didn't have to go to school the next day. Or the time my mom went on a date and I didn't like how close the guy was sitting next to her, so I jumped out of one car and into hers. Or the times I was allowed to stay up and make "pink squirrels" for my mom and her friends while they hung out.

Alice and Bill at his high school graduation, 1983

But I won't. They are my stories!

The one thing I will tell you; nobody will ever have a better relationship with their mother than I did and have, and nobody will ever have a better friend, mentor, or confidant. I shared things with her that very few kids would ever tell their mom.

Then again ... man, if she ever reads this book from beginning to end, it will probably break her heart. The funny part is, I believe she's always had a good idea of what I was going through and the things I was doing, but probably just refused to believe it. That's the kind of person she is.

She has embraced my life, my kids, and my wife. We had a really tough time getting along after my divorce, but we survived it and worked it out.

Since Pop passed away, Alice and John have moved to Georgia and live less than a mile from us. No doubt, she did it so she could keep an eye on me.

This lady deserves more than any fame, wealth, or money could ever provide. I have nothing but love for Alice Marie Galligan.

Mom, I love you and I am sorry I didn't turn out the way I should have, or how you wanted me to, but please know that every day, I try hard to do my best.

As I read the final draft of the manuscript, I thought, *"I must be crazy to share this information with the public. It's not flattering, it doesn't make me a star, and it doesn't always make me look too good."* The truth is, there are things I reveal about myself which make me look downright bad, but such are the memories of the life of William Charles De Mott Jr. In addition to the swell and stupid things I've done, I've had both good times (most of which I don't talk about) and bad times (most of which I brought on myself).

I didn't set out to flay myself in public, but the writing of this book has afforded me considerable insights. As my editor and I worked our way through my life, I learned a lot about myself. I hope you, the reader, understand that, as you read, I am making the journey with you. My family may not be comfortable with it all, but I suspect they'll "get it" by the time they get to the end. I've learned it isn't so much about how I began the journey, but how I am going to finish it. Hopefully, those gleanings will help me get through the next 45 years (or more) of my life.

And, just for the sake of argument, let's "pretend" I am keeping a diary of my new adventures with WWE, *Tough Enough* (2011 season), and life. Maybe I can convince my man Scott to get involved again with me on this because even he has been perplexed by what the two of us have created here between the front and back covers.

I am a blessed and saved man. At the beginning of every meal and at the end of every day, I thank God for what he has done for me. Most importantly, I'm thankful he has a sense of humor because, even while finishing this section, I get THE LAST LAUGH.

God bless you all.

Chapter 1

Cow Tipping

"Didn't you used to be Bill De Mott?"

Anyone who has ever made a name for themselves in the pro-wrestling/sports-entertainment business has been asked the same questions over and over.

For example:

Is wrestling fake?

How often do you guys practice?

Nobody really gets hurt, do they?

Where did you learn to "act?"

These are just a few of the questions I'm asked on a regular basis. Granted, people plunk down their hard-earned money to see us wrestle, and for the most part, they're just curious about what it is we do. However, every once in awhile, I run into someone who is looking for attention he can't get in his everyday life. That person gets his kicks out of heckling the boys. I always try to be polite and thank the fans for being supportive of the business, but as long as there are sports, there will be a small group of people who hate anyone involved in the entertainment business. And for some reason, professional wrestlers seem to get more unwanted attention than other athletes.

The funniest things happen to me when I'm a guest at one of the "legends" conventions. I spend the day signing autographs and having my picture taken with fans. At every convention, there will be one person who has followed wrestling his whole life. That person will walk up and tell me about my whole career. I'm both amazed and flattered to think someone cares enough about the wrestling business and me to remember those facts. They wrap themselves up in our lives (at least the ones they read about and watch on TV) and feel like they know us intimately. I worry a bit about whether or not they know what kind of underwear I have on (or if I have any on at all). I get a bit pissed, however, when they go on to say they have "been watching me since they were little kids in school," when I know good and well that when they were watching wrestling, I was flunking out of Spanish at East Brook Middle School in Paramus, New Jersey.

And while I was taught that without the fans, I wouldn't have a job or the opportunity to be famous, there has to be a line drawn in the sand. I have found that with some fans, the line doesn't exist, but I also have learned that I treat people the way I would want to be treated, the problems are few and far between. And to that end, I can honestly say I have never had a "run-in" with a fan.

Well, except for the sick bastards who shot at me in Puerto Rico.

Oh, yeah ... and the assholes who threw urine on us in Mexico.

Did I mention the guy who pulled a knife on me when I left the ring in the Cayman Islands?

Other than those incidents, my interaction with the fans has been pretty good.

But getting back to the main question ... didn't you "used to be" Bill De Mott? That has to be my all-time favorite. People have walked up to our table when I was eating dinner at a restaurant with my parents, wife, and kids, and asked that question. I heard it while we were shopping, when we were at a park, and just about every public place you can think of. Everybody seems to want to know if I used to be ... ME!

If any of you who are sitting there reading this are wondering whether or not I am really ME, then just keep reading. This book should answer that question and many others you might have.

First of all, I was born a poor, black child.

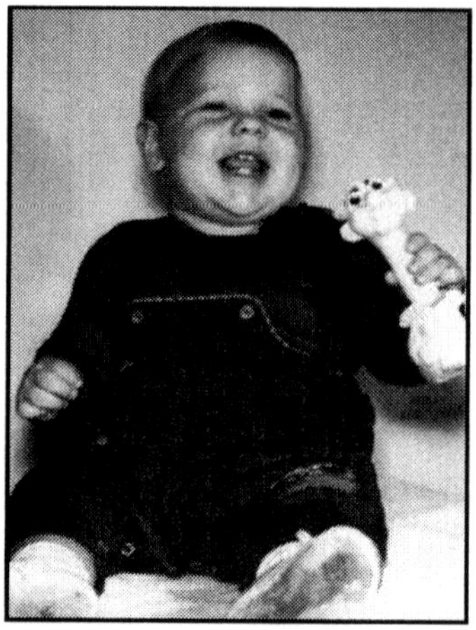
Bill De Mott, 1 year old

Just kidding. That line came from *The Jerk*, the movie which starred Steve Martin. I always thought it was hilarious and couldn't resist using it.

Actually, I was born William Charles De Mott Jr. on November 10, 1965 to William and Alice De Mott.

As a child/kid, I was called Billy, but some people referred to me as Butchie, a name I later used for my son, William Charles De Mott III. I think I was saddled with the name because I had a "butch" haircut. When I was older, a family friend named Jay Hayward (who I considered to be my big brother) began calling me "Wilbur." That name stuck with me for many years, and to this day, when I go home to Jersey, I occasionally run into someone who will call me Wilbur. I hate to admit this, but I believe I was given the name because I had/have somewhat of a pig nose!

Growing up in Paramus, New Jersey, I was a quiet kid who really didn't have many social skills. I just enjoyed sitting in my bedroom listening to music. Just about the only time I was away from the house was when I was at my grandparents' house in Wyckoff, New Jersey. I wasn't keen on talking to people outside of my little family circle. It's not that I didn't want to interact with others. I just never could relate to other people. I also had to be home most of the time because my mom was always working two or three jobs and we had a "sitter." The only people outside of my family that I did "hang with" were my mom's friends. I didn't worry about what they might be thinking about me. They were cool and let me tag along when they went out. At times, they even let me mix a drink with them. Eventually, I became really good friends with a kid named David Spangler. We would hang out together and he turned me on to different kinds of music. Dave was a good cat and we stay in touch to this day.

We didn't go on a lot of vacations or weekend getaways, and we didn't go out to eat very often. Vacations were a luxury we simply couldn't afford, although we would occasionally go to Cape May, New Jersey (southern part of the Jersey shore) with my grandparents, or take a day trip to Darlington Lake to swim and picnic. I can't express how hard my mom worked to make ends meet. I didn't take part in school functions or trips, either. My brother Darryl and I hung out with a group of guys once in awhile. Later in life, I came to the realization that we were all nerds, and in that circle, Darryl and I were cool. The two things I did like to do was bowl and fish, both of which I did with my grandfather.

Having to raise three kids on her own, my mom did everything imaginable to make a living, including working in a bakery and retail stores. She worked long hours and did whatever was necessary to keep the family together. My biological father was a cop, as was my Uncle Eddie, a man for whom I have the utmost respect. I love him and my Aunt Carol very much. They were a big help to my mom in the early years and they never abandoned us.

When I was fourteen years old, I began working after school and on weekends, the first of which was at a thrift store where my mom worked. I didn't need the money because I didn't do anything other than hide in my bedroom. As I grew older, I filled my time with work and became a "workaholic."

I dreaded high school and I don't remember much about my first two years, other than hating it. My sister, who was a year older, was making a name for herself in the school and around town (read into that what you'd like), and it wasn't easy to dissociate myself from that. She had her own issues and, along with some other girls from the neighborhood, began hanging out with a group of troublemakers. By themselves, they were just insecure and not sure of what they were looking for in life, but they were strictly followers and the guys they hung around with were nothing but trouble. As for myself, I remember skipping classes a lot, primarily because I didn't feel comfortable being around a lot of people. It was around that time that my mom was getting serious with John.

I didn't get involved in organized sports until my junior year when I convinced my mom (with the help of Charlie Bauer, the coach) to let me play football. That was an experience which helped break me out of my shell and, basically, was the foundation of the person I would become. I also ran track and became a male cheerleader (that's right, I said cheerleader), thanks to Ms. Bostonian, my psychology teacher, who made me realize that being different could be a good thing. Ms. Bostonian wanted to "liven things up" in the cheerleading program, so she kind of dared me and two other football players to do it. I had joined the wrestling team, but the sport just didn't click with me, so I looked at her challenge in a positive light.

Sports helped pull me out of my shell, although I had a lot of catching up to do when it came to interacting with my peers. I didn't know what was cool or

9-year-old Bill De Mott and Alice at a cub scout meeting

in style, and I didn't know what to say and how to act. I wanted very much to fit in and try to find myself, but it was a tough go. Being involved in three sports, I had to deal with a lot of new people, so that was a big thing for me to overcome. I didn't have a lot of confidence, but the forced interaction with others played a big part in developing my personality and teaching me to deal with situations that came up in my life. Hey, if I could be a male cheerleader, the rest should have been easy, right?

I continued to work part time and gave most of my money to my mom, but as I got older and began to go out with friends, I needed some spending money now and then.

Outside of those activities, even in my "new skin," I was still very uncomfortable, and there was a time during my junior year when I wasn't sure if I wanted to be around at all. My mom was dating and the "piece-of-garbage sperm donor" who was supposed to be my father had walked out on his family, leaving my mom and three kids to fend for themselves. I was just five years old when he left. My sister Debbie was six and my brother Darryl was four. I struggled a lot with the issue of not having a dad, especially during high school. Most of my buddies were tight with their dads. Their dads took them camping and fishing, and taught them sports, and when certain functions took place at school where a boy needed that father figure at his side, I began to realize how I had been cheated in the "father" department. Everything I learned was self taught or taught to me by my Pop. I can count on one hand the number of times the sperm donor tried to contact me, and that was only after I began wrestling on TV and became "famous." I am not, and never will be, interested in having a relationship.

The man I call my "Pop" is my grandfather, David A. Wilson. When I was a kid, he was the only father figure I had, and he worked hard to help me become a good person (even though I feel like I have let him down). People don't realize the psychological damage kids suffer when parents do things like that. Many times in my life, even into my thirties, I struggled with thoughts of not wanting to be "around." It's not something I'm proud of, but I do admit I had those thoughts. I never went so far as to come up with a plan to "off" myself, but I never was concerned with problems my actions might cause for myself.

Fortunately, a group of people "took me in" and accepted me for who I was. Those guys and girls were the "boys" to me long before I ever got into the wrestling business: Mike Hornidge (The Horn), Paul Kalksma (The Bear), Brendon Winters (Splint), Tommy Cangimilia (Mumbles), Tommy Miani (my cousin), Debbie Winters (Brendon's wife), Paul Bachia (Rock Head), and Bobby Guidettie (Bobby G). I'm sure there are more, but those were the cats who helped me survive a very tough time, and I'm proud to say we all remain friends to this day and we get together as often as possible. I love those guys and I cherish their friendship. They never blow smoke up my ass and they're not afraid to tell me what's on their minds. They are the best people I know and I would trust my life and my family's lives to them. I hope someday they realize just how much of a part they played in my life. I know I'm terrible about calling and staying in touch, but that's just a part of me that is hard to explain. To this day, I go through bouts of anxiety and I pace the floor a lot. I get anxious thinking about things I need to do, or what people want me to do, and I withdraw into myself. Even writing this book takes me to places I really don't want to go. The reminiscing about certain times in my life makes me very uptight. The good news is that I no longer try to solve my problems with booze, pills, and drugs. I simply tell myself to get my head out of my ass, fix the problem, and move on. I have a saying I often use: sobriety can be a bitch. Someday, I probably should address my problems with a psychiatrist. Right!

I'm proud to say I no longer have those thoughts. I found myself infused with a purpose when my daughters were born. That might sound corny, but kids are needy. They look to us for things they're unable to do for themselves. If nothing else, I didn't want to become the asshole who left me when I was young. I can never say it enough. If it wasn't for Lacey Storey, my girls Casey

Bill De Mott (#77) playing high school football

and Keri, and my son Butchie, there's no telling where I might be today, if anywhere. So, yeah! I'm over those feelings of not having a place in this world. Those thoughts, talks, and cries I had with myself made me stronger emotionally, mentally, and most importantly (especially lately), spiritually.

When I was in high school, my mom began dating John J. Galligan, a man who was a delivery driver for Entenmann's Bakery. John met my mom when he began making deliveries to the thrift store where she worked. After they had a few dates, he showed up at the house on Valentine's Day and my mom introduced him to us. They dated for a long time and he would occasionally stay overnight. Eventually, he moved in with us. John came into our family with a lot of his own baggage, much of which we learned about as time passed. He was separated from his wife, but not divorced, and he had four sons. The two I got to know, Steven and Gary, were (and are) cool guys. In fact, Gary and I share the same birthday. At first, my siblings and I weren't too happy about John moving in. I had a good relationship with my mom and I didn't like him coming between us and possibly stirring things up. Up to that point, other than my grandfather (Pop), we never really had a male figure in the house. In the months that followed, I began to realize that John made my mom happy, and that's what really counted. All things considered, John was good for my mom, and he did his best to guide us. We had (and still have) our issues because we're both Type A personalities, but I consider him to be my dad. It's funny, but people who met him would say, *"Hello, Mr. De Mott,"* not realizing the situation. We never corrected them. I don't remember exactly when they got married, but that doesn't really matter. They have been together for so long that we always introduce him as our dad. I guess he earned the title because he *was* there for us when we needed him.

From here on out, I'll refer to my mom as Alice. I began calling her "Alice" at about the same time I began calling my grandfather "Pop." I wasn't being disrespectful, but I can't really say why I began calling them by those names. I believe it was because our relationship was more of a friendship than it was "mother-son" or "grandfather-grandson." I was closer to my mom than my brother and sister were. It was almost as if we grew up together. We were both trying to figure out where we were going in life. We had some great talks and cried on each other shoulders from time to time. So, I began calling my mom "Alice."

The Horn, Bill, Splint, Bobby G, Jimmy, and Tommy Miani

Bill, John Galligan, Pop and Bill's brother Darryl

When I was a junior in high school, John (who I then accepted as my "dad") pulled some strings and got me a job at the local "Shop-Rite," a big supermarket. I bagged groceries, collected shopping carts, and did just about anything I was asked to do. As I got more and more involved with sports (and more importantly, girls!), I began to curtail my work activities and quit my job. Needless to say, John was pretty upset. I know my parents were more than a little disappointed that I was no longer enthused about working, but I was trying hard to fit in with my group of friends. I wanted to do whatever it took to be a part of the group and I didn't want to miss anything the rest of the cats might be doing. My work ethic continued to decline as I got more and more involved in sports, school (socially, not studies), and chicks. My entire focus was on being "me." Of course, that was the way I've always done things. It's either "all" or "nothing." I'm happy to say I still have an excellent work ethic, which I account to Alice, Pop, and John. Even during the worst periods of my life, when I was out of control and doing things which were not beneficial to my life, I kept my work ethic.

In June 1983, just two weeks after I graduated from high school (which was a small miracle), I left for Kutztown University in Kutztown, Pennsylvania. I had no idea why I was going to college, other than the fact that I was going to play football for the Golden Bears, a Division Two team. My friends were going, as well, so it seemed to be the thing to do. I had to take summer classes at Kutztown because my grades were barely high enough to get me accepted.

I had never been further away from home than the Jersey shore and, for the first time in my life, I was going to be alone in Amish country without friends and family. At a time when I was just beginning to find myself and feel comfortable with people at school, I was off on a new journey and starting over.

I struggled through my classes and barely comprehended what the professors were talking about. They might as well have been speaking a foreign language. Once again, my focus was on football and fitting in with everyone. That was a tough time for me, but I slowly made a name for myself on the football field and around campus. At least, I was "somebody" with the freshmen and the few girls I went out with. I'm not sure why, but people began calling me

"Psycho." It might have been because they thought I was a little "different," and I suppose that was the case, or it might have been due to my heavy consumption of alcohol. Regardless, other than the fact I was going to flunk every one of my classes, everything seemed to be going well. Until ...

During the last week of the summer session and on the night before our final exams, several of us decided to go downtown to a local bar. I was only seventeen years old at the time. From what I can recall, I had one too many. Okay, I was drunk. At some point, we decided to leave the bar (which was located on the main street) and go "cow tipping." I didn't know what that was, but we never got that far. As we walked out of the bar, the first thing we saw was a car, so someone decided we would have a contest to see who could do the most damage to cars (that's plural) with their body, head, feet, or hands. And, of course, being the "psycho," I had to live up to the challenge.

We did an amazing amount of damage to windshields, trunks, doors, and hoods. As the night went on, "damaging cars" turned into "turning cars over." We called it "car tipping," which was our alternative to "cow tipping." As the night wore on, we made our way back to campus ... one car at a time. We finally decided to move a car into the cornfield behind one of the dorms, oblivious to the fact that we were making enough noise to wake the dead. The last thing I remember (actually, the last thing I was told) was getting a car in my sights ... at the same time a cop had me in the sights of his pistol. One thing led to another and we were all handcuffed and taken to jail.

High school senior photo, 1983

Did I mention I was only seventeen years old?

Well, I had granted the obligatory "one phone call" and I chose to call my brother, who was in Maywood, New Jersey, where my family was living at that time. He then took it upon himself to call Alice and Pop (unbeknownst to me). "Scared" does not come anywhere near to the feeling I felt when I looked up the next day and saw Alice, John, and Pop looking at me through the bars of the jail cell. I was embarrassed to have my mom and dad see me, but I was absolutely ashamed when I saw my grandfather. If I had been given the choice, I would have chosen to stay in that jail cell for the rest of my life rather than see the disappointment on his face. That vision haunted me until the day he died.

After posting bail, they took me to the dorm to get my personal possessions, and by the time we pulled onto campus, everyone had heard about the incident. Of course, that just added to the reputation of the "psycho." After an appearance in court (where I plead guilty), and a meeting with the dean of students (where I plead stupidity), I was fined and put on probation. The worst part of it was that I took the rap for the others, all of whom were over eighteen years old and, as "adults," would have been facing federal charges. I had been caught red-handed doing the damage to the cars, while they had been standing by when the police arrived. Since they weren't caught in the act, they were considered accomplices and charged with criminal mischief.

To sum up my college days, I flunked my classes, partied my brains out, met a large contingent of women, none of whom I can remember, left school after my freshman year, and disappointed my family. For years after that, it seemed like whenever the family got together, someone would bring up the incident, and I was always embarrassed. On the bright side (if there was such a thing), the remarks were always presented in a humorous manner, but even so, my family and friends weren't going to let me forget the time I screwed up my college experience. I'm just glad they never learned of the other times I was in a similar situation.

Okay, so now they know.

The moral to the story is to always ask ... "What do you mean by "cow tipping?"

Bill with fellow college football teammate, Shawn Grignon

Chapter 2

Learning to Crawl

After I left college, I had a lot of jobs. I was a line cook at a place called "Bobby Rubinos", a barbeque franchise which was run by some "interesting" gentlemen. I don't want to go into detail, but some might say they were a "family." I wasn't there too long before I was running "errands" for them and building a reputation as a "go-to" guy. I was "morally challenged" at the time, so it wasn't beyond me to locate safes, people, or other things which needed to be found … or lost. I was called into the office from time to time, or stopped in the back room, and asked to do things like transferring safes from one apartment to a house, or moving other "things" from one place to another. I never gave any thought as to why they sent me to somebody's house in the middle of the afternoon when they wouldn't be home, to remove a large, heavy safe, and take it to another house where nobody was at home. I just did what I was told. I also began my long and adventurous career as a bouncer and "trouble-shooter." I would be invited to bars and restaurants to remove people, or to make sure certain people "didn't get in." I didn't worry about retaliation or legal problems for strong-arming people because I knew the "family" was protecting me. Nobody ever asked for details about the way I had handled a job. It was simply, *"Everything good?"* My answer was just as concise: *"Yes."* I don't remember being paid for my services in those early days, but I never had to pay for drinks (or drugs) and I was always welcome and treated well in the clubs.

My involvement with the "family," or people who were involved in "family business," didn't hurt my popularity with the ladies, either. That was another job where I made friends for which I did "favors." I also pumped gas, worked for a towing company, drove a truck for a paper company, and worked in my father-in-law's print shop. One job I had for a long time was painting stripes on parking lots and highways for Park Rite Striping Co. The company was owned and operated by Jesse Winters. Jesse and his family were always great to me and his son, Brendon, was one of my best friends.

During that time, I met Rose Azzolino through her cousin, Tommy, who was one of my best friends, and her brother, Vince. We got married just before I turned 21 years old.

Paul Bachia, aka "Rockhead," got me involved coaching football for the Paramus Recreational Football League. I was the line coach for the Pee

Wees and it was strictly a volunteer position. It was something I took on initially just to kill time, but working with the kids was very rewarding, not to mention a lot of fun. It made me feel good to do something positive after screwing up my college career. I still hear from some of those kids. The funny thing is, even though they're all grown men now with families of their own, they still tend to call me "Mr. De Mott." I would like to think they grew up and I stayed the same.

As far as professional wrestling goes, I never paid much attention to it when I was a kid. As I got older, I remember seeing it on WWOR-TV, Channel 9. The only wrestlers I remember seeing in those days were Bruno Sammartino, Pedro Morales, and, of course, the midgets. When the WWWF came to my high school, I walked to the school in a snow storm to meet up with a girl. The main event that night was supposed to be Pedro Morales against Jesse Ventura, but I didn't go for the wrestling. I wanted to be with the chick. When I got there, a sign was posted which said the show had been cancelled. While I stood there, a pink Cadillac pulled up to the curb and Ventura stepped out. He was really pissed because nobody had told him the show was cancelled. He gave me a little push when I walked up and asked him for his autograph. He was hot and didn't want anything to do with a snot-nosed kid. I wouldn't attend another wrestling event until several years later when I went to Madison Square Garden with my girlfriend Rose, Tommy, and Vince. That night, I caught the "wrestling" fever.

My first actual exposure to professional wrestling was when my dad John took me to Brooklyn to "look into it." John was from New York and he knew his way around, so he took me to Gleason's Gym at 77 Front Street. We walked into the gym and met "The Unpredictable" Johnny Rodz, a professional wrestler who trained wannabes at the gym. Johnny was very sure of himself and he had a lot of students in the building that day. Until that time, I didn't have any interest in becoming a professional wrestler, but there was something about what the kids were doing in the ring, and the way in which Johnny presented himself to me, that caught my attention. After making the obligatory small talk, Johnny told us about the gym and that it cost $3,000 to join with $1,500 up front. He said the gym was open every day and we could come as often as we wanted. He also let us know that wrestling wasn't for everyone, that not all of his students would "make it," and of those who did, not everyone would get the opportunities that others would get.

John and I went back to Wyckoff to talk about it with Pop, Alice, and Rose. My dad was excited about the possibilities, but $3,000 was a lot of money. I was making enough money to pay my bills and live a normal life, but I was newly married and I didn't have that kind of cash lying around the house.

Pop finally agreed to loan me the money to get started based on the condition that I would give him ten percent of my future wrestling earnings. He also gave me money for two pairs of boots, eight pairs of tights, and any other equipment I might have needed. I was never sure if Pop really believed I could make it in the wrestling business, but he backed me whole heartedly and never expressed any doubts to me. I think he did it because he knew it would be something on which I could focus. My family knew I would never go back to college, but they wanted to help me succeed at "something." They were a bit skeptical at first, but they all backed me.

At least, my immediate family supported me. My in-laws were a bunch of assholes who thought wrestling was going to be a big waste of my time. They said I should be learning a trade and become a "normal man and husband." It didn't matter what job I had. All I heard was I should have a normal job with security and health benefits. Nothing was good enough for them. When I was working 80 hours a week for Park-Rite Striping, they said "you work too much." It didn't matter what I was doing if they didn't approve of it. Even when I worked with my father-in-law at the print shop where he worked, I couldn't make them happy. They were straight off the boat from Italy and refused to accept me or anything I did.

On October 10, 1988, within a week of my initial visit, I returned to Brooklyn with the cash and paid Johnny in full. Not too many of his students did that, so it sort of endeared me to him. We spent a lot of time talking and getting to know each other, and a camaraderie and trust rapidly developed between us. Of course, that built up some animosity between me and the guys who had already been there for awhile, but that happens in life (and especially wrestling) every day.

The first wrestler I knew on a personal level was a cat named "Diamond" Jim Brady, a.k.a. Steve Cooper. I continued to work the jobs while I was training and commuting to Brooklyn. Steve and I worked together for a towing company of which Steve was a partner. We became good friends and stayed in touch even after I quit working for him. Steve actually tried to talk me out of getting involved with wrestling. I'm so glad I didn't take his advice. I first met Paul Heyman through Steve. They were buddies and I would tag along with him to wrestling shows. I actually sat at a show with Paul's girlfriend to make sure nobody messed with her.

Bill De Mott, 1988

At the time, Rose and I were living in an apartment in Hackensack, New Jersey. It was a 45- to 60-minute drive each way to the gym. Most of the time, I would ride my motorcycle through the city and tunnels. That wasn't the brightest thing to do. It's dangerous enough in a car, but riding a bike through New York City was verging on suicide. If it was raining, I would borrow a car or drop off Rose at work and leave the gym in time to pick her up.

I would train two times a day at the *Strong and Shapely Gym* in East Rutherford, New Jersey, beginning early in the morning around four o'clock. Bob Bonham, who would later become a big name as a bodybuilding show promoter for the National Physique Committee [NPC] and the International Federation of Bodybuilders [IFBB], had just opened the gym. He took a lot of grief from people for the name of the gym, but he wanted to own a gym which would appeal to both males and females. His plan worked because the gym has grown from the original 2,500 square feet of space to 25,000 square feet, and most of it is filled with equipment. In later years, I enjoyed going to Bob's gym when I wasn't on the road. Bob was very much a support system when I began wrestling. I still hear from him from time to time.

From noon until whenever I decided to leave, generally six to eight hours a day, I would be at Gleason's Gym. The wrestling gym was in a big warehouse adjacent to the boxing section of Gleason's. That warehouse would later become a parking garage. I trained until I couldn't walk, and then I would go home, sleep, and go back to do it all over again. My goal was to become better than anyone else. I know this will sound strange, but I became addicted to being thrown around and beaten up. I had been bitten by the wrestling bug. Eventually, I either quit or was fired from my daytime jobs. Several of my employers told me I couldn't keep missing days and changing hours. I agreed with them wholeheartedly ... so I quit! I wanted to go to Brooklyn every day of the week, so I kept working as a bouncer at night and doing "favors" for my friends. I worked at two different clubs. One was a local bar (more of a hangout than anything else), and the other was a strip joint called Shakers near Giants Stadium.

Sleep wasn't really a requirement back then. If I wasn't bouncing at night, Rose and I would go out and party with our friends. If she wanted to stay home, I would go out with the Horn and my other friends. I was wrestling, weightlifting, partying, or spending time with the family. Sleep was an afterthought.

Johnny Rodz was constantly telling me about wrestlers and telling me stories about things that had happened in the business. I didn't know anything about what he was talking about, but unlike my time in school when I didn't understand what my teachers were talking about, I hung onto every word Johnny said. I wanted to know everything there was to know about professional wrestling. He would make me sit in front of a television.

"Watch this match."

"Pay attention to this guy."

"Find yourself!"

"Look at what these guys do and how they do it."

That's exactly what I did, and when I wasn't actually training, I spent hours watching video tapes of the veterans in action. I wasn't sure what I was looking for, but they made me want to imitate them. Anything other than ring training was done on my own time. It was up to me, and me alone, to do my "homework," studying tapes and learning moves and holds. None of it was mandatory, but Johnny made suggestions which some guys picked up on.

I'm sure listening to me talk about my new life was contagious because my family and friends supported me completely and became more and more interested in my new career path as the days went by. However, I wanted to be at the gym so badly that I eventually quit even my night jobs, which led to a bit of friction because money was tight in our home. Pop helped me out quite often. Looking back, I realize it was selfish on my part, but I expected a lot from everyone else in order for me to pursue my dream.

Johnny Rodz taught me about the business from the ground up. He prepared me for everything that could, would, and should happen to me. He taught me the basics and fundamentals, and how to survive and play the game. As he says, *"First you need to crawl, then you learn to walk, and only then will I teach you to run.* The most important thing he taught me, however, was to *respect* the wrestling business. To this day, when I train students, I teach them the Johnny Rodz method. I"m sure I've added a little bit of "Bill" to the training, but Johnny is the foundation for what I do when I train, teach, and speak about the business.

I think the biggest misconception in wrestling, even to this day, is that we all spend so much time "rehearsing" what we are going to do. I'm somewhat ashamed to admit that I believed that when I first began training. I thought the wrestlers all "talked" and "choreographed" their matches in the dressing room every night. Boy, was I ever wrong! I don't think anyone who has never been there can ever appreciate the "magic" that goes into a match.

The first thing I was taught was *"the wrestling business is no fucking joke,"* which were the very words used. There were no money-back guarantees, either. Johnny said (in so many words), *"if you pay your money and you can't cut it, too fucking bad!*

Another thing a good trainer will do is to work a new student so hard that he will quit. We were roughed up every day, and at the end of the day, nobody sat us down and said, *"You did a great job today, kid."* The rough handling was a test to determine how badly we really wanted to be in the wrestling business. Johnny didn't try to injure me, but he was constantly stretching me. He would lock me up and explain why and when to do things. He wanted me to believe that everything that happened in the ring was real because whether people believe it or not, there are holds which, when applied in the right manner, will do legitimate damage. That's why I've always been a big fan of working "snug." When I work in that manner, my "opponent" doesn't have to "sell" what I do to the people in the audience. I "work" the holds, but use them in such a way that the fans can tell he's genuinely fighting against me. Having that mindset worked to my advantage in future years because the veterans knew my work was believable, but at the same time, they never had to worry about me hurting them.

In my opinion, the thing I had "going for me" in the beginning was that I was a quick study. I watched carefully and did things over and over until I could do them without thinking. I began to get comfortable in the ring when I was told it was time to learn how to chain wrestle and to learn specific moves and holds. That was when everything began to fall into place for me. The two most difficult things for me in the early days were hitting the ropes and getting my ring legs [wind].

Johnny advised me to get as many video tapes as possible and to watch them over and over until I knew what each man did well. I would report my findings to him and he would tell me whether I was correct in my analysis or not. If I was wrong, he would explain why I was wrong and show me what I had missed. It was a good mental workout. I learned a great deal from watching people like Jimmy Snuka, Nikolai Volkoff, and the Samoans. I also was going to shows to study people like Paul Orndorff, Sgt. Slaughter, Greg Valentine, Honky Tonk Man, and Koko B. Ware.

Wrestling was an education and I was brought along slowly. Nobody sat me down and formally smartened me up, or told me anything about the inner workings of the business. Unlike today, in a time when everything is on the Internet, we had to figure it out for ourselves. If we were lucky enough to spend some time with the guys who had been around for awhile, we learned to keep our ears open and our mouth shut. And whenever somebody told us something, we quickly learned to "believe half of what you see and none of what you hear."

I never really picked up on anything when I watched the matches, other than the fact that the guys were talking to each other in the ring. But there would be other matches where the guys never said a word. It was a mind game. It made me wonder, *Are they talking TO each other or AT each other?*

It didn't take me long to become a full-blown "mark" for the business, which, in my opinion, is a lot different from being a "mark" for yourself. During our training sessions, I began having short matches and I tried everything under the sun I thought I could do.

When Johnny decided I was ready to wrestle, he walked up to me one day and said, *"You're working the show tonight. You need a name and a character."* Johnny never was able to say my last name (De Mott), so he called me "Williams" and introduced me to everyone as Bill Williams. For some reason known only to himself, Johnny began calling me "Big Sweet Williams," which I later discovered was the original wrestling name of Luke Williams [Brian Wickens] of the Bushwhackers. Sweet William is also the name of a flower, so on my shirts (once again, funded by Pop), I had the picture of a flower on the front and "Big Sweet Williams" on the back. I wasn't portraying a homosexual character, but I wore pink tights and a vest. The color by itself got me good heat. Later, I would come to the ring wearing other colors, like yellow and purple, which wouldn't normally be worn by a 300-pound man. I wrestled as Big Sweet Williams until I went to Germany for the first time. I still say Johnny gave me that name because he wouldn't pronounce "De Mott." To this day, whenever I call Johnny at home, he will call out to his wife (who he calls Mama), *"Mama, Williams is on the phone!"*

My wrestling debut took place on November 26, 1988 at Gleason's Gym, where Johnny presented shows at least once a month. I had taken part in a few workouts that were "match-like," but that night was to be my first actual "match." I was going to be wrestling Bialo the Giant [Allen Bialo], who everybody called Herbie. That cat stood 6-foot-5 and weighed 400 pounds. He looked intimidating and acted as if he had been a main-event guy his whole life. The truth is, I had never heard of him, but he was a graduate of Johnny's earlier classes. The problem was that he was dangerous. He had no finesse and he didn't think about protecting his opponent. With it being my first match, the only thing I was concerned about was getting out alive and not looking like an ass in front of my family and friends. Johnny had made sure I could take a body slam, and that I could bump and run the ropes, but other than that, I was on my own. Besides, Bialo had his own persona and things in mind. I was so nervous. I didn't really know how to breathe, but I didn't blow up because my nerves and adrenaline were overpowering. I didn't talk to Bialo before the match, so he gave me the "follow me, kid" speech when we met in the center of the ring.

The match went well and I was relieved when it was over. My parents and friends were really excited to see me wrestle, and I think the fact that we had

(top l.) First publicity photo of Big Sweet Williams, (top r.) Big Sweet Williams, (bottom l.) Big Sweet Williams, (bottom r.) Big Sweet Williams vs. Johnny Rodz

a full house made it seem better than it was. Johnny was happy with my performance and a few of the other guys had some great suggestions and criticism. I listened to everything from everyone because there was always something to learn. Regardless, I was happy to get my feet wet. My mom told me something that night which she would repeat many times in the years that followed: *"You were meant to do this."* The most important thing I discovered that night was that I enjoyed being someone other than myself. When I was in the ring, I didn't have to worry about what people thought about Bill De Mott. I was "Big Sweet Williams." As I left the gym that night, all I could think about was getting back to the gym the next day and getting back to work.

There was an incentive to working the monthly shows at Gleason's Gym and getting in front of people, that being we made one dollar for every ticket we sold (which if I'm not mistaken was ten dollars a ticket). Since I was from New Jersey, and not just a ten-minute car ride away, it should have been hard to get people to come watch me wrestle. Well ... it wasn't!

I said earlier that my friends and family were all very supportive of what I was doing (even if they didn't really understand it). Well, one night, I was going to wrestle none other than Johnny Rodz himself ... in the main event! I sold 200 tickets to the show. And not only did I bring 200 people (all of whom bought tickets) to see me, but I made a $200 payday. That was unheard of at the time. I didn't work hard to get so many people there just to make money, though. I wanted "my" people to see exactly what it was I had chosen to do as my life's work and get them involved in my career. It was so funny because Pop had actually rented two Greyhound buses to shuttle all the people from Jersey to Brooklyn. It was quite a sight to see the bus pull up in front of the gym and more than a hundred people get off and make their way into the gym. I will never, *ever*, forget the feeling that washed over me that night.

Johnny was a little taken aback by the reaction he received that night because he was the babyface and I was supposed to be the heel, but I had the numbers in the crowd. It changed the dynamic of the match when the people got behind me. Of course, I didn't change with that dynamic because I had no clue about how to react. It was Johnny who took the reins and steered the match in the direction it needed to go.

I was more nervous in that match than I had been in my debut match because Johnny Rodz was the biggest name there at the time. I had been in the ring with him as my coach/trainer, but never in a real match in front of an audience. I know I must have done some things that looked hokey, but for the most part, the match went well. I didn't do anything to lead anyone to believe what we were doing was "fake." I understood early on that wrestling was an art, and if it was done correctly, you left the ring with the people either loving or hating you. When in doubt, a good bump will take all doubt out of anyone's mind, which is why I was taught to "bump and bump well." And besides, I was working that night with Johnny Rodz, and he *never* had a problem working snug.

I still have the very first dollar bill I ever made, which came from the ticket sales for my first match. The bill and the flyer for the show have been framed and are hanging on the wall of my den.

Chapter 3

Key to the City

After my first few matches, I wrestled up and down the east coast, taking every booking Johnny could get me. Johnny also sent Mondo Kleen [Phil Theis] and me to work on every World Wrestling Federation [WWF] card he could. Mondo, who later wrestled as Damien Demento, began training with Johnny long before I got my start in the business. Johnny was very high on Mondo. When I began training at the gym, Mondo took me under his wing and helped me along. He became my first tag team partner.

Mondo was very intelligent and he had a unique way of looking at the business. After Mondo had a taste of working for the independents, and Johnny tried to get him booked with one of the big promotions, Mondo developed his own, somewhat distorted, theories on the business, and I got the feeling he didn't care for the way Johnny was using him. Granted, Mondo was a good talent and everybody was talking highly about him, so I guess he thought he deserved more. It's possible Johnny didn't think Mondo was ready and was holding him back, but Johnny was doing right by me, so I kept my mouth shut. I was happy with the direction my career was moving. I listened to the things Mondo said, but thought to myself, *"I don't ever want to begin thinking that way."* We gelled well as a tag team and I enjoyed working with him, but as time passed, Mondo began looking for the big payday. There was nothing wrong with that, but *everybody* who had been around for a few years thought they were the next big thing.

Every WWF show was the same. Mondo and I would stand in awe of the superstars, only to be told, *"We don't need anybody tonight."* That was okay by me because I was nowhere near ready for the WWF. It was all pretty intimidating. I had caught on quickly, but I was still learning how to bump and hit the ropes. The most humiliating trip to the WWF was when Chief Jay Strongbow, who was the agent, told us, *"You guys aren't much to look at, but if you brought your trunks, you can put my boy over."* That was the first taste of *"Fuck you, kid"* that I got from wrestling. Strongbow came across as a real asshole. To this day, I can't remember who the kid was that we were asked to put over, but I know he didn't get much of a push. Strongbow could have had a better delivery with his words, or at least feigned some interest, rather than looking down at us and being insulting. I made a mental note to always remember that incident so I would never treat anyone in that manner. I never had a great opinion of Strongbow after that. I ran into him several times over the years and he always came off as a prick, but I made a decision to "act" professionally by saying "hello" and "thank you." Other than that, screw Strongbow.

We didn't get to work that night, but we met Jose Estrada and Jose Luis Rivera, both of whom would play a big part in my life a few years later. That evening, most of the talent there walked past us at one time or another, mostly out of curiosity to see the two 300-pound guys. I had a Mohawk and Mondo was bald with a little ponytail in the back. We looked menacing. We were awful, but we looked menacing. Nobody seemed very cordial or welcoming. Only later did I learn that new guys were always considered a threat to someone's spot, and were treated as such.

I began to get noticed and promoters around the area would ask Johnny for me. I wasn't making big money. In fact, the payoffs on average were only twenty to twenty-five dollars a show, and after driving six hours each way, buying gas and food (and, of course, beer), and taking time off work, I went into the hole for a whole lot of money. All the while, however, I was learning and taking in everything I could from each show.

I never actually worked any WWF shows before I left for overseas tours. I would say that between Mondo and myself, we attended less than a dozen shows, most of which were as a favor to Johnny. If you didn't know any better, we looked like we belonged on the shows, but we stayed in the background and kept quiet. Perhaps we were never given an opportunity because we were too quiet, but it never bothered me. I was just happy to be there and let the guys see me.

During that time, I continued to train with Johnny. I was working almost every night, but I would still get to the gym more than anyone else. I loved it there. No matter how often I wrestled, I always learned something more from Johnny. I got a lot of help from a lot of the guys who worked with me, as well. The guys in the clique at Gleason's were helped and looked after. On the other hand, there were guys we destroyed because they had a bad attitude, or carried themselves in a cocky manner. We were a tight group back then and we treated each other with respect. I later came to the realization that it wasn't me the other guys were helping, but themselves. They knew the harder I worked, the better they looked. Everyone knew I would bump my ass off and give a hundred percent to the match, even if I was only paid gas money, for the opportunity to work and get better. If I tagged with someone, they knew I didn't mind taking the brunt of the bumps.

I had the greatest class of guys training with me, many of whom went on to become big names in the business:

Tommy Dreamer [Thomas Laughlin], who was a big wrestling fan, came in looking like the typical New York stud. Man, he was in shape! Tommy's first match was at a Gleason's Gym show and I was his first opponent. He was going to be presented with the "Rookie of the Year" award that night, so his entire family was there. During the presentation, Mondo and I hit the ring, destroyed the trophy, and put the boots to him. We left the ring pretty quickly because the heat got pretty intense. Tommy's family was pissed for what we did to their boy. I'm not saying they were normally violent people, but that was the first time I ever encountered wrestling fans actually getting angry with me.

It was funny to watch the people who were wearing Big Sweet Williams t-shirts and hats. They hid that stuff fast because Dreamer's family was out for blood. That story is still one of my favorites. Tommy and I talk about that every time we get together. It was a great time because we treated everything as if it was real and we did everything we could to make the people mad (or happy when the situation warranted).

Kid Krush [Peter Senerchia], who would later become known as Tazmaniac, or simply Taz, always knew how to carry himself. He had confidence in everything he did. I have the utmost respect for Pete and I enjoyed the time we spent together through the years.

Vito Joseph LoGrasso, a.k.a. Big Vito, who I helped train, went on to work for all the major promotions: WCW, WWE, ECW, and TNA. When he first came to Gleason's, he had that typical "Hey, yo!" attitude and acted as if his shit didn't stink. He wasn't shy about giving people a resume of things he could do. That was all well and good, but before you were allowed to boast about who you were and what you could do, you had to train with us and go through the same tank of shit we did. I remember Vito's very first workout. We rode him like crazy, taking turns wrestling him and roughing him up. He literally wrestled himself out of his clothes. Well, maybe we had something to do with that. We yanked at his shirt and shorts until we had ripped them to pieces. When he left the gym, he looked half naked. We figured that was the last we'd see of him. Imagine the surprise we got when he walked through the door the next morning and every day after that, ready to train and learn. I'm so happy for the success Vito has had in the business, although it would have been even greater if he had just learned to keep his ego in check and not let his mouth overrun his brain and get him so much heat. Vito is a good guy who I like very much, and to know him is to appreciate him.

Devon Hughes, who later wrestled as D-Von Dudley, now works for TNA as Brother Devon. With his "brother" Bubba Ray Dudley, Devon has etched his name in wrestling history as one of the greatest tag teams of all time.

We all went our own way in this crazy business, but I thought it was funny when most of us wound up working for Vince McMahon in the early 2000s.

During the early part of my career, Johnny took care of my bookings. He would book me on independent [indie] shows for guys like Tommy Ganette, who promoted shows in northeast and upstate New York, Boston, Pennsylvania, and New Jersey. Most of the indie shows featured veterans who had worked for the WWWF during the '50s and '60s and supplemented their cards with guys like me who were hungry and worked cheap. Independent promoters were always glad to use talent from Gleason's because Johnny could guarantee we would be there and do what we were asked to do.

After branching out of Gleason's Gym, I began working for guys like Dennis Galamb in Woodbridge, New Jersey, and Joe Savoldi [Joe Fornini] in Jersey and Pennsylvania.

I was introduced to Dennis Galamb by Ted Petty. Dennis worked hard to produce a quality show and eventually produced a local television show. I loved working for Dennis and his family. They treated me very well, always paid me what they said they would, and kept me as busy as possible and always in the thick of things. I learned a lot during that time just due to the fact that Dennis gave me the opportunity to work on a regular basis. I was featured in some articles in wrestling magazines when I was working Dennis' shows, as well as local newspaper coverage. I also saw my first trading card produced during that time. That was a big deal in those days. Well, maybe it wasn't to anybody else, but it was to me.

(right) Referee Dick Woerle declares Big Sweet Williams the winner of a match in Woodbridge, New Jersey, 1991

On the other hand, working for the Savoldis' International Championship Wrestling [ICW] promotion was a nightmare, but in hindsight, it was a good learning experience.

I began working ICW shows through my friend, Tony Rumble. Tony, who was a great guy and a fan for the business, did everything possible for his friends. He did everything he could to help the young boys in the northeast. If it wasn't for Tony Rumble feeding them talent from his own Century Wrestling Alliance, the Savoldis wouldn't have had half the talent they had. At every show, Tony promoted the "story" for the event which would follow, and he built a company of wrestlers who could tell stories and make the fans buy a ticket for the following week. We were all a bunch of green, independent wrestlers, but Tony treated us like we were full-blown pros.

The ICW promotion used a lot of stars, both past and present, on their shows: Koko B. Ware, Ivan Putski, Jimmy Snuka, Tony Atlas, and "the world famous team" of "Jumpin'" Joe Savoldi and Vic Steamboat (please note the sarcasm), and on one particular night, Tito Santana.

I had the privilege of getting to work with Tito that night and I was excited about the possibility of learning something from him during our match. As anyone can tell you, most dressing rooms were filled with young guys who would talk loudly ninety-five percent of the time, but who learn nothing in the process. I was always more than willing to just sit and listen to the veterans.

When Tito was told he would be working with me, he decided he would bless me with his knowledge and speak to me. When I asked him if there was anything in particular he would like to do during the match, he sized me up and said, *"Do you know how to take an arm drag or a hip toss?"* I was stunned for a moment. I thought he was kidding, but I eventually came to the realization that he was dead serious! It might not have bothered me if we had been having a private discussion, but he did it in the locker room in front of everyone else. In effect, I felt like he was kind of "punking me." My shock quickly turned to anger, although I didn't show it. My reply was, *"Uh ... I've seen it done on TV."* It was total sarcasm, and the expression on my face was like that of a deer in the headlights. All the other boys in the locker room were listening and thought it was hilarious, but Tito was somewhat flustered. He didn't pick up on the sarcasm, and from what he said after that, I could tell he didn't want to work with me.

Tito was very careful not to put himself in harm's way during the early stages of our match. When he realized I did know what I was doing, he relaxed somewhat. I made it a point to see him after our match. I simply held out my hand, said *"thank you for the opportunity,"* and walked away.

I had all the respect in the world for the veteran wrestlers, but that was my first inkling that some of the guys were full of themselves and believed their own press. I was never a fan of Tito Santana after that. In the few times we met during the years which followed, I would do little more than say hello and shake his hand. I don't believe he ever put two and two together, but it's a story I will never forget ... the night Tito Santana "taught me how to work."

The Savoldis did things which would benefit nobody but themselves, like claiming the gate wasn't as good as they would have liked, and they coined the phrase, "the check is in the mail." They were always working some kind of an angle with ticket sales and the "finishes" in matches. They gave me the old line of "give us about 30 promotional photos so we can send them overseas for shows we plan to run." None of that ever happened. I was told they were selling our photos to the fans. I never questioned it because the guys who worked for them were friends of mine and I was happy just having the opportunity to wrestle. It was work, but it wasn't steady and they became difficult to deal with. It was never enough to just go to the building and work. I always felt like they were blowing smoke up my ass just to get me to stay and work for peanuts. I eventually told them to go screw themselves.

One time, when I was offered a tryout with the WWF, the Savoldis called Pat Patterson and told him I was still green and not ready for the "big time." They told him it would be better if I stayed with them so they could get me better prepared, as if I was their "boy" and they were training me. Nothing could have been further from the truth. I worked on their shows, but they taught me nothing.

The last straw was when Tommy Savoldi called my house one night when he was drunk. He began to read me the "riot act," telling how he was this, how he was that, and if I didn't respect him, he would ruin me in the business. Needless to say, his comments didn't go over very well with me. After a few choice words, I hung up the phone and never did business with them again. More lessons learned.

I worked a lot of independent dates, but whenever I went out, I would always come back to Johnny to learn more. Unlike a lot of trainers, Johnny Rodz *never* took a percentage from my payoffs. He might have worked something out with promoters when he booked me out, but if he told me the payoff was 25 dollars, that's exactly what I got. The contract I signed when I first began training simply stated I would pay $3,000 to learn how to wrestle. There were no other stipulations. It was plain and simple ... you pay, you play.

Sometime during the months when I was learning my way around the ring, one of the funny things that happened to me was being presented with the "key to the city" of Paramus. During the time I was coaching recreational league football, I met a lot of great kids and their families. Two of the boys I had the pleasure of coaching were Eddie and Joey Skiba, and their parents treated me like one of their own. The boys' dad, Eddie Skiba, told someone in the city government that I was a full-fledged "pro wrestler," and before I knew it, I received an invitation to receive the "key to the city" and was asked to ride in the Fourth of July parade.

It was funny because I had not yet made a name for myself in the wrestling business, and I certainly was nobody of importance in the town. And yet, all of a sudden, I was riding down Farview Avenue in the same parade my uncle Eddie had marched in for years with the Paramus Police Department, as well as figure skater Elaine Zayak. Now, here I was, wearing my neon pink tights and sporting a Mohawk haircut, and being handed the "key to the city" by the mayor of Paramus. I wasn't sure what to make of it all, and I was scared to death, but I gladly went along with it. I even arm wrestled the mayor at the podium. I don't know how he did it, but after a long "struggle," he "beat" me. The story made the newspapers and it became a big deal (at least for that day). That was when I began to realize that it wasn't that Bill De Mott was of any great importance. It was my Big Sweet Williams persona and the fact that I could "become" someone important that made people stand up and take notice. This would be the beginning of me figuring out that "it isn't who you are, but who others think you are," or at least, who they think you will become. That's not to say I wasn't flattered. I was very proud of the recognition and thankful for those who supported me, but in the big scheme of things, Bill De Mott would never have received the "key to the city."

Everybody in my family was very excited because of the things that kept happening for me. My in-laws could have cared less. They were still of the opinion that wrestling wasn't going to get me anywhere and their daughter deserved better. They never supported me until years later when I was wrestling for World Championship Wrestling [WCW]. Suddenly, now that I was a star on national television, I was "their son-in-law." They wanted pictures and wanted to know all about my travels. They bragged to everyone who would listen about their son-in-law being on television.

I also was with Johnny Rodz when I did my first TV interview on a show called *Good Day, New York*. We wrestled a little, but basically, we stood on the set and tried to look like "tough guys." I was really nervous and I wasn't sure what to do. I never got rid of the nervousness until I went to work for WCW where Arn Anderson and Jimmy Hart told me to *"just be yourself"* and that *"the truth is a lot more entertaining than anything anyone could write for you to say."* Arn was very believable. He was a wordsmith. His interviews were so convincing that he could make the people buy into everything he said. During my career, I probably let a few "damns" or "hells" slip out onto the airwaves, but I was told cursing was the cheap way out because anybody could get on TV and curse. The mark of a professional was someone who could bring the people to the arenas with their words and actions.

In 1990, I went out on my first overseas bookings, so I wasn't destined to remain with Johnny for too long. That year, I met a wrestler named Eddie Mansfield at Gleason's Gym when he came to see Johnny about potential talent for a movie screenplay he had written. Eddie's biggest claim to fame was exposing the secrets behind "blading," the process by which a wrestler gets blood during a match, on the television show *20/20*. That was in the 1980s, a time when most wrestlers would allow their kids to be shot and their wives raped before they would admit to professional wrestling being anything but a legitimate contest. Eddie even demonstrated the method for the cameras by dragging a razor blade across his forehead during the interview.

Eddie's screenplay included two characters named "Bash" and "Crash." He invited me to play the part of "Crash" and I signed a letter of intent. Unfortunately, the movie never came about, but I used the name "Crash the Eliminator" when I was wrestling in Europe as the tag team partner of Ted Petty, who wrestled as the Cheetah Kid. Road Warrior Animal [Joe Laurinaitis] no-showed the European tour, so on the first night of the tour, the promoter promised me a bonus if I would shave my head and wrestle as a Road Warriors type of character. On the first night of the tour, Teddy shaved my head with a moustache trimmer. We worked in Austria, Sweden, Germany, and (if I remember correctly) Switzerland. Afa Anoa'i, the Wild Samoan, was on that tour, along with Tom Brandi, Mike Durham (aka Johnny Grunge), Misty Blue Simmes [Diane Syms], Kat LeRoux, Tiger Jackson [Claude Giroux] and another midget (who stole things), Michael Lane, and the Power Twins [Larry and David Sontag]. I never did get that bonus pay and I made a lot less than I had been promised. However, I was wrestling in another country in front of a lot more people than at Gleason's. I was a fat kid from Jersey who had never been out of the country ... a "nobody." But outside of the United States, I meant something. I felt like a star.

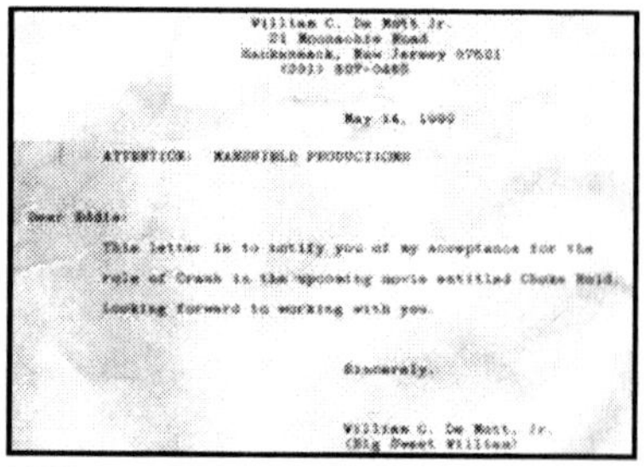
William C. De Mott Jr.
21 Moonachie Road
Hackensack, New Jersey [illegible]
[illegible]

May [illegible]

ATTENTION: MANSFIELD PRODUCTIONS

Dear Eddie:

This letter is to notify you of my acceptance for the role of Crash in the upcoming movie entitled Crash Hold. Looking forward to working with you.

Sincerely,

William C. De Mott, Jr.
(Big Sweet William)

Bill's agreement letter to appear on the movie *Crash Hold.*

A side story about Larry Sontag: he was an All-American football player at East Stroudsburg University, the school I originally planned to attend before deciding on Kutztown. Larry had given me a tour of the school. We would later become roommates when we were both living and wrestling in Puerto Rico. Go figure! It's a small world.

The fans in Europe were brutal. They would always whistle, which was the equivalent of saying "you suck." They didn't have any qualms about letting us know if we were the shits, but they also got behind us if when we were good and believable.

When we arrived home from Europe, Teddy kept me in bookings all over the northeast. I continued to work as "Crash" during the remainder of my independent run, as well as subsequent tours of Puerto Rico, Japan, and Mexico, where the name was often changed to "Crash the Terminator" (Puerto Rico and Japan), or "Crash the Eliminator" (Mexico), depending on who submitted the information for the posters, arena programs, or newspaper articles.

To sum up my early days, I lay the credit for my success in the wrestling business at the feet of Johnny Rodz. I will always tell everyone where I came from, and that it was Johnny who got me to the dance. After all the Internet rumors and stories floating around about my reputation, I'm not sure if Johnny wants to be associated with my training, but I hope I made him proud. I will always remember the "lessons" that were "learned," not "taught," and I will continue to pass them on.

So, thank you, Poppi!

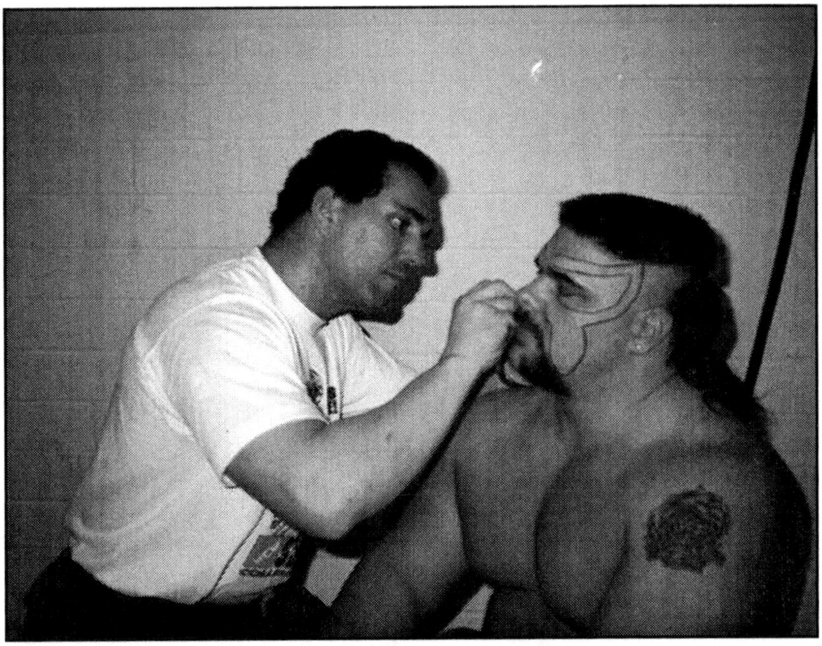

(above) Ted Petty applies makeup to transform Bill De Mott into Crash the Eliminator during their first tour to Europe; (below) Crash the Eliminator

Chapter 4

Dog Meat

In the summer of 1990, a wrestler named Hercules Ayala came to Johnny's school. I had no idea who Ayala was, but Johnny introduced him to Mondo and me. Ayala said he was going to produce several TV shows for a new wrestling promotion in Puerto Rico named All Star Sports, which would run in opposition to Carlos Colon's established World Wrestling Council [WWC] promotion. Ayala said he had seen me working with Black Gordman, who had been a big name in Los Angeles and Texas in the '70s. He was impressed by what he saw and wanted to use Mondo and me in Puerto Rico for two weeks. At the time, I weighed 320 pounds and I was gassed, but I don't know if I had anything more spectacular than any of the other guys, other than the fact that I wanted it ... and I wanted it badly.

We were told we would make $500 a week and we would live in a resort hotel on the beach. I was making more money than that painting parking lots, which was what I was doing at the time, but this was "wrestling." I didn't care if he paid me or not. I've heard guys training today say they want gas money to drive to a town 100 miles away. Bite me! Ask anybody who worked in the business during the '80s and '90s (and long before that). They'll all tell you ... you worked and you got skunked. I went to Europe and came home with no money. I was newly married. My wife said, *"What the hell are you thinking? We can't live like this!"*

But Ayala was going to pay me and I was going to live on a beach? *"Okay. We'll go."* We didn't sign a contract and there was nothing in writing. The deal was set up exclusively on a handshake. In fact, during the more than two years I would work for them, I never signed anything. Mondo, however, threw everyone a curve ball when he went back on his word and went to work for Eddie Mansfield's IWF promotion in Florida. We were supposed to be a team. Things worked out better for me since he didn't go because they used me more as a single. That was the last time I saw or heard from Mondo.

The three-hour flight from Newark International Airport to San Juan, Puerto Rico was an easy one. David and Larry Sontag, the "world famous" Power Twins, were on the flight with me. When we disembarked, we were met by Chicky Starr, who told us the wrestling office had taken care of all the details and had set us up in a great resort hotel with all expenses paid. For the two weeks I was there, I didn't pay for anything. It was fantastic. We had access to great food, booze, and hot Latin women ... and we were going to be "big stars." One of the first things Ayala and Chicky asked when we arrived at the hotel was, *"Where is your partner?"* I didn't have an answer because Mondo hadn't told me he wouldn't be there. All I knew was that he had planned to fly out of New York.

When Mondo didn't show up, Ayala showed me a picture of a wrestler and asked, *"Do you know this guy? Since Mondo won't be coming in, do you think you could get him to come to Puerto Rico?"* It was a picture of me as "Big Sweet Williams." When I told them it was me, they thought I was kidding.

Chicky Starr and Crash the Terminator

Chicky would become my manager. The first thing he did was teach me a phrase in Spanish that I would say on television ... *"Telemundo tu canal siempre."* That's all I was told. A couple of hours later, I appeared on television. Chicky let us get in our "one line" and pushed the idea that we were three big guys who were there to destroy the islanders.

Those two weeks passed by faster than I could believe. Before we left, the Power Twins and I were paid our guarantees and we were asked to continue working for the company for an indefinite period of time.

When I returned to Puerto Rico as a regular talent, I was told I was getting over, although I didn't really understand what that meant (and still don't). What I did know, however, was that I had gone from being listed on the window posters as "And Many Others" to main event status as Crash. I always said I had fat guy's luck. There was never a time in Puerto Rico where I didn't draw or they weren't interested in me. I was always included in the mix. The Twins came back, as well, but they shot themselves in the foot. As time passed, they became big-headed and began telling the office who they would and wouldn't put over. Shortly before the first Christmas break, they were told they wouldn't be returning. I don't remember anyone actually getting fired in Puerto Rico. Talent would leave because they weren't being paid enough, but the Twins figured out a new way of getting off the island.

At first, we were working three times a week, but as business picked up, the company began running four or five times a week. That gave me the experience I needed to pick up on the things I needed to learn. We ran shows in every town that Carlos ran, but we also went to small towns. Some of the trips to the other side of the island were terrible. We drove up and down mountains and through small towns which were located in the middle of nowhere. We really enjoyed going to Bayamón because it was an easy trip. That was the first town where I was billed in the publicity as "many others." When we began drawing good crowds in the smaller venues, Carlos began booking shows there, as well, and business became very competitive. I can't remember the guy who was working in the office for Carlos, but when we ran a show in a baseball park, he climbed up a pole to watch the show and see what kind of a crowd we had drawn. It was funny. Ayala, Chicky, and the boys loved it.

While they were there, I traveled with the Power Twins because we lived together, but most of the time, we rode with a paramedic named Robert. He became our "unofficial" personal chauffeur. He enjoyed taking us to the shows. It made him feel like he was "one of the boys." Ayala allowed him to hang around because that meant nobody else had to go out of their way to pick us up and drive us. I got sick many times riding up and down the mountains in his ambulance, which wasn't air conditioned. I laugh when I think about it now, but at the time, I was miserable.

There were the expected cultural differences between Puerto Rico and the United States, but we didn't have many problems when it came to adapting to the new environment. Since we (Larry, David and I) were the first Americans there for the promotion, we didn't have anyone to help us, so we made a few mistakes. For instance, early on during my first trip over, the three of us (David, Larry and me) went out to find a place on the outskirts of San Juan where we could buy household items like pots and pans. Boy, did we ever wind up on the wrong side of town! The office had warned us that the cops didn't even go into that part of town at night, so we needed to finish our business and be on our way home before dark. Our interviews had already aired by that time, so we already had heat with the people. When we stepped off the bus in a neighborhood, the locals began throwing eggs and rocks at us. I never did very well in school, but I learned quickly that we should ask for information before leaving the vicinity of the hotel.

Crash vs Hercules Ayala

When I returned to the island as a regular, we lived in a condo which was located just ten yards from the beach. Las Gaviotas was the name of the building in Isla Verde, a resort area located about 20 minutes from the airport and down the street from the San Juan Hotel and Resort.

The island had a lot of food choices, but we decided to be frugal (cheap). We lived on chicken, tuna, bologna, cheese, and pasta with chick peas. That was our diet most of the time, but once a week, we would splurge and go to the Sbarro restaurant for pizza. I always looked forward to pizza night. There weren't any restaurants in the smaller towns, so when we made trips to them, we had to eat the food which was cooked by vendors in the street corner huts, which was usually either chicken or pinchos. Occasionally, the meat in the pinchos was dog. That's right. Dog!

During those early days, the company "office" was at the house of a lady named Gloria, who was the money lady behind the project. I don't know for sure where she got her money, but I believe she owned another business.

We were invited to her house a few times and occasionally had to stop by to pick up something or someone on the way to a show. Eventually, the company bought office space in a "strip-mall" type of building where we could tape our promos. The wrestling matches for the TV show were being filmed at the arenas and buildings where we held the house shows.

Gloria took care of the payoffs, which were always in cash, and we were paid every week on time. I've heard the old-timers talk about making "draws" on their pay, but I never had to do that. When I got paid, I budgeted my money so it would last until the next pay day. There were a few times where my pay might have been light for a couple of days, but for most of the time I was there, they also paid my rent and utilities. Guys like Rex King, who were working for the WWC told me they were digging ditches during the day and busing tables in restaurants to make ends meet.

The only problem I had with Gloria was her "boy toy," a guy named Medina. He was an asshole who wanted to be the boss, but the only thing he had going for him was he was "boning" the boss. At best, he was an errand boy. He convinced her that we should pay our own bills. They continued to pay my rent and the water bill, but the rest was split between my roommates and me.

One of the people who worked in the office (and might have been a partner in the company) was Hugo Savinovich, a former wrestler who had been a partner of Carlos Colon. Hugo and I became friends. I enjoyed listening to his thoughts on the wrestling business. He was very passionate about things in which he believed. He also was very good on TV commentary. Many years later, when I went to work for World Wrestling Entertainment [WWE], Hugo was doing the live broadcast commentary in Spanish. Whenever I wrestled, he spoke highly of me. He took care of me while I was on the island and I always considered him to be a straight shooter.

The day-to-day details of the business were handled by Chicky or Ayala. The only part of the matches planned ahead was the finishes, but they were not long and complicated. High spots were called in the ring on the fly and they happened as they happened. I did my promos in English, but every once in awhile, I would learn a phrase in "Spanglish" with which I would insult my opponent. That was funny to me because I took one year of Spanish in school and failed it miserably. I didn't learn anything (and didn't care). Now here I was, years later, in a country where a majority of the people spoke Spanish, and I understood almost nothing of what was going on around me.

I learned a lot during those years because there were a lot of egos on the island. There might have been an occasional squash match on the TV show now and then, but for the most part, everyone on the card meant something at one time or another. There were several guys who had jumped ship from Colon's WWC promotion and they weren't happy about the three big American cats stealing their thunder. They acted friendly to our face, but in the ring, they worked stiff and tried to take liberties with us. I quickly let them know that I wanted to work with everyone, but I wasn't afraid to give receipts when the situation warranted. As a result, I never had a problem with anyone in the ring.

I remember when Steve Strong [Steve DiSalvo] left the WWC promotion and came to work for Ayala. I had never heard of him, but the boys told me he worked stiff. That was when I first learned that comments like those were matters of opinion. I enjoyed working with Steve. He was a punch-and-kick guy who didn't do fancy high spots. We didn't do long, drawn-out finishes, either. We just went at it tooth-and-nail and let the shit fly. Steve and I had several matches and every one of them was very physical. We wanted to make everyone else very leery about getting into the ring with us. That was my first experience in "working the boys," wanting them to wonder about how much of our match was a "work" and how much of it was two monsters not caring about what they did to each other. It was all in good fun, however. I enjoyed the reputation of being a stiff worker, but everyone knew they could trust me and that I wouldn't intentionally hurt anyone ... or at least, anyone who didn't deserve it.

Steve Strong and Crash

For the most part, Steve was a quiet, intelligent guy, but he intimidated the hell out of everyone. He had an imposing, physical look, and slicked-back hair. Even his ring gear and demeanor outside the ring were menacing. But he was so easy to do business with.

Another good talent was Tom Brandi [aka Salvatore Sincere], who I first met back home in the northeast. He was an awesome roommate while we were there together. He also had some great ideas on the business. Tom was the first guy who ever asked me to shave his back! That's right. I said it. I used to shave Tom's back in Puerto Rico. I never knew a guy who could attract more women, and yet, be less interested. It was unbelievable to see the girls flock to him. He would talk for a while and be "cutesiest," and then he would never want to see or talk to them again. He had loads of potential. I remember when he got the call to go to WCW and become Salvatore Sincere.

"Kayfabe" was important then, so we didn't often interact with talent from Carlos Colon's promotion. However, we lived just ten yards from the beach and I saw Frankie "The Thumper" Lancaster and Wendell Cooley all the time, so we occasionally got together to drink a few beers.

For the most part, All Star Wrestling was an easy company to work for, and unlike many promoters, they always asked for input and ideas. I didn't feel like I had been in the business long enough to give my opinion, so I usually sat quietly and learned. Ayala was a cool character. He was laid back and tried very hard to make everyone happy, at least in my dealing with him. He was honest and treated us exactly as he said he would when he hired us.

Puerto Rico was where I got my real education in "heat" and fan reaction. When I worked independent shows at home, the fans would yell "yay" or "boo," but the fans on the island either loved or hated us. If they hated us, they would throw things. The worst heat I had experienced in the States was at an independent show when my Pop was with me. The fans got so mad at "Big Sweet Williams" that they waited after the matches and threw stones at our car. That was when Pop said, *"Holy shit! This is real!"*

That was nothing compared to what took place in Puerto Rico. The fans were constantly drenching us with cups of urine, and it wasn't unusual to get hit in the mouth with batteries. I had trouble with the islanders even when I was away from the arenas. The Power Twins and I had rocks thrown at us, and there were a few times when people tried to flip over our van ... with us in it. I'm not complaining. We considered that to be "good" heat. That changed one night when someone fired a gun at me ... while I was in the ring! I was ready to leave the island, but Chicky Starr talked me out of it. The next night, I got shot at again. Those fans lived and breathed wrestling. To them, it was real. And perhaps it was. It was sure real to me. The last time I checked, I don't remember hearing about anyone shooting a gun at Hulk Hogan.

When I was in the Cayman Islands on an independent tour promoted by S.D. "Special Delivery" Jones and Mr. Haiti, a fan sitting at ringside pulled a knife out of his shoe as I attempted to leave the ring after "cheating." That was scary stuff for a green kid from Paramus, New Jersey.

I originally went to Puerto Rico for two weeks ... and those two weeks morphed into more than two years. I was on the island the entire time, only going home one time for four days ... for the Christmas holidays. Again, I was newly married. The television in Puerto Rico wasn't like what was seen in the States. It was work. We had to work hard to make the people get with us or hate us ... whatever the case was ... so we stayed on the island and put our relationships in the States on hold. I lived and breathed the wrestling business. To me, there was nothing else. Rose, who worked a regular job, came to visit me one time during those three years and flew back home after seven days. I was sending most of my paycheck home, keeping only a minimal amount so I could buy bologna or something to eat, but she had had enough. One day, Rose called and said, *"I'm going home to live with my parents."* It was a wake-up call for me. At the time, I was living with Tom Brandi, David Heath, and Luna Vachon. We had a great time together, and in the ring, I was having the time of my life playing the part of a vicious heel ... but it was time for me to go home.

I never had the opportunity to work territories. I worked for Smoky Mountain Wrestling in 1993, but I never worked the territories the way Arn Anderson or Kevin Sullivan did. Puerto Rico was as close as I was going to get to it, and I understood that, so I made the most of it. I loved it. Puerto Rico, though, destroyed my personal life.

As I said earlier, business always was conducted verbally and with a hand shake. I would later work in Japan and Mexico, but I wouldn't have to sign a contract until years later when I went to work with World Championship Wrestling. I worked in Puerto Rico for almost a year before I ever thought about asking for more money. The one or two times I asked for more money, it was done face to face, and when I left the territory for good, I sat down with Gloria and Chick and I said, *"I'm gonna finish up in two weeks."* I did it the right way ... and they understood. I was really lucky to have been given the opportunity to make my bones in Puerto Rico and I will always be grateful to them for taking a chance on a green, fat kid from Jersey.

Gangrel (David Heath), Luna Vachon and Crash in Puerto Rico

In February 1995, I went back one time for Carlos Colon's promotion. I was worried about that because he was the opposition and I was known. Eddie Gilbert, who was booking for Carlos, called and asked me to come in. In fact, it was the week Eddie died. He said, *"Will you come down for us?"*

I knew Eddie, so I asked, *"How do you think that will work? Do you think I can get the heat I once had?"*

He said, *"You just show up and I can almost guarantee you'll get heat."*

I wasn't sure whether he meant heat from the fans or heat from All Star Sports. I went, anyway, and the heat was there.

Eddie Gilbert died shortly after that. During that time, he was trying to quit drugs cold turkey. He struggled with a lot of things, but when he walked into the dressing room or stepped into the ring, he worked hard as if nothing was wrong. He missed the last show of my tour there. When I walked into my rental house in Jersey, my phone rang. They had found Eddie dead in his apartment. That was sad. I liked Eddie very much. He was one hell of a talent and he had a good mind for the business.

I was in Puerto Rico when I was first introduced to "the blade" and "juice." I wasn't there too long before Chicky Starr approached me about getting "color" [blood]. I hated to look stupid, but I had to be honest. I told him I had no idea about how to do it. From what I had seen of others, I wasn't too anxious to learn that particular lesson, but as with anything I did in wrestling, I took it head on and considered it to be another branch of the "learning process." I was spurred on by stories I had heard about referees doing it for guys who didn't know how to do it, and cutting them from ear to ear in the process. I had also been told the guys would carry blood-filled condoms in their mouths, which they would bite down on during their match to make it look as if they were hemorrhaging. And then there was the story about Eddie Mansfield giving away the "secrets" of the business, including "how to get blood," on the *20/20* television show.

When Chicky said he would do it for me, a big, red flag flew up. If my forehead was going to get cut by a razorblade, I was going to be the one doing the cutting. He showed me how he made his blades and how he taped them to his finger. I remember sitting in my condo on the night before the show, lightly pulling the blade across my forehead to see how it was going to feel. To be honest, blading is one of those things you don't practice or try to get used to. You just do it.

On the night of my "juice debut," I was wrestling Hercules Ayala. We were involved in a good program. On that particular night, I was supposed to take a bump outside the ring, hit my forehead with the blade, and get back into the ring, where Ayala would hit me with brass knucks. Being my first time to get juice, I wanted to make sure I did it right, so I dragged a ditch from one side of my forehead to the other. Man, did I ever get color. I was gushing blood so freely that Ayala kept hitting me with the brass knucks in an attempt to stop the bleeding. I lost a lot of blood, but the fans went home happy, having seen what they came to see. The office wanted me to get stitches, but I had seen how the doctors had botched the job on some of the other guys, so I passed on the idea. I wasn't big on doctors and stitches, so as you can imagine, I never took stitches when I was cut. I did use Super Glue a few times, though.

Getting color was like nothing I had ever done before. I was excited about donating some of my precious blood for the "storyline." Needless to say, my forehead was sore for weeks. I had cut deeply, so it took several weeks for it to scar over. Until then, all it took was a stiff punch to the forehead and off we would go. I wore that wound like a badge of honor. It made me feel like I was finally "one of the boys."

One night, while I was working with Hurricane Castillo, I got my blade in position to get some juice. Just as I placed the tip of the blade on my forehead, he smacked me in the forehead with a board, pushing the blade across my face and close to my eye. It was a scary moment, but I was able to get the color and continue the match without serious injury. When I cleaned up after the match, I saw just how close I had come to cutting my eye. After that, I always made sure I didn't put myself into a position where that could happen.

In a related story, when I was in Japan with the W*ING promotion, there was an ongoing rib with the guys who got drunk. When we would be sitting in a hotel lobby, or on a train, we would suddenly find blood running down our face. After several weeks of this happening to different guys, we began to get spooked. As it turned out, Miguel Pérez Jr. and Ricky Santana would walk around with a bottle top or another sharp object and "gig" the drunk guys. Since alcohol thins the blood, it would flow out quickly and they wouldn't realize it until they felt a warm sensation on their face. It was a funny sight, but it wasn't too humorous if you were the object of the rib.

Victor Quiñones loved to have blood in almost every match, and that was what W*ING became known for, but it lost its appeal when every match had juice. When the other promotions began pushing barbed wire matches, chair shots, and getting color, those things became passé and overdone. When the time is right and the storyline calls for it, there's nothing like "getting color," but there's a time and place for it.

It's no big secret that entertainers and celebrities have a following of special "friends." "Groupie" is the general term for these friends. In wrestling, we called them "arena rats," or "ring rats."

My first experience with "fan appreciation" took place when I was in Puerto Rico. I had a female "friend" there who told me her mother wanted to meet me, but her mother didn't want her there when we met. Apparently, mom wanted to "get to know me." I also was on the island when Luna Vachon, my good friend and roommate, explained to my wife at the time that there is a "50-mile rule" in wrestling. If a wrestler was married, but was more than 50 miles from home, then a blowjob didn't count as cheating. I don't remember my wife's exact words, but they were something along the line of, *"Is she kidding?"* Hey, rules are rules, and they're meant to be followed! Who am I to argue?

When I was working in Japan, I had the honor of having a "fruit girl." A fruit girl is someone who takes it upon themselves to make sure you eat healthy during your travels in the country. I'm not kidding. That's exactly what she did. I had the same girl for the three years I was over there. She was just a fan who showed up in most of the towns. Years later, when I went back to Japan with World Championship Wrestling [WCW], she showed up again. I never really got to know her, mainly because she didn't speak English, but I think she was a bit intimidated by my look and persona. She did, however, have a sister who was … well, let's just say she was a "massage girl." Now her I knew!

When I was in Mexico, I didn't want to know the women. I hated being there, and if I couldn't enjoy the water, why would anyone think I would enjoy a Mexican woman?

When we made tours overseas, I found the women entertaining. It became somewhat of a hobby to see who I could get to come to the hotel with us, and to see how far she would go to "entertain" us. My favorite story would have to be the time Tom Brandi brought some girls to see a sleeping Tiger Jackson [Dink the Clown]. Tiger had a "third leg" that made him a novelty. He had no qualms about showing the women of the world his bar. His stock line was, *"Hey, baby! Wanna see my bar?"* Before they had time to respond, he would whip it out.

By far, the most eye-opening experiences occurred when I was with WCW. By the time I did my first TV in Dalton, Georgia, I was already on the radar of quite a few young ladies (and a few not so young). I had never been exposed to so many upfront women in my life. I never would have received so much "attention" from the ladies if I was towing cars, bouncing, or painting parking lots.

Don't misunderstand me. It wasn't all about sex. I made many lifelong friends who just happened to be women. I spent a lot of time on the road, and it was nice to have friendly faces waiting for me when I arrived in the towns. They were people I could talk to and hang out with. I wanted to surround myself with people whom I could trust and become friends, not just acquaintances who were only interested in the moment.

The bottom line is this: Attention does not always equal Affection.

(above) Bill on the beach in Puerto Rico; (below) Crash the Terminator

Chapter 5

Urinal Balls

While I was working for All Star Sports, I met a promoter named Victor Quiñones. At one time, along with Carlos Colon, Victor Jovica, and Abdullah the Butcher, Quiñones owned shares in the WWC promotion in Puerto Rico. In 1991, when the company was hemorrhaging money, he left the company. Later that year, along with Kiyoshi "Mickey" Ibaragi, Victor formed a new wrestling promotion in Japan called Wrestling International New Generation [W*ING].

I didn't meet Victor by chance. Ricky Santana was working for Carlos Colon while I was still with All Star Sports. While I was talking with Ricky, he mentioned that Victor was looking for guys who wanted to work in Japan and had shown some interest in bringing me over. Puerto Rico was the first company I worked for outside of the States and I wanted more, so I told him I was very interested. I didn't know either Ricky or Quiñones, but Ted Petty told me it would be a place where I could get more experience. If nothing else, I could go one time to see how they treated me.

When I asked Ricky what they required from me, he said they needed a copy of my passport before I left for the States because they needed me later that week. As I flew home from Puerto Rico, I thought, *"Oh, God! If I tell Rose I'm going to Japan, she's gonna leave me. But I've gotta go."*

Two days after I walked into my house, I left for Japan. To my surprise, Rose didn't act upset over the fact that I was leaving again. My guarantee was more than I had been getting in Puerto Rico and it was just a two-week gig (or so I thought), so for the time being, her threat to move back with her parents was just that … a threat.

I had flown to both Germany and Puerto Rico, but the flight to Japan was horrendous, taking more than thirteen hours. I couldn't sit still that long. I drank everything I could get my hands on, mostly due to the encouragement of Ricky Santana and Miguel Pérez Jr. They kept putting drinks into my hands until I was snockered. Halfway through the flight, I dozed off and didn't wake up until everybody was getting off the plane. During the flight, Ricky and Miguel had filled my head with the notion that it was disrespectful to appear in public without my face paint. They said it was very important that we be in character at all times, so when we landed, and I didn't have on my face paint, I thought, *"Oh, no. I'm fired my first day."* What I didn't realize was that Ricky and Miguel had been screwing with me. You never traveled in your paint unless you were an idiot, but I was so worried about screwing up my deal that I instantly sobered up. It was a good rib.

I was greeted at the airport by someone who worked for the office and he drove me to the hotel. After being on the plane for such a long time, I wasn't too enthused about the drive, but it was nice to know the office had sent someone to pick me up. At the hotel, I hung out in the lobby with the guys, but since I didn't really know any of them, I kept to myself.

My first appearance for W*ING was on September 18, 1992. I wrestled a young Japanese boy named Masaru Toi. I don't remember what we did in the match, but I do remember Toi being pissed about having to put over "the new guy." Fortunately, I remembered conversations I had with Japanese wrestlers in Puerto Rico. They told me the Japanese boys would work stiff and hit hard in order to determine what kind of heart you had. I went to the ring that night intent on sending a message: Crash the Terminator isn't a guy you can mess with!

The office put me in matches with young Japanese boys who were machines and I spent the whole tour fighting for whatever I wanted to get. I didn't give any quarter, but in the back of my mind, there was the niggling, *"I don't know about this."* By the end of the tour, I put my own twist to the Golden Rule: Do unto others before they do unto you.

Mickey Ibaragi was the boss, but as far as I could tell, even though he was the majority owner, he was just a figurehead for the company. I believe he made occasional decisions on the style of the matches, or a finish now and then, but Victor Quiñones was the "go-to guy" who ran the day-to-day operations of the company. Victor was a merchandising genius, but he had his hands in everything. He booked the talent, made the travel arrangements, and scheduled the TV programs. Victor also was the person who booked me, so he was the guy I answered to. I worked for him for almost three years, and in all that time, I never had to buy a plane ticket or pay for a hotel room. Whenever I traveled by bullet train or subway, they would always reimburse me. I was very well taken care of while I was there.

As was the case in Puerto Rico, I never signed a contract while working in Japan and we did business on a handshake basis. The only time I had to sign anything was when I applied for my work visas. I wasn't interested in paperwork and I took people at their word. They knew they could trust me, as well. I liked doing business like that. The only thing I had to sign for was my payoff at the end of each tour. Ibaragi and Victor guaranteed me $1,000 a week (American money) for the first tour and they gave me a bonus, as well. During the next three years, there was never a time when I didn't get whatever I had been guaranteed plus a bonus. They did good business and they were honorable men who lived by their word. On subsequent tours, my pay increased to $1,500 a week. Again, that was supplemented by bonuses and gifts (money) from sponsors and Ibaragi.

If I needed to make a "draw" during a tour, I would get it at the very beginning and make it last until the end. They made us sign for the every draw because there were always a few who "forgot" what they had taken and claimed they didn't draw the amount recorded. A lot of the guys were workers twenty-four

Bill with Ryo Miyake from the W*ING promotion

hours a day! When I left for the airport at the end of a tour, I was almost always paid personally by Ibaragi, who handled the money. Ibaragi never failed to thank me for working for them. The two of us had some good discussions about the business and he never failed to ask about my family. I really liked him. When Casey (my first daughter) was born, they sent hundreds of dollars and gifts to my wife.

Victor also was very good to me. He made sure I was always booked. We had a good business relationship and, while I know a lot of guys had problems with him and he had issues with other people, Victor stayed true to his word in everything he promised. Thanks to Victor for using me as well as he did, a lot of doors were open to me when I left Japan, so I owe him a lot.

Victor was a "mover and shaker." In other words, he made his money on merchandise, bringing things from Mexico to well in Japan, and vice versa. I only went to the office a couple of times during my time with the company, but it wasn't very big. From what I can remember, it seemed to be more of a storage room for merchandise than a place of business. Victor made sure that everything we did was taped for a possible sale on DVD. I had several really good matches that never made the DVDs, and yet, other matches that I thought really sucked, did make it. Victor was compensated well for the talent he represented and he did good business for himself and the guys he took under his wing (no pun intended).

In the early days, I remember hearing guys say, *"Oh, W*ING is a gimmick promotion. It'll never last."* Well, when W*ING folded, Victor created the International Wrestling Association [IWA] and he had another good run. You can't knock Victor's promotional skill. If it hadn't been for promotions like FMW [Frontier Martial-Arts Wrestling] and W*ING, or IWA, there never would have been an ECW [Extreme Championship Wrestling].

I was sad to hear when Victor passed away on April 1, 2006. He was only 46 years old.

I was never worried about how I would adapt to life in Japan, but during the first few tours, I was definitely treading lightly. I've heard people say that "you either love Japan or you hate it." I loved Japan! I looked forward to every trip and it didn't take me long to fit in with company and the country.

The tours were of different lengths of time. Some were short, maybe eight days, but the average was four weeks. For the first few months, I went home after every tour and worked independent shots during the interim. When I began wrestling in Mexico, though, I would leave Japan at the end of a tour and go directly to Mexico for several weeks. When the Mexico tour was over, I would go home to the States to see the family for a few days (maybe a week), but I was never home for long. As a rule, if I had less than five days between tours, I would stay in Japan (or Mexico) before returning for the next tour.

I never learned to enjoy the plane flights to Japan. My consumption of alcohol, which began in the Crown Room at the airport, moved to a whole new level. As the weeks went by, I knew how much booze (or pills) I needed before I got onto the plane that would allow me to sleep through the entire flight. My goal was always to wake up when the plane was landing. It was a science project of sorts.

We traveled to the towns by bus. During my first few trips, when we stopped to eat, I would order soup, or the old standby, ice cream. I didn't want to spend too much money, especially knowing that when we arrived at the arenas, the office would provide us with a bento box, which was a box lunch consisting of rice, chicken or fish, and vegetables. When I realized there were McDonald's and KFC franchises in Japan, I thought I had hit paydirt. As I became acclimated to the Japanese culture, and learned a few phrases to use in restaurants, I began to try the native cuisine. Of course, at two o'clock in the morning, when I had completed a heavy night of drinking, good ol' Mac was always an option. They were always open late. To be honest, by the time I went to Japan, there weren't many differences between food choices in America and those in Japan, but I did learn to enjoy authentic Japanese dishes.

Ricky Santana and Miguel Pérez took me under their wing (so to speak) and made me feel at home in my new surroundings, but at the same time, they screwed with me to see where my head was, but I never did crack.

I later became close to Mike Kirchner, Doug Gilbert, and Tracy Smothers. Mike Kirchner wrestled as Leatherface, a takeoff on the character from the 1974 movie *The Texas Chainsaw Massacre*. He brought a chainsaw to the ring. That was scary because he didn't remove the blade. I love Mike, but he was a gimmick as Leatherface, much as he was when he wrestled as Corporal Kirchner. As Crash the Terminator, I had a gimmick, as well, but I always retained my roots as a wrestler. Whenever I thought Crash was pushing the envelope, I would bring my matches back down to meat and potatoes and grabbed the interest of the people again.

Mike spent about six months in jail over an incident that took place in Japan. One of the wrestlers, Mike "Canadian Tiger" Lozanski, pinched the ass of a Japanese girl, but her boyfriend thought it was Kirchner, so he got in his face.

Lozanski melted into the background and let him take the rap. When the guy put his hands on Kirchner, he laid him out with one punch to the face. The guy was a businessman and had money, so he decided to make an example of Kirchner to show the American wrestlers [gaijins] they couldn't do things like that. That was one of the few times when I had a disagreement with the office. They didn't fight it and let Kirchner serve his time. Mike and I talked a few times after that, but I never saw him again. Our paths took us in different directions. I remember him telling me about his terrible divorce from what he called a "filthy animal" and that he sold his house for a dollar. He made sure he gave his wife her full share — fifty cents.

I learned early on that most of the Japanese boys could speak and understand enough English to know what I was saying, especially when it came to calling spots in the ring. It was funny to watch them around other gaijins (foreign wrestlers), acting like they didn't understand what they were saying ... until they wanted to do something they needed someone to comprehend. That scenario repeated itself in Mexico, too, so it was twice as entertaining when the Mexicans came to Japan. They tried to "work over" the Japanese boys, and the roles were reversed when the Japanese went to Mexico. I worked hard to learn enough of the Japanese language so they couldn't mess with me. I bought a few books and asked some of the young guys to teach me. I had decided that since I was going to stay in Japan as long as I could, I was going to learn about the country and their language. To this day, I use some Japanese around the house and when I'm training young talent, but I'm really out of practice.

There were a few times when I had to let the Japanese boys know I wasn't as stupid as they thought. When I realized they were talking about me, I would bide my time until I could "smarten them up" in the ring where we all spoke the same language ... although some of us spoke more loudly than others. I realized the same things held true in most other countries. Everybody thinks foreigners are stupid until they're answered in their own language. I had always been of the mind that people who come to this country should learn to speak English, so I didn't think I should be any different when it came to learning to speak Japanese or Spanish. Besides, I had to eat, get drunk, and find places to go, so it was important for me to learn the language.

For the most part, the finishes for our matches were handled by the boys themselves, except for the top matches when a specific finish was necessary to continue a storyline or program. When there was a problem communicated a finish due to language barriers, referee Wally Yamaguchi would step in to translate and explain salient points. Those communication problems were what really made me aware of how lucky I was to have been given quality training by Johnny Rodz. I didn't have to rely on a series of choreographed spots which had been discussed beforehand. I could go to the ring with confidence and take things as they came.

Most of the guys would give their opinions or ideas on the direction a match should go, but given the nature of the wrestling business in which the guys have big egos, some of them thought they knew what was best for everyone ... and that usually translated into what was best for "them." Ego and self-direction was nothing new in the wrestling business, but when the hard-core style of wrestling became popular, everybody began to think they were match experts. The truth was, in most hard core matches, all they did was hit their opponents and refuse to sell. Every character became the "strongest in the company" and someone was always trying to shut someone up.

In the ring itself, the specifics of a match were kept simple and basic: "Clothesline … duck." If a specific sequence of events was expected to take place, the two (or four) competitors would spend time together discussing it in the dressing room. As a rule, though, our matches were created "on the fly" and "in the ring." The result of that spontaneity, however, often forced you to enforce your will on your opponent. You had to let them know you weren't a pussy and that you were willing to fight for position in the ring and the right to do your spots.

One of the things that struck me as very strange was that the Japanese wrestling fans sat very quietly during a match … until something big happened, like a powerful or acrobatic move. When it did, they popped big and went nuts. As a result, I spent a lot of time trying to figure out what it was that elicited the big oohs and ahhs. It was one hell of a rush to hear an entire arena chanting, *"Terminator! Terminator! Terminator!"* They wouldn't put over just anything. They wanted the true "cowboys" and "Indians" mentality. Whenever we would kick out or make a big comeback, they would get with us. We always knew when we were getting over because, when we did, our pictures would appear in the newspapers and magazines.

As they did in All Japan Pro Wrestling and New Japan Pro Wrestling, the wrestlers traveled from town to town on a bus, but unlike the "Big Two," we all traveled on one bus (most of the time) and closed the curtains when we got

Crash the Terminator and Tarzan Goto

close to town. When we worked at Korakuen Hall, we would ride the train because it was cheap and easy to access. When we weren't on the road, I lived in Ikebukuro, the commercial and entertainment district of Tokyo. The train and subway stations were located at the center of Ikebukuro.

I think my favorite memory of any of the titles I held during my career was that of the W*ING tag team title. Perhaps I felt that way because it was my first title. For the most part, though, I didn't get off on holding titles. I was more interested in just being part of a storyline. Titles never made me more money or got me anything I didn't already have. It did feel good to realize that someone in the office thought I was worthy of representing the company as a champion. Mr. Pogo and I won the straps from the Headhunters in Sapporo on November 6, 1992. When it came time to drop the belts, I had to do it with another partner. Pogo had a bit of an ego and thought he walked on water, and yet, I never knew a guy who was in such bad physical shape as he was. He was over, though, and I got the rub from him when we became the tag team champions. Pogo didn't feel like he was as "over" as a tag team champion, though, and he didn't like sharing the spotlight, so he talked the office into sending him in another direction, leaving me with both belts. Four months after Pogo and I won the title, they put me with Mitsuhiro Matsunaga and we dropped the belts to Freddie Kreuger [Doug Gilbert] and Leatherface [Mike Kirchner] in Hakata on March 30, 1993.

One night, when Kevin Sullivan, Mike Kirchner, Jimmy Delray, Doug Gilbert, Steve Collins, and I were out wandering around Japan looking for something to eat, we came across a "soup house." We weren't as interested in the soup as we were the beer. Just after Sullivan left the table to get his first round of beer, Jimmy came out of the bathroom with a "urinal ball," one of the deodorizer blocks found in urinals, and plopped it into Kevin's soup. We were laughing hysterically, but didn't give it up to Kevin when he came back. Kevin sat down, took a spoon full of soup … and wouldn't you know it? The "piss ball" was on his spoon! We thought the rib was over before it began, but without looking, he opened wide and sucked it right off the spoon. He realized immediately that he had taken in something he shouldn't have and spit it out. We fell out of our chairs and rolled on the floor with laughter. Huge tears were coming out of our eyes. Kevin screamed, *"How the fuck do I tell my wife I got Aids from eating a piss ball?* His wife at the time was Nancy, who later became Nancy Benoit.

What we all forgot was that Kevin was the devil incarnate. We continued to party at the hotel and let our guards down as we drank ourselves into stupors. Everyone, that is, except Kevin. The next morning, we all woke up with no eyebrows, mustaches on just one side of our faces, and beards on the other side. Poor Jimmy got the worst treatment of all. Kevin had shaved him from head to toe … and there was a "huge" pile of red hair at the foot of his bed. That night, we were supposed to appear on the biggest show of the tour, and we looked like we had escaped from an insane asylum. Needless to say, Ibaragi (the boss) was hot! On the biggest day of the tour, when magazine and newspaper photographers were at the arena in droves, we showed up looking like mongrels.

July 7, 1993 is a date which will remain etched in my memory until the day I die. That was the day I missed the birth of my first child.

Mike Kirschner, unknown man, Jimmy Del Ray, Crash the Terminator, and Kevin Sullilvan (note the lack of eyebrows)

Five days earlier, I left the States for another tour of Japan. Casey (my daughter) wasn't expected to arrive until September of that year, so that was to be my last tour until after she was born. I wrestled that week in Sushima [July 4] and Ichihara [July 6]. The next day, my mom called to tell me Casey had been delivered by C-section. My wife had fallen down and the trauma induced labor. There were four days remaining on the tour. When I told the office about it, they tried to get me out on a flight. When they were unable to make the connection, they said, *"We can get you home tomorrow … or you can wait."* That was typical of wrestling promoters. There was always that little, subtle, *"Or you can wait."* That was one of the unspoken rules of the business: you never left a tour … even for family. Being the "wrestler" I was/am, I finished the tour before returning home.

I walked into Hackensack Hospital to find my baby daughter in an incubator. She weighed less than four pounds and had feeding tubes in her. She was healthy, but she was too premature to eat. I spent the next ten days waiting for the doctors to tell me we could take her home. While there, I bought Casey a stuffed bear with a music box inside which the doctor allowed me to put in her bed. That bear was bigger than Casey. From that day on, we called her "Bear."

Casey is seventeen years old now. She will never fully know how much she means to me. We have a special bond and I'm proud of what she has achieved in life so far. I admire her for her compassionate heart. Casey never asks for anything for herself and is always concerned for others. She is sweet, sensitive and beautiful. And, yes, even if she wasn't my daughter, I would say that. We are very proud of Casey and everything she does. I feel sorry for the poor bastard who tries to "get over" on her. Having grown up around me and the "boys," she can smell bullshit a mile away.

When Keri, my second daughter, was born, I made sure I was home when it happened. Since then, Casey has taken every opportunity to remind me (usually when we're in big crowds of people), *"Hey, remember the time when you were in Japan and I was born?"*

"Shut up."

It's a good (and deserved) needle. I hope my story helps the young guys of today realize that being on the road could cause them to miss important events at home … events which can never be recaptured. On the other hand, you have to understand that wrestling waits for nothing and nobody. You must have a strong commitment and love for the business and be willing to sacrifice those times with your family. If you don't, someone else *will.* Wrestling stops for no one and nothing at any level of the game.

I enjoyed my time in Japan. At times, the travel wore on us, but the work was good. I've often said, you either love it there or you hate it. I loved it and would go back anytime.

Chapter 6

Batteries and Pesos

During my time with W*ING, I made trips back and forth to Mexico. Those were the worst experiences of my life. I HATED Mexico. I was wrestling five nights a week and making decent money (better than the guys who actually lived there), so I went back whenever Quiñones booked me out, but every time my flight landed in Mexico City, I could think of nothing more than wishing I was somewhere else.

One of the major complaints I have about Mexico was that I lived in a seedy part of town. The first night I was there, I was worn out from the long flight from Japan, and all I wanted to do was lay down my head. I popped a handful of Valium and, without even taking off my clothes, I laid down on the bed and went right to sleep. Minutes later, a loud commotion sounded directly below my window. When I looked out, I saw an army marching down the street. They wore fatigues, carried rifles and guns, and marched in lockstep. I couldn't believe what I was seeing. I went downstairs to ask what was going on and was told, *"Oh, they're patrolling the area."*

I had heard so many daunting stories about the food and water in Mexico that I was afraid to eat or drink anything the next day. As in all wrestling companies, I was the new guy, so the boys all got together and said, *"Let's rib the gringo."* One of the guys walked up and, with concern in his voice, told me that under no circumstances was I to drink the water. He then handed me a bottle of Hi-C, which I took gratefully and guzzled immediately.

They made the Hi-C with their water. Of course, it goes without saying that I got the shits. Every time I went to Mexico, I lost 35 pounds and returned to Japan looking like hell.

I also was the only "gringo" on the tour. That was common practice. A second American might show up at the end of the loop, but most of the time, I was by myself. All the other tour guys were booked together, or at least had one other guy with them. My one saving grace was one of the boys, a guy named Ray Richards, who was one of the regulars for the company. He was a Mexican worker, but he was given the task of getting me from show to show. He was a good guy who went out of his way to be sure I was comfortable and taken care of. He would pick me up every day and drive me to the towns in his van. The greatest thing Ray did for me was to take me into the town square one night. He introduced me to a man who cooked and served food out of the back of his car. If that happened in the States (or anywhere else for that matter), I would say, *"There's no friggin' way I'm gonna eat this,"* but believe it or not, it was the best meal I ever had in Mexico. I'll never forget the experience of eating barbequed (not sure what and don't really want to know) out of the back of an old Toyota.

As much as I hated Mexico, the work there was the best. For my first match, I was told to go out and do fifteen minutes, which I did. I worked hard and put everything I had into that match. By the time I got back to the dressing room, I was breathing heavily. When I sat down to take off my boots, Miguel Pérez walked up and asked, *"What are you doing?"*

"I'm gonna change clothes."

"We work two-out-of-three-fall matches here."

I had to go back out and do two more fifteen-minute falls. That had never been explained to me. Once again, earn as you learn. Miguel Pérez had a way of teaching me things like that. He liked to have his fun with me.

I wrestled for forty-five minutes every night, but how could I complain? There were local guys there who were making the equivalent of ten or fifteen dollars a night. I was making $1,000 a week. Who was Bill De Mott to make a thousand bucks a week? I was just in the right place at the right time and I drew well for them.

The wrestling fans in Mexico were almost as bad as those in Puerto Rico. In some ways, they might have been worse. They hated "gringos" and anyone else who would come into their arenas to beat their heroes. I don't recall which arenas we were in, but I worked a double shot against Vampiro [Ian Richard Hodgkinson], who was getting his first big push. He said he didn't know much, but if I would beat him around the arena, the women would get worked up. So, I did just that. We weren't ten feet away from the ring when those crazy Mexican women began smacking the hell out of me and ripping my hair out at the roots. Vampiro was grinning the whole time, so I'm pretty sure he had known that would happen. Needless to say, I pulled him right

Scorpio Jr., Crash the Eliminator and Dr. Wagner Jr. in Mexico

back to the ring, where he beat me with a clothesline off the top rope. When the referee made the three-count, the women went crazy. They loved him.

Many nights, the fans threw cups of piss on me as I walked down the aisle. When I got into the ring, they threw batteries and pesos. Some of those pesos hit so hard it left the imprint of the coin in my skin. Don't get me wrong. I'm not complaining. That was "good heat."

I also worked under a mask a few times during my time in Mexico. The reason I did was so the promoters could sell masks designed with the face-paint patterns I wore. That didn't last long because I wasn't a big fan of the "hood."

I spent a lot of time in Mexico and went there after every Japan tour. The only person I dealt with there was Senor Minus. I couldn't even make a guess as to who owned the company or made the decisions about matches and programs. My business arrangements were all taken care of by Victor Quiñones and I never had to worry about anything. I didn't even have to get a visa or working papers. I went as a tourist. Victor said, *"Don't worry about it. Just walk in like you belong there."*

I had a good run in Mexico ... until I ran into "the biggest asshole in the world:"

Mil Mascaras.

Don't get me wrong. Mascaras is a legend and I respect that. There are a lot of people who sing his praises, but I had a chance to work with a legend and he pissed in my coffee.

One day, Senor Minus booked me to wrestle "The Great Mil Mascaras" on an afternoon show. At the time, that's how I thought of him. I thought, *"Holy shit! What a great opportunity."* I had to ride on a bus for hours to a place in the middle of nowhere called Aguascalientes, but I had a plane ticket to return to Mexico City because I had a double shot that day. That was kind of cool because most guys didn't get that.

When I got to the arena, I went directly to the dressing room to change clothes. Mascaras took a shower before his match, and as he walked out (wearing his mask), I stood up and tried to introduce myself (emphasis on the "tried"). He had nothing to say to me and came across as an arrogant ass.

When we met in the center of the ring for our instructions from the referee, Mascaras said, *"I am the big man here, Amigo. I will do all the big moves."*

Wrong!

I wasn't having any of that. At the time, I was working three shots a day with Vampiro, and that kid was really over in Mexico. The first time I wrestled Vampiro, he said, *"For the finish, I'd like to jump over the top rope and give you a clothesline."*

"Okay ... and what are we gonna do for the first twenty minutes?

He said, *"Do you wanna beat me up?"*

I said, *"Done."*

That was how things would go with Vampiro, and he was a major star in Mexico. When we got back to the dressing room after our first match together, he thanked me and asked if we could work together again, but with Mil

Mascaras, on a show which was more than 300 miles away from Mexico City, he wanted to beat me and give me nothing. I didn't say anything. I figured I would give him what he wanted and get in what I could. I was halfway correct. I took bumps and flew around the ring for him, but that old man wouldn't put over *anything* I did and blocked everything I tried to do. He paraphrased what he had told me earlier. *"I am the strong man here, Amigo. I will not sell for you."*

Wrong again!

All my thoughts about respect for the "legend" left my mind. *"Fuck you,"* I thought, and I began doing what I wanted. I gave him a beating. I'm not talking about beating him in the working sense. I physically beat him down. He was putting over stuff that he never would have put over. Even though it was bad business, I was pissed that the guy had no respect for me whatsoever. I knew he didn't dare leave the ring until we went to the finish and he got his hand raised. He would have looked like a pussy if he had walked out while I was beating him, so he was forced to endure it. I beat on him and no-sold his weak, goofy-looking stuff for more than five minutes before I let him do his thing and beat me.

When I got back to the dressing room, almost everybody else was gone and my plane ticket was missing. Someone had taken it from my bag. The promoter of the town said, *"You beat up a legend. You wouldn't give him his due."* I was stranded in a one-chicken town in the middle of nowhere, I knew nobody there, and I had no idea about how to get back to Mexico City. Blue Demon Jr. saw how pitiful I looked and helped me by getting me a seat on a "goat bus." I'm not lying. It was a goat bus! If I hadn't been wide awake, I would have thought I was acting with Dan Aykroyd and Chevy Chase in a scene from the 1985 movie *Spies Like Us*. It was like a traveling petting zoo. Goats and chickens walked up and down the aisle, feathers were everywhere, the seat covers were ripped to shreds, and it was as hot as hell. Needless to say, the odor alone made me nauseous.

It took almost eight hours to get back to Mexico City. I was very thankful for Demon's help, but all I could think about was that I hated Mexico even more than I did before, and how Mil Mascaras, the so-called "legend," was an arrogant piece of shit.

When it came to finishes, I don't remember having problems with anyone else while I was there. Most of the time, when the time came to decide who would go over, we took turns. Winning or losing was *never* important to me. In fact, I made a career out of getting other people over. But there is a difference between "losing" to make someone look good and looking inept or weak by someone who thinks he's better than everyone else.

Other than the incident with Mascaras, Mexico was a great learning experience. I was never one to collect things, but on more than one occasion, the towns were papered with life-sized posters of "Crash the Eliminator." I thought that was the coolest thing in the world to see my image plastered all over walls and buildings. I asked for a few and I'm having one framed as I write this. It might be one of the few times I "popped" for myself. (I know, I know)

I loved the Mexican style of wrestling. I picked it up and became good at it ... but I've been there and I've done that. I will never, ever go back. Years later, I worked for both the World Wrestling Federation [WWF] and World Championship Wrestling [WCW]. If they had booked me in Mexico, I would have called in sick that day. If someone asked me today, *"Would you go back for one week of big shows and a big payoff?"* Hell, no! If the famous Aztec emperor Montezuma himself rose out of the grave and offered to paddle me across the Rio Grande in a canoe, I wouldn't go.

In September 1993, Eddie Gilbert called and asked if Miguel Pérez, the Headhunters, and I would like to work in Philadelphia for Eastern Championship Wrestling [ECW]. Eddie's brother, Doug, was a permanent fixture with W*ING at the time as Freddie Kreuger. He acted as the middle man between Eddie and me. Eddie said, *"We'll fly you into Philadelphia and pay your hotel expenses."* Philadelphia was smack dab in the middle of my backyard, so it didn't take much thought for me to agree. Miguel had his own personal reasons for going. He wanted to get booked by the WWF and thought it might be an opportunity to talk to someone in Connecticut. Miguel could really work. His problem was that he just wouldn't conform. He wouldn't shave his body, get into better shape, or do things the way the bosses wanted. He just wouldn't play the games by their rules. The WWF didn't use him then, but in June 1997, he and Juan Rivera would go to work for them as *Los Boricuas.*

The ECW show, which was called *UltraClash*, took place on September 18, 1993, during the time before Eastern Championship Wrestling was renamed Extreme Championship Wrestling. When I asked Eddie if he would let us do something Japanese style, he was all for it. We decided to do a barbed-wire baseball-bat match, the first of its kind to be held in the ECW Arena, with Miguel and me against the Headhunters. We had done that gimmick in Japan many times.

When we got there, we were told the person in charge of bringing the barbed wire had forgotten it, so we asked one of the "girls" who "helped" the boys to go get it. The boys watching in the back couldn't believe what they were seeing as we wrapped the barbed wire around the bat. During our match, the four of us beat each other all over the building and we got four-way juice. For fat guys, the Headhunters were good workers. They could do some agile stuff. The rest of their stuff sucked, but it was amazing to watch 400-plus pounds guys do things like moonsaults and diving leg drops.

I remember being outside the ring with one of the Headhunters and knocking him through a wall. As he fell, he knocked Abdullah the Butcher off his chair and onto his ass. That was cool to see. Where else but ECW could someone like me get away with knocking Abdullah on his ass and have him look up at me with a smile on his face? The people in the audience had never seen anything like that. They were on their feet.

After the match, Axl Rotten came over and asked me if I could show him how we used the barbed wire. In the years to come, he put barbed wire to good use, using it with all kinds of gimmicks, including baseball bats and chairs.

The coolest part about the whole thing was that my friends from Jersey were all there. I remember thinking, *"The fat kid from Jersey is back! Hey, here's what I've been doing for three years."*

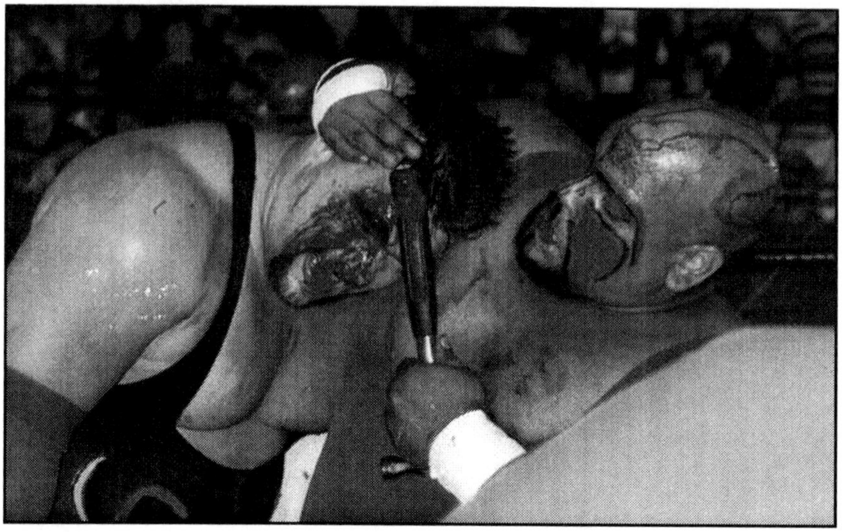

Headhunter works over a bloody Bill De Mott, Philadelphia September 18, 1993

I knew Paul E before I ever got into the business. I was a big kid and I knew a few of the wrestlers, so when I went to Meadowlands Arena, he let me hang around. I would act as a bodyguard for his girlfriend at the shows. For some reason, though, Paul E and I just never clicked when it came to business. There was some heat in 1994 when Paul used me a few times. Early that year, he brought in a guy named Al Poling, who wrestled under the name "911." I was supposed to be "911," but before that time, Paul had asked me if I would forgo a tour with W*ING and stay home so he could use me on a combined show they were going to do with Jim Crockett's World Championship Wrestling [WCW] promotion. I told him I would happy to stay if he thought it was a solid deal. I had a baby and one on the way, so I thought it would be a good way to make a payday and stay at home. I had never done much at home other than the independents, and working on a high-profile show with WCW would give me some good exposure to audiences in the States. The ECW/WCW combined effort never happened. For whatever reason — some say I had my head shaved for a Japanese tour, others say I didn't show up for a booking — Paul decided to quit using me. *"You shaved your head for Japan when you should have stayed home,"* he said. As a result, Big Al [Poling] became 911. Paul E did use me later as Mikey Whipwreck's bodyguard. I dressed in all black and I wore a mask. It was supposed to lead to something, but it didn't. I was told that when the blowoff came, Reggie Bennett would be under the hood. Paul E and I always had a tentative business relationship, but nothing ever panned out. I lost a lot of money waiting around for him to find a spot for me. By the time things really began to roll for him, I was no longer working for W*ING and I was under contract to WCW. Ted Petty later told me that Paul was telling people he was going to teach me a lesson. That "lesson" came in the form of a payoff in an envelope ... for twenty-five dollars.

Paul and I couldn't get it together for ECW, but we get along well today. We worked together on many occasions in the WWF/WWE and we are friends.

Chapter 7

The Man of Question

For most of 1995, I was living at home in Elmwood Park. During that time, on January 9 to be specific, my second daughter, Keri, was born. Casey was the "Bear," but Keri was immediately named the "Beef" because she was so much bigger than Casey was when she was born. Keri was delivered by C-section, and this time, I was there! I made sure I was home before the due date and took off two months afterwards to stay at home with my daughters.

It was nice to come home and have people walk up and tell me what I did overseas. They would show me magazine articles: *"There you are in Tokyo."* I'm still dumbfounded by the things fans show and tell me. *"Remember when you did this with so-and-so?"*

One Sunday night, my good friend Adrian Byrd (one of the guys I trained with at Johnny's school) was visiting. I was telling him about my plans and how I wanted to stay off the road and spend more time at home with my family. While we were talking, the telephone rang and I answered it.

"Are you still fat?" asked the voice on the other end of the line.

I knew who it was instantly. Kevin Sullivan. Kevin was the booker for World Championship Wrestling [WCW]. I was shocked to hear his voice, but I wasn't surprised by his straight-to-the-point questions. *"Yes,"* I replied. Kevin was never one to mince words.

"Are you still wrestling?"

"Yes."

Kevin's next question was the one which changed my life forever. *"Can you be in Macon, Georgia tomorrow?"*

"What?"

"I need you in Macon tomorrow night for our TV."

It was all I could do to stammer out, *"Sure."*

Kevin told me someone would call later that day with my flight and rental car information. *"Okay,"* I said. *"What do I bring?"* I waited a full five seconds before saying, *"Kevin?"* After a few more seconds passed, I said, *"Hello?"* The line was dead. Kevin was never much for goodbyes, either.

I later discovered that WCW road agent Paul Orndorff had gotten into a fight with Vader [Leon White]. When Eric Bischoff told Vader he would have to pay a $250,000 fine and be suspended for six months, Vader told him to "stick it" and left the company. That opened to door for Crash the Terminator to make his debut.

After I hung up the phone, I looked at Adrian and Rose. *"That was Kevin Sullivan. They want me in Macon tomorrow night."* We spent the next hour celebrating ... although we really didn't know what we were celebrating about, other than the fact I was going to work for WCW for at least one night. Just minutes before the phone call, I had been talking about putting my gear away and finding a job locally. I was hoping to get back my job with Brendon and Jesse at Park-Rite Striping. Jesse was good to my brother and I and always found a place for us. Now I was thinking about what I was going to put into my "working bag" and what might be in store for me in Macon.

When I arrived at the Atlanta International Airport, I found my rental car and drove to the Ramada Inn, which the boys called "The Dungeon."

From there, I went to the Macon [Georgia] Coliseum and found Kevin, who took me to an empty locker room to meet with Eric Bischoff and Hulk Hogan. I don't care who you are. No matter what business you're in, or how well you've done in that business, you will always "mark out" when you meet certain people in your business. For instance, if I was a singer, I would be in absolute awe if I met Elvis Presley or Wayne Newton. It would be like, *"Holy shit! I just met Elvis."* There I was, a professional wrestler who had made a name for himself in Japan and Puerto Rico, standing in a bathroom talking to Hulk Hogan. I don't care what anyone else says about him. He's a cool guy.

Eric and Hogan introduced themselves (like they had to) and told me how highly Kevin had spoken of me. Hogan shook my hand and said, *"We like what you do. We want you to work for us."* I still wasn't sure whether or not I was being set up for a giant rib, but I was stunned when Eric said, *"We'll start you out at $85,000 a year for your first three years."* I thought I had been doing well in Puerto Rico and Japan, but I never dreamed of making $85,000 a year. I didn't hesitate to accept their offer and we sealed the deal by shaking hands. I didn't need a lawyer or an agent. That was the way I had always done business.

It really didn't sink in until I was watching the show that night from backstage. It was like a light had turned on inside my head. *"Holy shit! I've made it!"* I was being handed the opportunity that every wrestler hopes to get, and to top it all off, it had been offered to me by the boss and the biggest name in the wrestling business. Me! A fat kid and father of two daughters from New Jersey whose mother had to work three jobs and get food stamps to make ends meet.

By the way, the phone call from Kevin is what prompted me to begin referring to myself as "the fat kid from New Jersey." That didn't mean anybody else could get away with calling me that, but it was my thing. Diamond Dallas Page later told me that I shouldn't say that because people would begin looking at me in that way.

The day after I met Hogan and Bischoff in Macon, we did TV tapings in Dalton, Georgia. When I broke into the business, I had been taught that I should always be prepared when I went to a show, even if I wasn't scheduled to work. When I left Elmwood Park, I had no idea what Kevin had planned for me, but I automatically took my wrestling gear with me I didn't take it into the arena in Macon because I didn't want to overstep my bounds, but I had it in the trunk of the rental car, just in case. There's nothing worse than a green kid bringing his bag and taking up space from the boys that are actually working. To this day, I hate it when guys make themselves at home in someone else's locker room.

My first match with WCW took place in Dalton on September 7, 1995 against Barry Houston. Barry made me look like a true professional … much better than I could have ever looked. I used the moonsault to end the match. When I got back to the dressing room, Sullivan was laughing. *"Can you do that every night?"* he asked.

"Sure," I replied. *"I can also do the 450 Splash. Just tell me what you want and I'll do it."*

Sullivan thought I was joking. *"Oh, shut the fuck up."*

"I'm being serious when I say that. I can do it."

A few of the guys in the dressing room who had been with me in Japan said, *"He's telling the truth. He can do it."*

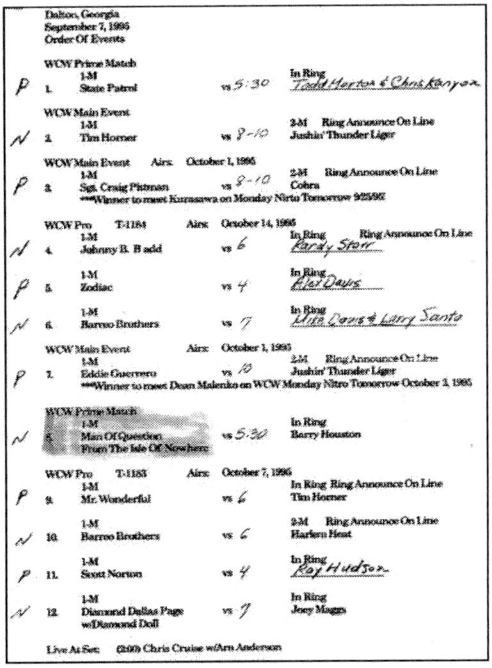
Dalton, Georgia
September 7, 1995
Order Of Events

WCW Prime Match
P 1. 1-M State Patrol vs 5:30 — In Ring: Todd Morton & Chris Kanyon

WCW Main Event
N 2. 1-M Tim Horner vs 8-10 — 2-M Ring Announce On Line: Jushin' Thunder Liger

WCW Main Event Airs: October 1, 1995
P 3. 1-M Sgt. Craig Pittman vs 8-10 — 2-M Ring Announce On Line: Cobra
***Winner to meet Kurasawa on Monday Nitro Tomorrow 9/25/95

WCW Pro T-1184 Airs: October 14, 1995
N 4. 1-M Johnny B. Badd vs 6 — In Ring Ring Announce On Line: Randy Starr

P 5. 1-M Zodiac vs 4 — In Ring: Alex Davis

N 6. 1-M Barrio Brothers vs 7 — In Ring: Mike Davis & Larry Santo

WCW Main Event Airs: October 1, 1995
P 7. 1-M Eddie Guerrero vs 10 — 2-M Ring Announce On Line: Jushin' Thunder Liger
***Winner to meet Dean Malenko on WCW Monday Nitro Tomorrow October 2, 1995

WCW Prime Match
N 8. 1-M Man Of Question From The Isle Of Nowhere vs 5:30 — In Ring: Barry Houston

WCW Pro T-1183 Airs: October 7, 1995
P 9. 1-M Mr. Wonderful vs 6 — In Ring Ring Announce On Line: Tim Horner

N 10. 1-M Barrio Brothers vs 6 — 3-M Ring Announce On Line: Harlem Heat

P 11. 1-M Scott Norton vs 4 — In Ring: Ray Hudson

N 12. 1-M Diamond Dallas Page w/Diamond Doll vs 7 — In Ring: Joey Maggs

Live At Set: (2:00) Chris Cruise w/Arn Anderson

It was funny (and kind of strange) that Kevin even asked the question because when he was in Japan, he made me do the moonsault every night I was there … and now it was like he was seeing it for the very first time.

I was actually in Puerto Rico when I learned to moonsault. One afternoon, we were drinking by the hotel pool. Actually, we were all pretty wasted and we acting like clowns. Ricky Santana and Miguel Perez knew one of my big fears was heights, so they dared me to jump off the diving board. I wouldn't jump from the board, but I began doing belly flops from the edge of the pool. After a few belly flops, Santana yelled, *"Come on, you fat fuck. Do a flip."*

I wasn't that drunk. *"Hell, no!"* But after a few more beers, I was doing flips. By the end of the day, I was doing a moonsault, an aerial move which I had seen Keiji Mutoh do in Japan. To perform a moonsault, which is generally executed from the top turnbuckle, a wrestler faces away from his prone opponent and executes a backflip, landing on his opponent in a press position. However, I believe I took the move to another level. Instead of doing a simple back flip from the turnbuckle, I would leap high into the air before flipping over. By the time I was beginning my descent to the mat, I was anywhere from ten to twelve feet in the air.

On my next tour of Japan, just minutes before a match in which Mr. Pogo and I would be challenging the Headhunters for the W*ING tag team title, Kevin Sullivan said, *"You and Pogo will go over tonight ... and you will use the moonsault for your finish."*

I said, *"What? I'm not doing a moonsault in front of all those people."*

Kevin said, *"You will moonsault tonight and cover one of the Headhunters for a three-count, and you will be the new champions ... or you'll be going home. It's your choice."*

I couldn't believe what I was hearing. Kevin was threatening to send me home if I didn't do exactly what he told me to do. I had never refused to do anything asked of me up to that point, but I did that night. *"I can't moonsault! That's fifteen feet up in the air!"*

Kevin said he had heard about me doing moonsaults at the pool and made me feel guilty for not wanting to do what they wanted, so I finally gave in. When the time was right, I bodyslammed one of the Headhunters into one of the corners and climbed to the top turnbuckle. The photographers must have sensed something was going to happen because the camera flashes began firing off. I closed my eyes and leaped out into the air. I did a backwards flip and landed across my opponent's chest. One, two, three. Pogo and I were the new tag team champions.

As crazy as it sounds, getting drunk and doing moonsaults at the hotel pool was what advanced my career. The photos of me doing that moonsault made the magazines, and from that night on, the people expected it. It was just one of those moments when I was in the right place at the right time. It wasn't something I planned. It was simply the fact that I didn't want to lose my job because, when push came to shove, Kevin didn't have that kind of power. Kevin wasn't in any kind of a power position at W*ING, but he had a lot of influence with Victor Quinones. If he wanted me fired, he might have been able to make it happen, so I was genuinely concerned that he could do exactly what he said. Even if I didn't believe he could do it, I still would had done what he asked simply because I respected him for who he was and what he had done in the business in the past. Kevin never had any problem expressing his opinion, especially with guys in whom he had an interest, and it would later become obvious that he was very interested in helping me.

On the night after the show in Dalton, I drove back to the Ramada Inn, which was where all the "boys" stayed when WCW had a show in Atlanta. I was now in the same bar as Ric Flair, Arn Anderson, and all the stars from WCW. I had watched those guys on TV, and like every other wrestler who wanted an opportunity to be them, I was now in the same bar. Yeah, baby!

The hotel was okay, but the bar belonged to the girl who ran the place and "the boys." It was a safe haven for the boys and a place where we could go and do our thing without worrying about repercussions or people prying into our business. The first time I walked in, I was amazed to see pictures of the famous WCW wrestlers that had been there before me. It was awesome! We went there after each show to burn off steam and unwind. The "official" motel was later changed to the Quality Inn, but every time I go to the airport, I pass the Dungeon and remember the many escapades I had there when I first joined the company. My very first adventure at the Dungeon took place that night when I met my first group (three girls) of wrestling fans.

While I sat at a table in the lounge, a brunette walked up to my table. I had seen her sitting at a nearby table with two blondes. As it turned out, the blondes were sisters and the brunette was their cousin. The brunette was the only one of the three that was old enough to drink, but they were *all* old enough to make their own decisions about other matters. Somehow, we all wound up in my hotel room and, one after the other, they "introduced themselves" more thoroughly. For some reason, they each wanted to be my "best friend" in Atlanta and they weren't going to let the others be better. After the four of us had a long "discussion" over who was the best, I decided the brunette and I had the most in common. At least, we did for a few nights, but after that, I never saw her again. For the next few years, though, the blond cousin would show up every time I was anywhere near Georgia.

The next day, I flew home and told my wife and parents. I told them I was going back on the road, not even thinking about the fact that "I was going back on the road." They both thought I was stretching the truth (especially about the money), but they became believers when the contract arrived in the mail that week. I signed it immediately and went to the post office.

I wrestled as Crash during my first match, but they hadn't yet decided on what they were going to call me. Brian Adams was working for the WWF as Crush, and Sting and Renegade were already wearing face paint, so WCW wanted me to be different and avoid any confusion. Sullivan called me and told me to send one of my wrestling singlets to the company seamstress in Georgia. I forgot all about it until, one day a week or so later, a box arrived in the mail. Inside the box was my singlet ... with question marks sewn all over it. *"What the fuck?"* In those days, you didn't ask questions (no pun intended). You just did as you were told. The next time I called Sullivan, he said they didn't know what they were going to do with me, so for the time being, they were going to call me "The Man of Question" from "The Isle of Nowhere."

During that time, Terry Taylor was running the TV show. He asked me, *"Can you do a promo and talk about Randy Savage?"*

Instead of answering with a simple "yes" or "no," I stammered and asked, *"Macho Man Randy Savage?"* I must have come off as a total mark. I couldn't help it, though. After all, I had only wrestled for three promotions [W*ING, Puerto Rico and Mexico] and they were relatively small potatoes compared to the WWF and WCW. I was now going to be working with "them." I don't care who you are. If you're an up-and-coming wrestler, your goal is to work with "them."

Terry's eyebrows creased in puzzlement (or irritation) as he said, *"Uh, yeah. Can you talk about him?"*

When I told him I didn't have a problem doing promos, he told me to be at CNN Center in downtown Atlanta on September 20. At the time, I didn't realize they employed people who wrote promos for the guys, giving them bullet points and details to talk about. I didn't need that because I had a natural gift of gab. I said, *"If you'll just tell me what you want, I can give you what you want in my own words. It will come off more natural than if I was trying to follow something that someone else has written for me."* Terry told me what he wanted and I gave it to them. I have a little laugh which I used during my promos in Puerto Rico and Japan. It's kind of off the wall, but it fits my personality (off the wall), so I used it. It really didn't matter what I said because the local wrestling fans spoke either Spanish or Japanese, but the laugh stood out in any language. When I was finished, Terry said, *"Can you do another one?"*

"Sure. What do you want me to talk about?"

"Talk about Randy Savage again."

The promos aired that week to promote the upcoming *WCW Saturday Night* television show which was going to be held at Center Stage in Atlanta on September 27, 1995. Terry told me I would be wrestling Randy on that show.

During that time, I made my last independent commitment in Maryland. I was booked to wrestle "Cactus Jack." That in itself was an honor, but when I saw Mick in the back that night, he made a big deal about me getting hired by WCW and getting a shot at the "bigs." In the back of the arena that night, a television was set up, and the WCW television show was airing. Just before Mick and I went out to wrestle, my promo on Savage aired. I was amazed to see and hear myself, and as I watched myself on the screen, question marks were flying all over.

It was so awesome to hear the announcers talking about me. By the time it ended, I was pumped and ready to go out and wrestle the "hardcore legend," Cactus Jack.

I had been watching *WCW Saturday Night* for a long time, so when I walked into the theater, I was completely taken by surprise to realize the auditorium was no bigger than a movie theater. Some of the greatest wrestlers of all time had wrestled there, and now ... I was going to work there. What an incredible feeling that was. I was at Center Stage with a "Who's Who" of wrestling: Eddie Guerrero, Meng [Tonga Fifita], Jim Duggan, Bubba Rogers, Lex Luger, Road Warrior Hawk, Scott Norton, Mike Rotunda, Alex Wright, and Paul Orndorff. I was even in awe of the guys whose only purpose for being there was to "do a job" in order to help someone else get over.

The members of the Dungeon of Doom — Taskmaster [Kevin Sullivan], Meng [Haku], Shark [John Tenta], Zodiac [Ed Leslie] — came to the ring during my match. That really got my blood flowing. They were cats I had watched on TV for a long time. I always enjoyed listening to King Curtis Iaukea, the "Master" of the Dungeon of Doom, who opened his promos with *"Sullivan, my son."* He had such a distinctive voice.

After my match with Randy Savage, I was told I would be given future opportunities to talk. Unfortunately, politics reared its ugly head, as it often does in the wrestling business. People wanted to know what the "new kid" had done to deserve to get air time. After that, I did a few segments with Mean Gene Okerlund and David Penzer for commercial spots and fillers which were specifically designed to introduce the "Laughing Man" to certain markets. They also flew me to Atlanta to do a commercial for a pay-per-view where I played a prisoner in a jail cell. That was easy. I had real-life experience playing that part. But other than those few occasions, I wouldn't find myself doing promos again for four years, which was a long, frustrating time. That was politics, though, a game I've never played well.

The main problem was I never knew what I was going to be allowed to do. Sting had the "Stinger Splash," which was a lot like a move I called Squishers, which was actually a running splash in the corners I couldn't do the "elbow off the top rope" move because Randy Savage used it. I was a 300-pound guy doing dropkicks, spin kicks, and moonsaults ... and that ruffled feathers. Kevin sat me down and told me I was strictly a "punch-kick guy." *"Hey, when the time is right, we'll turn you loose. Until then, hang tight. We know what you can do."* That didn't sit well with me because I had learned several different forms of my craft: Japan, Mexico, European, and American. But what could I do? I did what I was told.

The Dungeon of Doom, WCW Magazine, November 1996

I got a lot of attention at the "Dungeon" after the matches that night, especially from the "local welcoming committee," better known as "arena rats," wrestling's version to "groupies." That's all I have to say about that.

I didn't wrestle again after those first two matches until October 25, when I wrestled (and was disqualified) against Dwayne Gill on *WCW Saturday Night.* I also was introduced as the newest member of the Dungeon of Doom, which consisted of the Shark [John Tenta], Zodiac [Ed Leslie], Meng, and Barbarian [Sione Vailahi]. After seeing my promos on Randy Savage, Terry Taylor's wife said, *"He has a strange sense of humor. I think he's quite humorous."* For the match that night, I was introduced as "Humorous," which was later changed when the announcers, Tony Schiavone and Dave Penzer, read it as two words: Hugh Morrus. At first, I didn't care what they wanted to call me. I was working for World Championship Wrestling. But when people didn't seem to understand the joke, I took my concerns to Terry [Terry Bollea, aka Hulk Hogan], Kevin and Jimmy Hart. At that point, the people in charge of the promos and advertising added "The Laughing Man" whenever they mentioned or advertised my name.

I had heard so many stories about the legends abusing the young guys, but I could not have been given a better reception during my early years in WCW. Johnny B Badd [Mark Mero] was always very cordial and made me feel at home with the company. Mike Rotunda, who wrestled as V.K. Wallstreet, was another guy who would help and give me a "heads-up" on things pertaining to the road. Diamond Dallas Page was very helpful and took time to sit down with newcomers to give them his theories on the business. Dallas, who was one of those rare larger-than-life characters, always had the appearance of being in complete control.

Lex Luger had his moments of "acting" like the star he was, even when he was just around the boys, but on occasion, when he didn't feel the need to act like a prick, he was a pleasure to talk with. Lex got mad at me one night when I "didn't get up" for his finish. He couldn't lift me and felt like I should have done more to put him over. My attitude was, *"It's your finish. Pick me up and do it!"*

I enjoyed hanging out with One Man Gang [George Gray]. When we were both members of the Dungeon, he was a different guy from what I had heard about his earlier years. I had heard stories about how wild and "outgoing" he was, but when I was around him, he was calm, soft-spoken, and on a different path in life. He didn't even drink. I never would have guessed he had been a hell-raiser. I'm not saying he had been, but I was making the assessment based on the stories I had heard. The most important thing George taught me was to "never be late for a show." That lesson stuck with me throughout my career.

I had worked with Dick Slater in W*ING, so we already had some history together. During our time in Japan, we made a trip on a huge ferry. The water was very choppy and caused the boat to tip and sway from side to side. It was funny to see "hard-ass" Slater laying on the deck of the boat and screaming, *"We're gonna die!"* That was definitely a lasting moment.

While I'm on the subject of Japan, years after WCW went out of business, I learned that New Japan had asked for me several times, and they had been told I was too busy. That was during the time when I was sitting at home a lot. It wasn't an issue of money because the boys who were sent over to New Japan by WCW didn't make anything over and above their guarantee. Sonny Ono told me the office kept the money that was supposed to be for the boys. I didn't care about that. I just wanted to work.

Alex Wright was a good guy. On November 16, 2000, we won the WCW world tag team title from Mark Jindrak and Sean O'Haire on the *Millennium Germany* show in Oberhausen, Germany. Disco Inferno [Glen Gilburdy], who was called Disqo at the time, was supposed to be Alex's partner in the match, but Disco "wasn't feeling well," so they asked me if I could wrestle again. I was blown up from wrestling Lance Storm, but I agreed to take Disco's place. I was told up front that even though Alex and I were going to win the title that night, by the time we got home to the States, Alex and "Disco" would be billed as the new champions. Just four days later on *WCW Monday Nitro*, Alex and Elix Skipper dropped the belts to Chuck Palumbo and Shawn Stasiak. How Elix got into the mix, I'll never know, but it didn't make a whole lot of sense. I just went about my business and did what I was asked to do. A lot of the boys thought it was ridiculous, as well, and the fact that I never lost the title became an ongoing joke. It would have been nice to have been recognized as the champion, but I didn't get into the business with the expectations of winning titles. I just wanted to be a part of things, and it was awesome to be a part of the title switch in Germany and to hear the reaction we got from the fans.

Disco was a freaking dummy, and I mean that affectionately. I could never figure out exactly how he got as far as he did. For all the charisma and talent Disco had, he chose to be the class clown and/or village idiot when he was in public. He was like the cool kids comic relief. He always acted like a nerd, or the dork of the group, and that got him a lot of attention. He seemed to be "in" with everyone, but not "all the way in." He was always hanging around with the top guys, but only when they needed a follower or someone to boost their egos. He was definitely a kiss-ass and he knew who he needed to befriend.

A funny incident involving Disco took place when we were coming back from one of our overseas tours. We were on the shuttle bus, rushing to get back to our hotel in Florida because we had to leave almost immediately for a TV taping. Disco just would not shut up. He wasn't saying anything, in particular. He was just talking. Arn Anderson told Disco several times to *"shut the fuck up,"* but Glen was Glen. Disco knew my girls loved his character, so he told me, *"Be sure to tell your girls that Uncle Disco said hello."* From there, he began prattling on about how Arn was "the baddest man to come out of Rome, Georgia." It was one thing after the other and everyone on the shuttle was annoyed. All of a sudden, Arn stood up and bitch-slapped Disco right in the puss. They say silence is golden. It was during the remainder of the trip. Nobody moved or put it over, but there were smiles on the faces of everyone. Well, it goes without saying that there was one person who wasn't smiling. Glenn didn't say another word until we arrived at the spot where we picked up our rental cars.

Steven Regal [Darren Matthews], who later wrestled as William Regal in the WWF, was easy to work with and fun to party with, but things changed later when we were both working for the WWE. He was still the same guy, but he was more serious and hung around with the "more important" crowd. He formed a tight friendship with Triple H [Paul Levesque], which kept him safe from the rest of the world.

Bobby Eaton was a great talent. He made our matches so easy. He was easy going and he always let us get our spots in. On the other hand, there were times when Bobby would get frustrated when the younger guys would try to take too much of the match and he would "light them up." He would remind them that he was the leader and in control of the match, not to mention the fact the he was the person being showcased. One time, when we left Sturgis, South Dakota, on a charter flight, Bobby freaked out when someone locked him in the bathroom and ripped the door off the hinges. He had that "retard strength," which is a term we used for guys who didn't appear overpowering or threatening. Needless to say, WCW didn't charter another flight for the boys for some time after that. Bobby was one of the most friendly, laid-back guys I ever met, but he would only put up with a certain amount of crap before he fought back.

I had some good times traveling with Bobby Duncum, Jr. I really enjoyed listening to him tell stories of when he was a kid and the things his dad did when he was a wrestler. On one trip, we were on the road doing a tour of the southern states. As a rule, everyone traveled with their chosen circle of guys. On this particular tour, everyone was looking for something to numb their minds, but nobody had thought to bring anything with them. Bobby finally stopped at a convenience store and bought a bottle of Tylenol. He went back to his motel room, drank a beer, and downed the whole bottle. Looking at it from the outside, you might wonder why I didn't stop him, but we were all in the same place as far as taking things to get "straight." Often, it wasn't until the next day that we realized how stupid and dangerous some of things were that we did, never mind worrying about what someone else was doing.

Months later, I ran into Bobby and his beautiful family at DisneyWorld during one of our rare weekends off. We said hello and talked for a few minutes before going our separate ways. It felt so weird to see each other out of our "element," but I remember thinking "this is so normal" to be a family man at home and a complete screw-up on the road. Not too long after that, they found Bobby dead of an overdose of a prescription painkiller. As I write this,

I feel the same way now as I did then ... empty. I remember thinking to myself, *"Why did he go so far and not be smarter about the things he did?"* Of course, that's a completely screwed-up notion from a guy who did more than his share of stupid things, even after Bobby died. No matter how many of my friends passed away in that fashion, I continued to do what I did best ... wrestle and get gooned out.

I don't mean this to be disparaging to Bobby. The fact is, I had (and have) the utmost respect for him and I enjoyed the time we spent together. It's simply that as I drift away from wrestling and live a sober life, I begin to remember and think back to what my life had once been like. It's to remind me that someone else could be writing a book and discussing the "fucked-up way Bill De Mott lived his life" (and Lord knows there are several people who could tell that story).

Luke McMasters, who was billed as the Loch Ness Monster, was huge. At that time, the company's main goal was to find big guys to feed to Hogan and Savage. I was told that at one time, Luke was a good wrestler for being such a big man. However, by the time he came to WCW, he had really slowed down. When he did a run-in, it took him a long time to get to the ring. It was brutal. We would get our asses kicked every night waiting for him to make his entrance.

One cat named Chad Brock was being paid while he was getting trained. Sullivan hated the kid. It had to do a lot with Chad constantly talking about the record contracts he had and how, since he was already famous, he should automatically be pushed as a top guy in the wrestling business. He was always talking smack about being a big singer-songwriter and rubbing the guys the wrong way. As a result, every time he was booked against someone from the Dungeon (especially me), it was "suggested" he get an ass kicking. One day, he got hurt pretty bad (or good, depending on how you look at it). I don't know if he quit or if the company let him go, but we never saw him again.

Chad did well after he left the wrestling business. In 1998, he released his debut single, "Evangeline." His follow-up single, "Ordinary Life," became his first major hit, peaking at number three on the Hot Country Song charts and number 39 on the Billboard Hot 100. In 2000, his single, "Yes!," hit the number one spot on the charts. WCW hired him to perform live at a show. I thought it was hilarious that he had been treated like crap, and a few years later, the company was falling all over him and having him headline a wrestling show.

After wrestling on October 25, I didn't hear anything from the company for several weeks. I was even more worried about the fact that from the time I went to work for the company in the beginning of September, I hadn't received any money. I had been taught that I should never ask for my money, but I was turning down opportunities to wrestle for independent promotions, so I began to think the people in charge had changed their minds. I decided to call Kevin at his office. When he answered the phone, I asked, *"Kevin, is everything okay?"*

"What do you mean is everything okay? You're getting' paid, aren't ya?"

"I'm bein' honest with you. I'm not getting paid."

"What the fuck do you mean you're not getting' paid? We stood there and made a deal."

"I agree with you, but I haven't gotten paid."

"Are you fuckin' kidding me? I'll get back to ya."

He hung up, once again forgetting to say "goodbye."

He really sounded pissed. I thought, *"De Mott. You've really fucked up now."* I had broken the rule and questioned the man who was handing me the "key to the city." *"Shit! I shouldn't have asked for money."*

Hugh Morrus

The next day, FedEx showed up on my doorstep with an envelope. Inside was (this is where you would hear a drum roll) a check for $12,000, give or take a hundred bucks. That was the amount owed from the day of the handshake to the day of the phone call. I had never seen that much money in one place at one time. From that day on, I received a regular weekly check.

On November 26, one of the feature matches was a 60-man battle royal. At the time, there was a lot of pressure put on the Dungeon to be ready for the cue to feed for certain guys, so Sullivan made it very clear as to what was expected of you. I remember being very nervous about "doing my job" in the battle royal, but I soon came to the realization that the sixty men were all about screwing around, especially when the camera was focused on somewhere other than where they were. What happened in the match really didn't matter until the field had been whittled down to the important players. I always had the opportunity to be in the final mix because I would bump for anyone, and I had no ego about doing it. I enjoyed any opportunity to be involved in a finish, so I did what I was asked to do. Besides, the more things I did inside the ring, the more I was being noticed "outside the arenas." (wink-wink)

For me, the highlight of those early years took place on November 27, 1995. We were in Salem, Virginia, and I was scheduled to wrestle Hulk Hogan. After I finished changing into my wrestling gear, I was approached by Brutus Beefcake (Edward Leslie), who said, *"The big man wants to see you."* I didn't say anything. Being summoned to Hogan's dressing room was very intimidating, especially considering the fact that I wasn't easily intimidated. I just followed him to the other side of the arena and sat down beside Hogan in his dressing room. He told me, *"Just do your thing as you would any other night. The only question I have is, will you promise not to kill me with your "no laughing matter" finish?"* I have to admit I had been nervous about flipping upside down and landing on Hogan's chest because he was "the man" in the company, but he really put me at ease when he grinned and asked me that question. That night, Hogan kicked out of my finisher and went on to beat me with a leg drop. That was awesome! Later that night, I was once again asked to see Hogan in his dressing room. As I made my way to the other side of the arena, in the back of my mind, I wondered if I had done something wrong. My fears were put to rest when Hogan held out his hand and said, *"Thanks, Laughing Man. I appreciate what you did."*

I repeat ... that was awesome!

Chapter 8

The Chubba Bubbas

In January 1996, Ted Petty and Mike Durham came to work for WCW. That was great news to me because I was excited about being back together with them. During the time they had been working for Extreme Championship Wrestling [ECW] as Rocco Rock [Ted] and Johnny Grunge [Mike], or more simply as "Public Enemy," they had built a name for themselves and a cult following. A lot of the talent in WCW had been a part of ECW at one time or another, but most of us knew each other. During our formative years in the business, Teddy, Johnny and I had been together in Gleason's Gym, so we had a strong bond which would keep us together for life.

When we reunited in WCW, Johnny began calling me "Chubby," which was funny since he was so round and in worse shape than any of us. In time, he would affectionately refer to me as "Chubba Bubba," and eventually, we all began calling each other "Chubby" when addressing each other. The boys all thought that was funny and we eventually became known as the Chubba Bubbas. The office had no idea about the force we would become ... more outside the ring than in.

At the same time, Teddy and I made it possible for a nice kid named Chris Ford to get a tryout with the company by introducing him to Kevin Sullivan. In those days, many of the boys would help the young guys find work. That changed in the future years. I also let Chris stay with me so he could save a little money. Chris worked at the time as "Devon Storm," but changed his name a few years later to "Crowbar." I first met Chris in New Jersey during the time when I was just breaking into the business. At the time, he was just a "kid." His energy and passion for wrestling was so powerful that it made me want to help him in any way possible. We became good friends and I'm so glad to know that he had a successful career in the business before retiring to become a physical therapist.

When we were working at the MGM and Universal Studios, we didn't have transportation. We didn't need it since the company took us to and from the studio in the company van or bus, and there was almost always someone around to take us wherever we wanted to go. The entire company stayed in the same complex when we were in Orlando for TV tapings, which made it easy for the company to shuttle us back and forth to the studio. The company eventually stopped taking care of the transportation to and from the studios and made us responsible for ourselves.

Joe D'Acquisto, Johnny Grunge, Rocco Rock and Hugh Morrus

On one particular night, Johnny and I wanted to go out on the town, but Teddy was partied out and decided to stay in. Since Chris was staying with me, we made him come along. At the time, Chris was the definition of a "good boy" and he wasn't yet corrupted into the things we did, although I did my best to introduce him to "the world." I'm proud to say Chris never did fall into the "hype" of being one of the boys (after hours), but every once in awhile, I would make sure he was in the middle of some of our hijinks. We went to the front desk of the hotel to try to scam a ride. When the clerk informed us that a company van was sitting outside, Johnny said, *"We work for the company, so we're allowed to use it."* Not!

Johnny had a way of making things happen and I'm sure I did my part in making things take place, so before we knew it, we had the keys to the van and we were on our way. We had no idea where we were going, but wherever it was, we wound up there. We had two strikes against us before we pulled out from the parking lot. One, we were already in no condition to drive, and, two, Johnny (who was driving) didn't have a driver's license. By the time we were headed back home, we were full of "recreational" drugs and alcohol.

As I drove back on the wrong side of the highway, Johnny decided he needed to pee. I didn't stop to let him out. I told him to piss out the window, which he did, leaving streaks of urine down the side of the vehicle and hitting Chris in the face as the wind blew in the spray. The drinking had made us hungry, so I pulled up to the drive-through window at McDonald's ... but I was headed the wrong way. They wouldn't take our order and told us to get lost. In the process of leaving, I drove over the curbing and took out their sign.

We made our way back to the hotel complex and I parked the van by the main entrance. I helped Chris walk to the room and we went to sleep. That's my version. More than likely, Chris helped *me* back to *my* room. Everything had turned out just fine ... or so we thought. As we got ready to leave for a show in Lakeland, a "buzz" began circulating. Nobody knew any details, but the word was out that *"the shit is going to hit the fan."* We eventually learned that the van we borrowed belonged to David Crockett, the executive producer for WCW television programming. He was a real tight ass who had no sense of humor, whatsoever. I also learned that after Chris and I went back to our room, Johnny had taken the van out again with plans to sample more of the Orlando night life. Unfortunately he asked for directions from a cop, who busted him for driving under the influence. As a result, the office called us (Ted Petty included) in for a meeting in which Crockett said we stole the van and damaged it. Okay, we did damage it, but we returned it. It wasn't our fault that Johnny took it back out and got arrested.

Kevin Sullivan was all but foaming at the mouth. He began screaming at us, telling us how he went on the line to get us our jobs and, in turn, how we made him look bad. *"You guys can consider yourselves officially fired."* Wow! We got reamed and fired just minutes before a live show [*WCW Monday Nitro*].

Teddy was really pissed. Now we had two guys screaming at us. He told Johnny and me that if we all got fired, he was going to kill us both. We had worked so hard, and in one night, we had pissed it all away. Keep in mind that none of the three of us had really been with the company long enough to screw up that badly. I didn't know if I was more afraid of Sullivan and Petty, or telling my folks. *"We just got fired from WCW!"* Teddy wasn't even involved in the incident, but the Chubba Bubbas were always together, so when one messed up, we all messed up. Thank goodness Chris wasn't called on the carpet with the rest of us. He was totally innocent and didn't deserve to be included in our mess. Sullivan eventually left the room, leaving us all sitting and staring at each other. All of a sudden, Sullivan barged back into the room and told Teddy and Johnny to get out. When the door closed, Sullivan got in my face. *"De Mott! You're a fuck up! Get your ass to the dressing room and get your gear on because you're in the main event. THEN YOU'RE FIRED!"*

That night, Kevin Sullivan and I worked with Arn Anderson and Brian Pillman. To make a long story short, Pillman refused to sell for Kevin and the match seemed to morph into a shoot. The match ended when Pillman rolled out of the ring and left the area. Reports came out afterwards that Pillman claimed Kevin hadn't been selling for him and they got into a heated argument in the dressing room.

Nobody really knew what was going on behind the scenes between Kevin and Pillman, but in matches during the next few days, everyone involved seemed to be on their guard. Things were confusing when we worked because we weren't sure just when or if we would have to go into "shoot mode" and kick someone's ass for not selling. We were ready to punch out anyone who might cross us. The Dungeon and the Horsemen spent a lot of time together when we were away from the arenas, so it was difficult to work stiff and not develop hard feelings. Besides our matches on television, we did a lot of live events together with all or some of our groups working against each other. Both groups were hot during that time and the matches were good. At least, they were good for the fans. Each of the guys would protect their own group, so "working snug" became the flavor of the month. Tempers flared with little or no provocation. I don't remember there being any outstanding incident, but the guys would get loud and tell each other to *"fuck off."* There were times when Kevin and Arn didn't see eye to eye and we had to keep them cooled down, but there were other times when we had to get physical in order to avoid being taken advantage of. Everybody wanted to make sure everybody else knew they weren't going to be "punching bags" for anyone. The "feuds" which were presented on television rolled into real life, resulting in friendships and working relationships suffering.

In my opinion, we were all played into one of the greatest "works" of all time. To this day, I believe only Kevin, Pillman, and the bosses really know what went on, and I'm not entirely sure the bosses were smartened up until the scenario had played itself out. Disco was one of the first people to begin telling everyone who would listen than it was all a work. Most of us had already come to that conclusion, and some of the boys were offended at being played, but at the end of the day, it was just wrestling and we moved on.

Pillman left WCW and appeared on the ECW *Cyberslam* show on February 17, 1996. During an interview, he made some derogatory comments about Eric Bischoff, including calling him a "piece of shit." It had all been mapped out ahead of time between Pillman and Bischoff so Pillman could return to WCW with more heat. The plan backfired four months later when Pillman signed a contract with the WWF. He had a good run with them, but we rolled right along without him.

By the time we got back to the hotel complex, everybody had heard the news about us being fired. Most of them had trouble believing that the three "new guys" could cause all that trouble, but they also found us to be entertaining. They never knew what we were going to do next. Besides, wrestling was comprised of good, old-fashioned fun, drugs, booze, cops, and getting the boss pissed off.

The company was hosting a barbeque that afternoon after the tapings. As far as we knew, we were officially fired, and since we were going home the

Hugh Morrus

next day, we decided to get a beer and temporarily forget our troubles. When Eric Bischoff approached us, we prepared for a huge ass chewing session. It would take place by the pool in front of half the company, including their wives and girlfriends.

Eric, however, pulled us to the side and asked if we really stole the van. We hesitated for a few seconds before giving our side of the story (like we had a legitimate reason to take the van). We stood there for a minute waiting for the fireworks, but after a few seconds of uncomfortable silence, Eric began laughing. He said it was one of the funniest things he had ever heard. Eric went on to say that David Crockett was so pissed that he (Eric) couldn't let us go. *"You made me laugh,"* he said. *"You're going to be fun to be fun to be around."* He shook our hands and told us we weren't fired.

Go figure! Our boss enjoyed our sense of humor. We stole a van, did hundreds (if not thousands) of dollars of damage, one of us got arrested, three of us got fired, poor Chris was thrown into a complete whirlwind … and we were at the pool with the boss, Eric Bischoff, drinking beer and laughing about it … and we kept our jobs! Sullivan didn't let me forget about that for a long time, which, I'm sure, was to make me feel guilty in order to keep my loyalty.

Later that night (or early the next morning), a SWAT team showed up at our hotel. A man and woman had been arguing and the man had thrown her outside, naked, in twenty-degree weather. The SWAT team evacuated all the rooms so they could use tear gas to drive the man out of their room. At least, that was the story we were told the next day. We were so gooned out that we didn't really know what was happening. However, I do remember breathing a sigh of relief to realize they weren't there for me.

A few days after Johnny's arrest, when things were back to normal (if there really is such a thing in the wrestling business), we were boarding the bus to travel to the sound stage for the afternoon TV tapings. Doug Dillinger, the head of security for WCW, got onto the bus and told Grunge he needed to see him outside. Johnny stepped down onto the sidewalk to find cops waiting to arrest him. Ted Petty was really pissed over the fact that Johnny was being arrested first thing in the morning and in front of the whole company. After a few minutes, Johnny was released from custody and allowed to reboard the bus. It had all been a rib concocted by Sullivan and Eric Bischoff. We were still on a high from our partying the night before, but the incident sobered us up instantly.

When news of those incidents spread around the country, a lot of our friends and family called to ask about it. That was how the Chubba Bubbas made their name. Before too long, a lot of the WCW superstars wanted to be … Chubba Bubbas!

At the TV taping at Universal Studios on February 7, 1996, we had a meeting with Eric Bischoff. Due to the Summer Olympics being held in Atlanta, we weren't going to have camera crews available in many of the southern states, especially in Georgia. As a result, the company would begin filming at Universal Studios in Orlando. Everybody was excited about the move because it meant we would be getting paid to party in Florida and work in the same place every day. The move was especially good for me since I had moved to Florida in late 1995, not too long after my signing with the company. Until that time, the company expected talent to live in the Atlanta area. I was one of the first to be allowed to relocate to Florida. That kicked off a trend and a lot of the guys began to get permission to move to Florida.

I flew to Florida to look for a house, but after coming up empty after several weeks, Rose and her mother went down and found a realtor. They found a house for rent in the La Cita golf community in Titusville.

Rose and I each had our own reasons for moving to Florida. We both knew property in New Jersey was out of our price range, and she didn't want to move to Georgia, but Rose had family in Fort Lauderdale, so it would give her someone to visit while I was on the road. My reasons were more personal. I wanted to move because it would put 1,100 miles between me and her parents. I was overjoyed when we pulled away from our home in Jersey. Unfortunately, that joy didn't last long. Her parents visited a few times, and within a year of our move, they bought a condo *in the same town*!

One of the funniest (and scariest) things that happened during my time with WCW took place in Baltimore, Maryland on February 17. Meng was in the ring doing a "chop-chop" spot with Scott Norton, who was taking the place of Pillman in a six-man tag team match. When Meng began getting the upper hand, Norton tagged out with Arn. After Arn put a couple of moves on Meng, he told him he was going to kick him in the balls. For some reason, Meng didn't block the move and Arn punted him dead in the nuts. All Meng could do was yell, *"Oo-oosh!"* The color drained from Arn's face when he realized what he had done. Sullivan and I looked at each other and he said, *"Holy shit."* Of course, everyone in the arena popped for the move and Arn bailed out by tagging Norton. That was one of the funniest stories I've heard Arn tell. It never fails to remind me of all the fun we had between the drama.

I don't think I was brought into Sullivan's *Dungeon of Doom* because I was anything special. More than likely, it was because they needed someone to take the ass-whooping and bumps. I don't say that in a negative way because I knew what my job was and I was more than ready to do it whenever I was asked. The members of the Dungeon [Meng-Barbarian-Zodiac-Earthquake-Bubba Rogers-Sullivan] were the most bizarre group of men that ever lived. And yet, every member was handpicked for specific reasons, one of which was that Hogan trusted us to keep him safe in the ring and to not hurt him. In addition, we were characters who could intimidate anyone, both in and out of the ring.

One night in Tampa, Florida, shortly after I was introduced as the new member of the Dungeon, I was drinking at the Marriott lounge with some of the camera crew and a few girls. What I didn't know at the time was that the girls worked for the office. They didn't introduce themselves as such. They just sat down beside me to talk and have a drink. One of the chicks became really friendly and we began knocking back the drinks. One drink led to twenty or so and we began to get "friendly." To make a long story short, the next thing I knew, I woke up in her hotel room with the girl in bed beside me. I was still drunk and I had a killer hangover. When I told her I had to get on the road or I would be late for the TV taping, she told me she was one of the producers who was in charge of the Dungeon shoots.

She rushed me to the warehouse where we filmed most of the Dungeon scenes. After I got dressed for the vignettes in which I would be a part, I passed out on the floor of the dressing room. It was really hot in the building and I was worn out from "talking" to the girl all night. The "Dungeon" scenes were always filled with smoke and lights, a combination which wasn't conducive to a hangover. When Sullivan walked into the room, he began screaming at me. *"Get your fat ass off the floor and start working for the money we're paying you!"* I did all my spots without missing a beat and returned to the hotel bar to continue where I had left off. I never did run into that producer again. To this day, I don't know who she was because she never told me her name.

My position in the Dungeon made me a steady player in the company ... as fodder for Hogan, Lex Luger, Savage, and Sting. They all knew I wouldn't hurt them and would put over everything they wanted to do without question. That would be how I would spend the majority of my career with WCW, and I was more than willing to take on that role.

Unfortunately, not too long after Pillman left for the WWF, another work/shoot took place between Kevin Sullivan and Chris Benoit. I can only speak from what I know (or think I know) when I talk about the situation. Chris became the fourth member of the Four Horsemen in 1995, which at the time was comprised of Ric Flair, Arn Anderson, and Brian Pillman. When Pillman signed a contract with the WWF, Chris took Pillman's place and became embroiled in an on-air (worked) feud with Kevin. At the time, Kevin's wife Nancy, using the stage name Woman, was managing the Four Horsemen. In late 1996, a storyline was developed in which Nancy was supposed to be having an affair with Chris, which lent more interest to the feud between Kevin and Chris. The on-screen relationship, which required them to travel together, developed into a real-life affair off screen. The joke going around was that "Kevin Sullivan had booked his own divorce." That was the general picture of what went down.

Chris and Nancy were, indeed, spending a lot of time together, and no doubt, their closeness was what brought them together. Chris would later confide in me that the relationship between Kevin and Nancy hadn't been all "wine and roses" even before they got together. I don't know if that was the case or not. As with anything, there are usually two sides to a story, but in this case, there were three. All I knew was that I loved all three of them: Kevin, Nancy, and Chris.

I was amazed, however, at how fast things got complicated. The vignettes which showed Chris and Nancy together began to take on a more "personal" flavor, like sharing wine in a restaurant, and being together in a house. Wrestling being wrestling, storyline became reality and the talk in the dressing room began. I can't give an exact time of when the sides were drawn, but coalitions were formed with Benoit's buddies on one end and Sullivan's on the other ... or so it seemed. As always, when the boys were with Sullivan, they were "pro-Kevin," but when they were around Chris and Nancy, they were "pro-Chris." That was the way it was in wrestling.

Whereas before, where the Dungeon and the Horsemen worked snug with each other, everybody began tightening up. We really let the hammer drop when we worked with Chris. We had never worked as stiff with the Horsemen

(back) Chris Benoit, Scott Norton, Hiroyoshi Tenzan, Hiro Saito, Hugh Morrus and Masahiro Chono, New Japan 1996

as we did that night, especially with Chris. To be honest, it was understood by both sides that we preferred to work stiff, and everyone involved like it that way, but "stiff" took on a new meaning that night. Not only that, but it gave Kevin and Chris license to beat the hell out of each other — legally. Chris was a big fan of "working snug" and believability. He expected to receive as much as he dished out.

One night in Baltimore, after Chris had his "street fight match" with Kevin, we were told to wait in the bathroom to do an angle with him. He had already taken quite a beating during his match, but Meng, Barbarian, Konnan [Charles Ashenoff], Big Bubba, and I didn't show any mercy. We beat the hell out of him. It was very physical and believable.

As time went by, it became obvious that Chris and Nancy were a legitimate couple and they were accepted as such. I don't know what kind of a strain Kevin might have been under when he saw them (or Chris and Nancy, for that matter), but business eventually went on as usual. If Kevin was bothered by the situation, he never really let on. It was, however, a hot angle which became very, very real.

Side note: If you don't want to lose your wife or girlfriend, keep her away from your job, especially if you're in the wrestling business. In future years, I would see many more of these "true-life" breakups take place with other "men" involved.

Perception is reality!

In October 1996, Joe D'Acquisto became the fourth and final member to join the Chubba Bubbas. We all knew Joe from our days with Savoldi's IWCCW and I had worked with him in Mexico. Joe, a typical New York kid who wrestled as the Rochester Roadblock during his time with WCW, was a very imposing character. He could talk you out of your shoes and make you think you owed him money for their return. Joe wasn't into the "recreational" substances, but he could stir up a party anywhere and he loved (as did we all) the monkey juice.

There are several definitions for "monkey juice," but ours was what we called GHB, or as reported in media reports, the "date rape drug." It was legally sold as "re-nutrient" and we used it to build muscles and enhance our performance, but it was advertised as a fat-burner to use just before going to sleep. None of the boys I knew ever used it to drug women. We were too busy getting ourselves high to care about them, not to mention the fact that women were more than willing to give it away without the support of drugs. In my opinion, GHB is relatively safe, but when used in combination with other drugs like alchol, or in massive doses, it can become dangerous. The same can be said about most other drugs, including those prescribed by doctors. The other problem I can see with GHB is that due to government prohibition, most of the GHB available is produced in what the FDA calls "clandenstine labs." I even saw instructions on how to make monkey juice. There was always somebody making it (usually in bathtubs), or somebody knew a "friend" who could get as much as we wanted. When the Chubba Bubbas were hitting their stride, GHB was running wild in the wrestling companies among the boys *and* the girls. At one point, I was ordering it by the case from one of the big name gyms in Las Vegas. Everybody carried bottles of GHB in their bags. When it became a banned substance and the company told us not to be in possession of it, we kept it in mouthwash bottles.

I have to make this point: if you take GHB, even in small quantities, do NOT drink alcohol. The combination can result in respiratory arrest. More to the point, I would advise you to not take it at all. Of course, this is one of those things that falls into the "do as I say, not as I do" category. I had quite a tolerance for heavy quantities of alcohol. I would spend hundreds of dollars *every* night at the bars. I could drink vodka like it was water and I didn't know any limits. However, I would never advise anyone to do the things I've done because, in truth, I'm very lucky just to be alive.

GHB eventually became a problem for many of us. At any given time, whether we were at an airport, a restaurant, or in a locker room, one of the boys might pass out from overdoing it. I remember one time, in particular, in which a very popular man who was "in charge" of things had a bad reaction to the monkey juice (or at least, that's what everybody said it was from) and fell onto the floor. While we watched, things became a little more "real" as paramedics began working to save his life. When blood began pouring out of his mouth, they inserted tubes down his throat in an attempt to keep his air passages open. It was like something you would see in a horror movie. That was a wake-up call that made us all think about what it was we were doing to ourselves. Well, we thought about it at least for the remainder of the show. By the time we got to the bar, things were back to normal and we were once again overindulging ourselves in drink and drugs.

Since I've cleaned up my act, I always find it amazing to realize that no matter what went wrong, or how many times we saw a bad reaction (or even death), we never gave a thought to the fact that it could happen to us. For the better part of twenty years, the only way I could get through each day and night, was with the assistance of alcohol and drugs. I was "gooned out" all the time. I built up such a tolerance that it took more and more to get me loaded. I wanted to be "goofy" all the time and I lived in a fog. How I ever lived through that is beyond my understanding. To this day, I cannot drink Sunny Delight. It was the one thing I would mix the monkey juice with when I was off work and at home. I can't even stand to look at it in the store. Bad memories.

One night, we were in Atlanta at the Gold Club on Cleveland Street, one of our favorite "adult entertainment" establishments. Big Joe decided that since he was twice our size, he should have twice as much monkey juice as any of us. Since we aimed to please, we let Joe drink as much as he wanted ... and he drank it like water. Needless to say, Joe was laid out in less than thirty minutes. The bouncers and the girls were worried about him, but we reassured them that everything was okay and resumed the festivities. We eventually carried Joe outside and left him lying in the doorway. Our plan had been to make him comfortable on the back seat of the car, but he was as heavy as a tank and we couldn't carry him that far. When the joint shut down, we dragged and rolled Joe into the car and drove home to the Dungeon.

That scenario took place almost every night.

On another occasion, Teddy and I were partying with Dean Malenko, Eddie Guerrero, and Chris Jericho. We wound up at a "hole-in-the-wall" strip club at which we were just getting to know the bartender and "talent." Needless to say, I had been taking my "vitamins" and other assorted "fruit candies." While I was sitting at one end of the bar with Jericho (who was a lot of fun to hang out with, drunk or sober), a very unattractive lady was working very hard to get our attention. Simply calling her "unattractive" is being nice. She was the definition of being "rode hard and hung up wet." The worst insult you can pay a "dancer" is to not pay attention to them. After a while, I got sick of watching her flaunt her naked body around us. I do draw the line (sometimes) at the less-desirable women, even when I'm drunk, so I reached into my "fag bag" (the pouch which the boys all wore around their waist to hold their money, keys, and pills) and pulled out a dollar. After handing it to her, I turned around and resumed my conversation with Jericho. Before I could utter a word, she was cussing and yelling at me. When Jericho asked me what I had said to her, I told him, *"I looked at the dollar bill and said, 'I'm sorry you have to be a part of this, Mr. President. I'll fold you in half so you can't see where you're going.' I don't know why the bitch took offense."*

Several times during my run with WCW, we went to Sturgis, South Dakota, for the *Road Wild* pay-per-view. Those days were filled with motorcycles, naked women, alcohol, drunken men, more naked women, and great food.

During one trip to Sturgis, someone in the company arranged for several of us to be backstage guests at a Lynyrd Skynyrd concert. Teddy, Johnny, Meng and I got so drunk that we never made it to the concert. Instead, we decided to go to a local strip club. As usual, while the rest of us got to know the local dancers, Johnny began to wander. Johnny was never much for staying in one place too long, so we got used to him wandering and meeting up with us later. We didn't know where he went, but we knew he would find his way back to the hotel. When Teddy and I got back to our hotel in the wee hours of the morning, we saw Dave Penzer walking down the hallway with a mop and bucket. What we saw when we walked into the room was our bed linens and personal items covered with shit! That's right. I said "shit." I was so stunned that I couldn't say a word, but Teddy was so pissed that he launched into an outburst of obscenities. And the fact that Johnny was nowhere to be found was somewhat suspicious. We later learned that while we were in the bar, Johnny had brought a lady friend back to our room for a certain sex act which involved this lady's ass! It was that chick's shit that was everywhere. By far, that was one of the most disgusting things I had ever seen, heard, or been a part of, but it was pretty funny. I'm not sure why, but Dave Penzer didn't seem to find it amusing at all. It might have been due to the fact that, once again, he had been relegated to cleaning up after the boys. It was both gross and disgusting, but it was par for the course for the Chubba Bubbas.

During one of our days off in Sturgis, Jim Duggan, Grunge, Teddy, and I decided to go to Mount Rushmore. None of us had ever been there. It was one of the coolest things I have ever seen. For some reason, even with Mount Rushmore standing there in all its majesty, the bikers and tourists were gawking at us. We had been drinking (I promise, if there was ever a time we *weren't* drinking, I'll tell you about that, too) on the way there. While we were taking pictures and enjoying nature, I decided to tell the boys a joke. *"Who were the three most famous people who got shot in the back of the head?"* When I noticed the blank stares on their faces, I said, *"Lincoln, Kennedy, and the guy who sat in front of Pee Wee Herman."* We all laughed and went on our way.

A few minutes later, a park ranger approached us and told us we had to leave the park. She said that when I told the joke, we had been standing

Bill, Jim Duggan and Johnny Grunge make a visit to Mt. Rushmore

above the outside amphitheatre where they were presenting some kind of a show … and my voice had been picked up and amplified by the sound system. Several of the women in the audience took offense and complained.

How many people can claim to have been kicked out of a national park?

The four of us were inseparable. We all knew we could trust each other with anything. It was around that time that Konnan was busting Teddy's chops about how his "crew" was tighter than we were. It was harmless banter about how he and his guys were really brothers, while we were just hanging out with each other. Well, that upset Teddy so much that he decided he was going to do something he had never done before. He was going to get a tattoo. Ted Petty, a former professional boxer and all-around athlete who never felt the need to prove himself to anyone, was going to get a tattoo and show Konnan how devoted we were to each other.

One night after a four-day run of "Chubba Bubba-ness," we were all enjoying a home-cooked meal (for a change) at my house in Titusville. Teddy began to draw an image of a cross. We all decided to go into town to talk with the tattoo artist who was doing my work at the time. While there, Joey, Johnny, Teddy and I all decided to have it done and we got the cross with our respective names on it on the backs of our necks. When Teddy and Johnny were working as "Public Enemy," they wore jerseys with the number "00" and "69," respectively. Inside the cross, Teddy and Johnny had those numbers tattooed. Big Joe had "RB" (for Roadblock) and mine has "BP" (for Big Poppa). Below the crosses are the letters "L.O.C.B.," which stands for "Loyal Order of the Chubba Bubbas." Mongo McMichael [Steve McMichael] later had a version tattooed on his neck because he loved us and enjoyed hearing about the things we did. A Englishman named Colin, who was in charge of the company magazine at the time, got one, too. As silly as it might sound, everybody wanted to be a Chubba Bubba. We had "legendary status" when it came to the night life. Before Teddy and Johnny died, a picture was taken of the cross on my back which had Teddy's name on it. That picture was used in *Unscripted*, a WWE book of body art. Later, we had hats and t-shirts made. The shirts featured a picture of a fat, sumo wrestler on the front, and on the back were the words, *"We are not here for a long time … just a good time … the Cubba Bubbas."* The hats had an embroidered cross with our initials. They were a big hit with both the boys and our friends outside the business. After Ted and Johnny passed away, I had the dates of their deaths tattooed underneath the L.O.C.B. initials.

The next day, Konnan and Rey Mysterio Jr. brought us each a gift they had bought while they were on the road. It was a silver cross which the Mexican clique all wore around their necks. It meant a lot to us and we wore them all the time. I still have that cross. Whenever I feel discouraged or go on a trip, I wear it. It still means a lot to me. All kidding aside, both groups hung out together and we had a blast. Friends like that don't come along often, and I was honored to have known all of them.

There were other people who were considered part of the Chubba Bubbas — Chris Jericho, Eddie Guerrero, Chris Benoit, Chavo Guererro, Steve "Mongo" McMichaels, and Mickey Jay — but they were voted in through the "skinny guy clause," which was our version of the grandfather clause. We made them honorary members because we were always together and they were loyal and cared for our friends.

I was closer to Chavo than I was to any of the other honorary Chubba Bubbas. Chavo and I always traveled together. On one of the "loops" we made, Lacey (more on her later) was with us. After a TV taping in Tupelo, Mississippi, we began driving back to Memphis where we would fly home the following morning. Like most TV tapings, we finished late at night and, like most trips, I was driving "slightly" above the speed limit in order to get to the hotel and get the most sleep possible before going to the airport.

When we were about five miles from the Tennessee state line, we were pulled over by a state trooper who wasn't in a very good mood. Fortunately, it was one of the few nights we hadn't stopped for beer and we didn't have any in the car. When the trooper walked up to my window, he asked the usual questions:

"Where are you going?"

"Memphis."

"Do you know how fast you were driving?"

"No, sir." I had been driving 90 miles an hour and I knew it, but I wasn't going to implicate myself.

Then it began. *"Who do you work for?"*

"Vince McMahon."

"Do you have an agent?"

"Jimmy Hart." That wasn't true, but I didn't have an answer and I was feeling cocky.

At that point, we were told to step out of the car and present our licenses. My license was from Florida, Chavo's was from California, and Lacey's was from Iowa. Before we knew what was happening, the trooper was talking into his radio. *"Get a drug dog out here."* Minutes later, several other patrol cars pulled up. Several of the officers walked over and shook our hands. They knew who we were! They had to go along with the officer who stopped us, though, and we were taken to separate areas of the road, where we were questioned like we had just committed a bank robbery. Lacey was really shaken because she had never been in a situation like that. Chavo was very (as in extremely) pissed off. Me? I was just being me.

While we were being questioned, they had a drug dog search the car. While we watched, the dog sat down in the front passenger seat and put his snout into a bag that Chavo had at his feet. That was when I heard one of the funniest thing I had ever heard in my life. Chavo yelled out, *"That dog better not eat my doughnuts!"* He was dead serious.

In the end, they took my license and made me pay a ridiculously high fine. By the time we pulled into Memphis, we only had time for a couple of hours sleep before we had to leave for the airport.

Working for WCW was "party central" for everybody in the company. We ran wild. We went to work every day, partied every night, and occasionally went to bed. One of our favorite places to party was the infamous Baja Beach Club in downtown Orlando. When we went to the Baja, we owned the place.

That was good for the owners because people would come just because the wrestlers were there. On November 10, 1996, a few of us were there to celebrate my 31st birthday. I had piled up more than my share of monkey juice, so at closing time, Rey Mysterio said he would drive my old-school, big-ass, four-door Lincoln and take Jeff Jarrett, Chris Jericho, Chavo, Kathy Dingman, and me to our hotel. I was told Rey had so sit on something in order to be able to see over the dashboard. Rey wasn't sober, either, but he was less drunk than the rest of us. Somehow, we all wound up at "Pineapple Pete's," another infamous hangout for the boys, especially the Chubba Bubbas. After closing that place down, we went back to the hotel.

For those who don't know, Kathy worked for the WWF as "B.B.," WCW as "Papaya," and TNA as "Taylor Vaughn," but I called her "Bubbles." She was, and is, someone I consider to be a good friend. I first met Kathy in Daytona Beach when Teddy and I were out on the town after a show. Teddy and Kathy hit it off and I went to my hotel room with her friend (I can't remember her name). Kathy is a tall girl and that didn't sit well with Teddy, so we switched "interests." Kathy and I became good friends and spent a lot of time together whenever we worked in Florida. She is a good girl and a very big reason why I returned home to Florida after trips. Contrary to what "certain people" (okay, my ex-wife) thought or think, Kathy encouraged me to always go home to be with my family in Titusville. She got me through a lot of bad times, but even though she saw me in bad shape, she never judged me. We still talk and see each other on occasion.

On the night of my birthday, everyone insisted I go to my room. Kathy tried like hell to get me up, but I was so "gooned out" that I was content to sleep on the back seat of my car. That made Chavo mad (he also was drunk), so he went to his room, put on his gym clothes, and came back out to drag me out of my car. He began smacking me around, hoping to get me pissed off enough that I would get out of the car to get him. I told him, *"If you don't stop hitting me, I'll kill you and every one of the Guerreros."* I love them all and would never do anything to hurt them, but being drunk and pilled up makes you say thing you don't mean. It didn't help matters that Chavo was hitting me in the face, especially since I *hate* to have anyone touch my face. When Chavo whacked me again, I sat up and ripped the door off the hinges. The hinges popped off the car frame and the electrical connections all came off with it. Everybody scattered as quickly as they could. I don't think they had been expecting me to do something like that. In fact, I believe I might have scared a few of them because I don't remember Jeff Jarrett ever going out with us again after that. I threw the car door into the rear of the car and went up to my hotel room. When I woke up, it was mid-afternoon. I checked out of the hotel and drove forty minutes to Titusville.

When I walked into our house, my wife said, *"Kevin Sullivan called here looking for you. I told him you were at work."*

"Dammit!" I thought. *"Now I have to call the office."*

I called Kevin and told him I wouldn't be able to make it in because I had been in a coma for the past fifteen hours. He didn't say a word. He just slammed down the phone. I had been with the company for a very short time and I had already missed a day of tapings, which usually meant three or four matches.

Chavo Guerrero Jr., Bill De Mott and Eddie Guerrero

The next day, I was very hesitant about going to MGM Studios. When I walked in, the guys didn't say a word. Instead, they just looked at me like I was some kind of a lunatic (which I was). I was immediately told to report to the booking room where Kevin, Arn Anderson, Jimmy Hart, and someone else were waiting. As usual, Kevin didn't waste any time with niceties. *"What the fuck do you think you're doing? I went out on a limb to get you this job and you fuck up a whole day of tapings. We were going to put you over and start to build momentum."* Frankly, I'm sure it was all bull-hockey, but it worked at the time because I felt like a big heel.

When I just stood there looking like a dumbass, Kevin yelled, *"Don't just stand there looking like a dumbass! I wanna know why you weren't at the tapings?"*

"I did a little too much celebrating the night before and couldn't even think about working. I was in a coma."

For some reason, that probably wasn't the best answer I could have given them. To my surprise, however, Arn and Kevin both began laughing. Kevin said, *"If that doesn't beat all! I have never heard a response like that. You are probably the only guy in the world who would be so honest about being fucked up. Go get dressed. You're going to work today and make up for the shots you missed."*

I was in shock. All I could say was, *"I'm sorry ... and thank you."*

I only missed two shows during my entire career and that was one of them. Arn still tells that story today, especially to the young kids who are just breaking into the business. Chavo will let me know that he hasn't forgotten, either, and Kathy and I still laugh about it when we talk. It became one of the greatest stories from that time. After all, I was Hugh Morrus of the Dungeon of Doom, and I had a reputation to keep!

During a tour of Texas, we went to a big cowboy bar to drink and hang out. As always, there were rumors that if we went, we would be drinking and having "fun" for free, so we went. Someone was always working the towns to see where the boys could go and raise a little Cain. Many establishments would give us free food and drinks because our presence always drew crowds of paying customers. There were even times when we were "booked" to make appearances at bars and other nighttime hot spots. While the rest of us decided which side of the room we wanted to "work," Meng wandered over to the dance floor. All of a sudden, in the middle of a song where cowboys and cowgirls were thick on the dance floor, we look over to see Meng walking into the deejay's booth. When he tells the guy he wants to do the Macarena, the guy blows him off. Meng walks out, gets out in the middle of the dance floor, and announces in his loud, Tongan voice, *"I want to do the Macarena!"* He instantly had everyone's undivided attention. When everybody fell silent, the deejay shut off the "hootenanny music" and put on the Macarena.

There he was, in all his glory. Meng! One of the toughest and scariest men to ever step into a professional wrestling ring ... doing the Macarena. Wouldn't you know it? Within seconds, he had women coming over to him from every section of the dance floor. Women were standing alongside that big teddy bear, doing the Macarena. From then on, we understood that "what Meng wants, Meng gets."

I miss the Chubby guys. Somehow, most of us have lost touch. My editor put me in touch with Mickie Jay while we were working on this book, but I haven't heard from Joe in a long time. We traded a few Christmas cards over the years. I sure would like to see him again. I think about them all the time. Chris Benoit and Eddie Guerrero are gone and I don't get many opportunities to see Dean, Chavo, or Jericho. Mongo stays busy as head coach of the Chicago Slaughter football team, a member of the Indoor Football League.

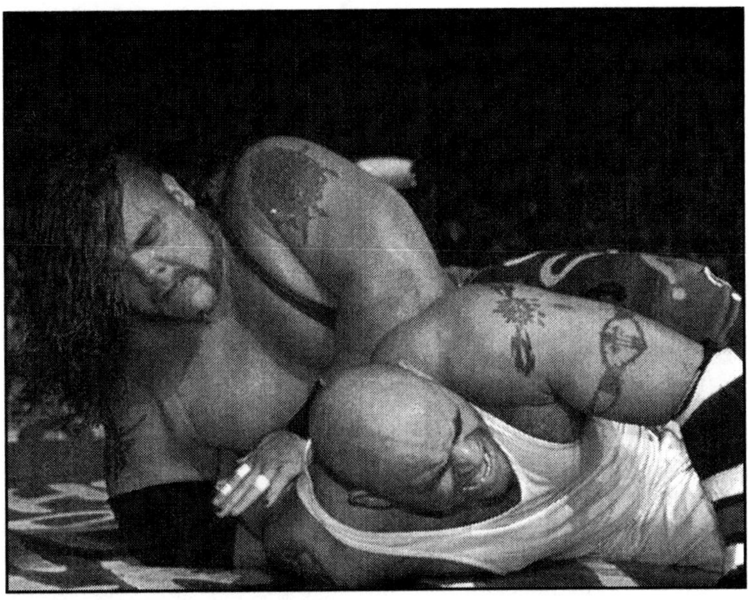

Hugh Morrus vs Konnan, 1998

Chapter 9

The Chemist

I was what they called a "journeyman" wrestler for WCW for a long time. As a rule, I would be given some good TV time where I could make my bones and get myself over. After a period of time, I would be asked to help someone else get over. That never bothered me. I made a career out of getting other people over. No matter what the circumstance, I always gave the fans one-hundred percent and I was in a good mood more often than not. I was happy to have a good-paying job and to be a part of the Chubba Bubbas. It's funny. It was easy to tell who was happy with the company and who thought they deserved more than what they were getting. For the most part, the guys who were making the big money were generally the most miserable.

There came a time, however, when I wasn't happy with the way things with my career were progressing and I wanted to get out of my contract. My unhappiness had nothing to do with money. In fact, throughout my career, money *never* was an issue with me. Everybody was responsible for what they made and for their own contract negotiations. If I had been worth more, I have no doubt that I would have been paid more. My hangup was that I wanted to be a bigger part of the company and to work more often. We had guys who would only work a limited number of days a year, while others wanted to work every night. I fell into the latter category. I didn't care whether or not I won my matches. Win, lose, or draw, I would get myself over. I just wanted to be working and in front of people. I wanted to be figured into storylines. There were times when I traveled to a town, but wouldn't be used on the taping, the live show, or the pay-per-views. It became really disheartening. I thought I had a lot to offer and I wanted the company to use what I had in whatever way they needed.

It was only after I got out of the business that I learned there were a lot of guys who felt that way … and most of them were the guys who worked on top. Chris Benoit, Eddie Guerrero and I would spend countless hours in locker rooms and catering talking about how the business was no longer fun. We talked and cried together about a lot of other things, as well. At different times, we all had marriage issues and problems with our kids. We made a pact that if we needed to talk to each other about something, we wouldn't hesitate. Our discussions always made me feel better and I think they felt the same way. It's funny how three guys, each with a different background and on a different level of the business, were able to keep each other going. Before

I knew it, they had left the company and were working for WWF. Chris and Eddie are both gone now. They died much too early. I miss our talks, but most of all, I miss them.

In 1997, I also had the opportunity to film a scene in the movie *The Waterboy* with Adam Sandler and Henry Winkler. It was a great experience. Alan Sharpe put my name on the list of people to audition. One morning at a TV taping at Universal Studios, I was handed a piece of paper and told to report the following day to a studio next door to where we were taping. I tried out for the part against guys like Dallas Page, Kevin Nash, and Jim Duggan. I think the producer picked me because I was the only guy who would bump for the Giant [Paul Wight]. I was treated really well. I even had my own trailer.

It's the story of my life, but when the movie was complete, the scenes with "Dr. Pain" (my character) were cut. After taking bumps for almost six hours and doing everything I could for them, I wound up on the cutting room floor. Boo! I did, however, frame my check and letter from the movie company as a keepsake. I'm also listed in the credits in an "uncredited" role.

Bill dressed as Dr. Pain in the movie *Waterboy*

When the Dungeon of Doom was dismantled in 1997, Jimmy Hart put me together with Barbarian, Jerry Flynn [William Brenneman], and Brian Knobbs [Brian Yandrisovitz], and called us the "First Family." Jimmy, who was our manager, both individually and as the mouthpiece for the group, proved to be the only normal person I would know in the company. Jimmy would help guide me through the rest of my career with WCW. Jimmy was the voice of reason, not to mention our babysitter. Jimmy had the best way of making us see the positive aspects of situations that we looked at as stupid and nonsensical. Time and again, he stressed how we had to be careful with our actions because we were important to the company. On more than one occasion, Jimmy saved me from myself during times when I was ready to self-destruct into the "why don't I get the push I deserve" attitude. Jimmy would talk calmly and say, *"Take it easy, big man. You've got to remember that you have a job and that your day is coming. You just have to hang in there long enough to reap the rewards."* Jimmy was a phenomenal motivator. He knew exactly what to say to encourage me to do my best each and every night. For the most part, I always believed in giving one hundred percent, but he was there to pump me up when I would get discouraged. I fed off of his positive energy. He always made me feel like I mattered and never gave me bad advice. I truly believe Jimmy Hart was my guardian angel. That might sound corny, but I don't think I would have survived those years, either personally or professionally, if he hadn't been there for me.

WCW First Family: Hugh Morrus, Jerry Flynn, Jimmy Hart, Barbarian and Brian Knobbs

Part of my problem was that I was very loyal to the people who brought me to where I was in the business, so I never had the balls to complain or ask for more. Kevin Sullivan was probably the most instrumental in the overall scheme of my career, so I wasn't going to gripe when he asked me to do something. I know I spent a lot of time bitching to Jimmy Hart, but he didn't make the decisions and was there only to reel me back in when I finished venting. When Vince Russo and Ed Ferrara came to work for WCW, I grew fond of them both. I even liked Eric Bischoff. Without them, I wouldn't have been given the opportunities I was.

Of all the things talked about between the covers of this book, this might be the most revealing and upsetting to people who are close to me. Contrary to popular opinion, I was already versed in the "drug scene" long before I entered the world of professional wrestling. For that matter, so were many others who have been involved in sports and entertainment. It's just easier to cast aspersions at an "athlete" or "actor" than at an "everyday Joe." When a regular person "overdoses," it's a tragedy because he must have been very troubled, but if a sports figure dies while intoxicated or high, it's because they are terrible people with a lot of money and nothing to do but get high.

I have "preached" to adults and children of all ages to avoid doing things which will hurt their bodies and minds. On the other hand, I never said I was perfect and I never denied I traveled a road that might have ended at a wall. In this chapter, however, I want to discuss a little of what took place in my life in regards to pills, alcohol, recreational drugs, prescription drugs, and whatever else I might have gotten my hands on.

As any other normal kid growing up in the early 1980s, I found myself with opportunities to indulge in things other than beer and grain alcohol. At the time, pot was the main drug being used. I tried pot on a few occasions when I was young, but I never really took to it. I didn't like the way I felt and smoking was never my thing.

During high school and college, I was exposed to a lot of drugs. I partied like a rock star. To me, at the time, it was unacceptable not to be accepted. The other college kids couldn't match my pace, which is why they called me "Psycho." I was usually drunk or wired and I was always willing to go further than anyone else. One of the things I learned about myself was that I am capable of adapting to the drugs I take. I have a ridiculous tolerance for drugs. I don't know if I was an "addict," but if I was, I know I could do more stuff that the average addict. I don't say that with pride, but I want to be honest.

When I was still living at home, I was less than 25 miles from New York City. As I grew older and became more and more adventurous, I began using drugs like Valium, cocaine, acid, mushrooms, and speed. When I was working in the bars and strip clubs, I ran into my fair share of people who wanted to know me, so they made sure I was happy and had "everything" I needed. In other words, drugs weren't hard to get. And while it wasn't any everyday occurrence, when Bill De Mott went out to party, he had no trouble staying out all night and going to work the next day with little or no sleep.

I know steroids and "performance-enhancing" drugs were being used before I got into the wrestling business, and they were readily available while I was involved, but I can honestly say I have never seen anyone actually use them in any locker room. Please don't think I'm stupid. I'm not saying it wasn't done. I'm just saying Bill De Mott never personally saw steroids being used in the locker room(s).

I also have openly stated that I used steroids during my career. I was knowledgeable of them long before I got involved in professional wrestling. I think it would be naïve to say the first time some of the guys used steroids was because they got into wrestling. That would be a "cop out" by someone who was full of bull. It would also be ridiculous for anyone to claim steroids were a prerequisite to making it in this business.

I was introduced to steroids when I was in my early twenties, right around the time I began serious weight training. I was a pretty strong guy, and when some of the guys in the gym realized that, they said, *"This will help you with your bench press,"* or *"This will make you recover faster."* At that time, I was looking for my niche. I had dropped out of college and I was just a "working schmo" who didn't have many goals. Lifting became an obsession. As time went by, my gym buddies pumped up my ego until I decided to dip into the world of steroids. I was strong, but when I was told I could be stronger, I didn't ask any questions about possible side effects. I simply began taking them. I also was big and I knew they would make me bigger.

It was so easy to buy steroids when I was working out in the gym. There was either a "gym rat" who had a hook up or guys who were "competing" and making money selling the stuff. When I was involved back home in Jersey, everybody who was training was taking something and knew someone who could get it: cops, contractors, students, and everyday Joes. I never got steroids from a doctor. Yes, I knew guys who were given scrips by doctors, but I wasn't a big fan of doctors, so I never approached them for their help.

When I actually got into the wrestling business, steroids were what I thought I needed to get a boost. I didn't do any major roids — just test [testosterone] and fat cutters like Winstrol-V or Clenbuterol. That wasn't too bright and I kept it a secret, but old habits come back. I honestly thought they were what I needed to get back into working condition. As it turned out, I didn't do enough for them to work, and quite frankly, I couldn't afford to spend the money necessary to do it right.

One summer, when I was training with Johnny Rodz, my focus was on becoming as strong and as big as possible ... until I became violently ill and had to be taken to the hospital. My body was dehydrated, my vision was blurry, and I couldn't speak or hold up my head. I also was exhausted. That wasn't so much from working in the sun or painting stripes on parking lots. It was from pumping iron and mixing steroids with my booze and blow.

I used steroids until I began working as a commentator on *WWE Velocity* in October 2001.

During the days when I was training with Johnny Rodz, my Pop asked me if I was on drugs. I had to lie and tell him a half-truth. *"Yes, Pop. I am. I've been taking steroids to build strength and muscle."* My parents aren't stupid, but I think they heard what they wanted to hear. Steroids were bad enough, but there was no way (until now) I would ever reveal to my mom or Pop that I was doing drugs.

At any given time during my wrestling career, I had a readily available stash of drugs: in my truck, motorcycle, fanny pack, travel bag, and gym bag. I had three or four pill boxes hidden in various spots in the house. Drugs were my blanket of comfort for more than 20 years. By the time I got into wrestling and left for Puerto Rico, I was well versed in the art of getting high.

When I wrestled in Puerto Rico, I lived in a condo by the ocean, I was surrounded by beautiful Spanish women, and I had a lot of free time on my hands. Enter ... the pills. Halcion, Soma, OxyContin, Percoset, Valium, Vicodin, Speed, downers, sleeping pills, and probably a few I'm forgetting. In Puerto Rico, they were all the "flavors of ice cream." Until 2007, I was on one or more of those drugs every day, but I'm proud to say I haven't taken any kind of a drug since then.

Puerto Rico was where I was really made aware of the guys getting messed up, either with drugs or alcohol, before their matches. The presence of the drugs didn't bother me, but for me, working the guys who were messed up in the ring was a whole new ballgame. I'm not throwing stones because I did my share of substance abuse, but I did all my stuff after I finished working. Just so everyone is clear, I want it known that I was never messed up before or during a match. I wouldn't put my friends into a position where someone might get hurt because I wasn't at my best. The same held true for 85 percent of the boys. They were professional enough to keep themselves in check during times when they were scheduled to work.

Traveling back and forth to Japan was always a opportunity to take whatever and be "wide awake" by the time we landed 13 to 14 hours later. It was common for us [wrestlers] to dope ourselves up before getting on a plane and letting it "kick-in" so we were knocked out for the entire flight. When the plane landed, we could walk out and be ready to enjoy life.

By the time I joined WCW, I was a full-blown drug user. Even though I never went to a doctor and I never had a prescription (except for when I got operated on), I could always get anything I wanted.

In 1999, the company surprised me with a drug test. In total, I must have taken ten tests during my time with WCW. Like most of the other "superstars," I knew when the tests were coming. That allowed us to prepare for the tests. We knew how long specific drugs stayed in our system so we could quit using them during the necessary time frame. There were also drugs we could take which would mask the presence of drugs. This time, however, I had an overabundance of cocaine, codeine, and morphine in my system. For some reason which I can't fathom to this day, those results sent up red flags. The failed drug test came at a time when I was a mess, both mentally and physically. I was gooned out all the time. I was always taking something: to wake up, to go to sleep, to work out at the gym, to lose weight, to stay strong, and to be able to party through the night. Most of all, I was always looking for something to dull the pain. Regardless of what anyone thinks, pain is a bitch. Most people will do just about anything to dull the pain in order to do what they do for a living. That was the common denominator with wrestlers. Some were very good at taking "just enough" of a drug to get by, but there are others who would go balls-out and take whatever was in front of them. I'm not sure where I fall in those two categories, but what I do know is I don't know how I lived through the things I did.

Hugh Morrus publicity picture

When my editor read the word "morphine," he knew it was important for me to explain my reasons for using such an addictive drug. Reasons not withstanding, it was seriously stupid for me to use it, but at the time, I wanted a way to get fucked up instantly. I didn't care about potential consequences. I was looking for something to make me feel better both mentally and physically. It came in a "sinus-inhaler" type of bottle that I could carry with me.

I don't want anyone to think I take the issue of drugs lightly, or that I'm proud of what I did in those days, but I can't undo what happened. I can't and won't speak for everyone, but I was well-versed in recreational drugs. Working, bumping, traveling, and partying took a toll on my body and my mind. I found a way to lay down and get up each day (and every day) by using Soma [a muscle relaxer] and narcotic pain relievers like Nubain, Vicodin, and OxyContin. I would take something to keep going all night, and something else to bring me down and help me relax. I didn't necessarily take anything to sleep, but I just needed something to take off the edge caused by the other drugs. As soon as I finished wrestling, I would get my bag and pop ten Somas into my mouth. I would chew them, wash them down with vodka and grapefruit juice, take a shower, and get ready to party. I never got on a plane without being drugged up in some way, shape, or form. I would get on the plane to leave the country with a pocketful of cocaine and a bottle of Somas and assorted pills. Guys who would come off the road with a one-day turnaround needed something to help them pass out on the plane so they could be rested and somewhat normal for the short time they had to spend with their family. When we made an overseas trip, we would stock up on pills and our "choice" of medicine.

There wasn't anything I wouldn't take and nothing I wouldn't mix. Stupid, I know, and I have to repeat that I'm not saying this to brag. For all intents and purposes, I should have died ten different times, but there is a purpose to this story. The fact that I'm still here makes me realize I was saved for a reason. I want everyone who reads this to know that drugs will make you think you need them to get through life, but they will kill you. Too many of my friends said "that won't happen to me," but in many cases, it did. I know full well that it is only by the grace of God that I am still around to tell my story. I carried around the torch of stupidity, selfishness, and disregard for my friends and family. I never stopped to think about how my actions affected them. It wasn't my intention to hurt anyone, but at the time, like everyone else, I thought I was invincible.

Strangely enough, whenever I was injured and required surgery, I was terrified. That seems stupid considering the drugs I took and the things I did, but I always worried about not waking up from the anesthesia. Even after the surgeries, I wouldn't use the prescribed medications because I was afraid of how my body would react to them. How ridiculous is that? I did and took everything under the sun without giving it any thought, but when something was legal and prescribed to me, I was scared about what might happen.

Wrestlers aren't bad people. We are family men and women, and speaking for myself, I never looked at drugs as hurting anyone other than myself. I used them in order to survive the pain, the headaches, and the pressure (that I put on myself), but I used them to excess. I'm sure the long-term effects of the drugs have taken their toll on my body and only the future will tell what troubles are in store for me. However, I was a chemist, and that made me more dangerous than most. I knew what to take, how much to take, and when to take it. I knew how to keep conscious long enough to get through whatever situation I found myself in. I knew what I needed to take to get "up" the next day. I even knew what foods to eat to make the drugs more potent. I reached a point where I didn't even have to think about it. It became a part of my routine.

For the most part, I was always under the radar. The boys who were close to me knew I was a mess and a party machine, but I never found myself in the headlines as "one of those guys" who acted up in airports, passed out in restaurants and parking lots, or pissed my pants in a hotel lobby. I knew what I could handle and still stay out of the limelight.

I can never imagine being able to live like that again. It wasn't something I did. To me, it was a way of life. I wanted to be the best. I never knew how to do anything in moderation. Today, I live with pain, both mental and physical, and the only drug I use is Advil. I want to survive to see my grandchildren. I drink occasionally, but I'm always aware that I can easily head in "that direction" again.

At the risk of sounding like I'm on my soap box, I want to let the young boys know there are other ways of dealing with problems. Don't put insurmountable pressure on yourself to succeed. If you're love the wrestling business and are good at what you do, you've already succeeded. And make no mistake. Eric Bischoff and Vince McMahon didn't make me take drugs. I traveled down the path I chose for myself. Anyone who says they were made to travel all year and do this or that for the company is full of bull. We are all grown men and women and we can make up our own minds.

Other than an occasional drinking binge, I have been sober since 2007. It's probably because I can't afford all those pills any more (see, always hugh-morous), but more importantly, I have learned to live with the discomfort and pain. I won't lie. There have been times when I was in a mood and wanted to get "gooned out," but I haven't followed through.

After I was told I had failed the drug test, I received the dreaded FedEx overnight letter from the company which gave me the information about what had been found in my system. It stated that I had to report to a rehabilitation facility in Melbourne to take another test. . J.J. Dillon then made a follow-up call to be sure I knew how seriously the company was taking it and told me I should be dead based on the amount of drugs in my system. I knew for a fact that my levels would be lower because on the night before the original test, I had just gotten back from a weekend run with several other familiar WCW personalities. By the time I took the second test, I hadn't been gooned out for several days. I reported as scheduled, peed in a cup, and then took a written test. I answered their questions honestly. Before I knew it, the doctor was enrolling me for a 90-day in-house visit. All I could do was say, *"Are you fuckin' kidding me?"* and I walked out. I know my levels were lower, but I never knew if I passed or not because they decided the test was faulty. One of the drugs they really looked for was Valium. Well, hell. I took Valium just to be able to take other muscle relaxers. To us, taking Valium was like eating Pez candy. We would take just enough to calm us down and stimulate our appetite so we could eat, which would then allow us to take something else. It was an art ... but it was dangerous. Many of my peers, as everyone knows, didn't live to tell about it, and yet, we never learn from our losses. We all think it can't happen to us.

I'm not trying to use this as an excuse to avoid punishment for what I did, but in my opinion, based on what I saw, the drug tests were used by the company only when needed for leverage. I believe certain people were notified about when they should be at TV and when they shouldn't (which was during times when drug tests were scheduled). It was obvious that it was a "numbers" test, and not a "talent" test.

One funny story about the drug test took place early in my WCW career when we were getting ready for work at the MGM Studios. We were told everyone had to be present at a company meeting, during which we were informed that there would be a drug test ... for everyone! When I arrived home in Jersey, I received a call from Gary Juster, who said I had failed the drug test. I had four hours to get to a drug-testing facility in Newark and take another test. As it turns out, twenty to thirty of the guys failed that same test. When the company execs went through the list, they came to the conclusion that the test must have been faulty because some of the "straight" guys (guys who didn't use drugs) had failed. Ted Petty failed and everyone knew he didn't do drugs, so they threw out the test and everyone was cleared. Rumor has it that someone (a big, blond, fat, nasty someone) had dumped something into the vat of coffee from which everyone had been drinking. He didn't want to be the only person to fail the test, and the more people who failed, the less likely it would be that the company would use the test. It worked and we all continued to work as scheduled.

I can't speak for anyone other than myself as far as who participated in what, but the use of Somas and Nubain was running rampant. Cocaine could be found anywhere and every pain pill imaginable was available to whoever wanted them. A few of the guys/girls made it a practice to ask the fans if they knew where they could get "hooked up." Many times, the fan would buy the drugs for the boys just for the "privilege" of being allowed to hang out with them. Even underneath card guys had people who wanted to hang with them. Our "girlfriends" had guys they could get it from and strippers had customers who would supply us. We could go to any town and get coke whenever we wanted. After we appeared in a town a few times, we could call the "townie" and let them know we were coming. When we got there, the drugs would be waiting. People loved the fact that the "superstars" were asking them for their assistance to get high. We had people everywhere, and when we didn't know anyone personally, we knew "someone who knew someone." For a long time, we bought Somas off the Internet. I would buy a bottle of 500 at a time and get more when I was on the road. I had a road stash, a home stash, and a truck stash. The same went for Vicodin, OxyContin, and coke.

When we couldn't get what we wanted through our contacts, we went to the doctors. It was so-ooo easy to convince doctors to write us scrips [prescriptions], although that practice has slowed down due to the spate of deaths of wrestlers over the past few years. I never went to a doctor's office, but I had scrips filled to get what I needed (or just wanted). It was a day and an age when anything goes.

On August 3, 1998, one month before my contract was due to expire, I approached Eric Bischoff in Denver to ask him if I could get a raise in pay and be more involved with storylines. Eighty-five thousand dollars was a lot of money, but there were also a lot of expenses I had to pay. When we made special appearances, such as autograph signings and charity events, WCW paid for our hotel and trans. For all other events, such as TV tapings and house shows, we paid for everything (hotel, rental car, travel, meals) except plane tickets. Eric said, *"You're lucky to have a job. You failed a drug test. You really aren't in any position to renegotiate."* I had great timing for things like that. I worked for six years without making any waves, and after I fail a drug test, I decide to ask for a raise. What an idiot! Bischoff was right. I'll be the first to admit that I was an alcohol and drug abuser, but it would be a safe bet for me to say more than half the roster was doing something, and the biggest offenders were the main event talent. That doesn't make it right, but it made me feel like I wasn't getting a fair shake. Nothing was done about my contract and it automatically rolled over for another year, which was common practice at that time.

Five months later, when we were at the Georgia Dome in Atlanta for the January 4, 1999 taping of *WCW Monday Nitro*, I told Jimmy Hart I was leaving the company. It was very rare for my character to get the nod, especially on TV, but on that night, I wrestled Glacier (the office loved that guy) and I was going to get my hand raised. That figured. When I was the most miserable, they put me over. That wasn't what it was about for me, though, so after my victory, I told Jimmy, Kevin, and Eric that I was through because I wasn't happy with the way things were going for me. The guys were always threatening things like that, so I'm sure they thought I was blowing smoke. Besides, a guy like me would have to be crazy to walk away from WCW when I was doing so well.

I left that night and flew home to Titusville. I didn't say much to my family about it because I hoped other options would come up. I had been talking with Jim Cornette about going to work for the WWF, so I thought an opportunity there might pan out for me.

Little did I know, the next phone call I would receive would be from J.J. Dillon, who was working as an agent for WCW. Those phone calls were never good. *Never!* When he asked me why I wasn't in Richmond for the January 7 *Thunder* tapings, I gave him the background information and explained that I no longer wanted to work for the company. I also told him I wouldn't be making any of my other scheduled bookings, either. To make a long story short, phone calls were made back and forth all day long, during most of which one WCW employee or another threatened to sue me for breach of contract. They said they'd take everything I had made during my time with the company and the money they "would" have paid me.

During one phone call, Bischoff reiterated the fact that I had *"no bargaining power due to the failed drug test."* I told him, *"Yes, I failed the test, but I've passed two tests since then and I won't be making my shots."* My remarks during that time reflected the fact that I really did have a problem. How screwed up was I to believe I was clean and didn't have a problem just because I had passed two tests?

By the end of the day, Eric convinced me to go to the house show so we could "work things out." I caught a last-minute flight to Richmond and went to the Coliseum where I explained my side of the story to Kevin and some of the boys. I didn't stay to watch the show, but went back to my hotel and packed for my early-morning flight to Atlanta.

The next morning, a car was waiting to take me to the airport. I was scheduled to meet Eric, JJ, their attorney, and Gary Juster at the WCW offices. When I walked into the office, the receptionist told me to have a seat and wait until they could see me. They knew I was there, but as usual, they did the old "waiting room" routine and kept me waiting for quite a while. It's like going to the doctor. They realize you're there, so they don't get in any hurry. When I was ushered into Eric's office, they didn't say a thing other than, *"Have a seat."* Before my butt had settled comfortably into the seat cushion, they placed a contract onto the table in front of me.

The contract was for $250,000 a year for three years.

I thought I had walked into an episode of *The Twilight Zone.* All I could think was, *"What just happened?"* They had been making threatening phone calls … and now they were offering me $250,000? *"Okay, where's Allen Funt?"* Where's the candid camera? *"You don't have any bargaining power. You're lucky to have a job. You should be happy we're paying you $85,000 a year. Oh, and by the way, here's a contract for $250,000."* Not only were they offering me a ridiculous amount of money, but they were telling me about the plans they had for me, and how valuable I was to the company, and what a star I was about to become.

I want to repeat myself. It was *never* about money. I was more concerned about being a part of something. But on the other hand, "my mama didn't raise no dummy." Who was Bill De Mott to be making a quarter of a million dollars a year. More importantly, the heads of WCW were telling me to my face about the big plans they had in store for me: a push, merchandise, and getting me to that "superstar" status that every wrestler dreams about.

Of course, I signed on the dotted line, and why wouldn't I? Who would pay me that kind of money if they didn't mean what they said? I was on my way to living my dream more than ever. Things were finally going my way and I was going to take full advantage of the opportunity. I went directly to the airport and flew to Winston-Salem to wrestle that night.

Unfortunately, even though the size of my paycheck increased, nothing else changed. I was stuck in the same spot and wrestling sporadically. In 1999, I wrestled an average of five times a month. It made me sick to my stomach to get on a plane and start off every loop knowing that by the time I got to TV, I would be hearing the same bullshit. *"You're off tonight,"* or, *"We need you to get this guy over."* You can only hear that for so long before you begin to doubt your abilities. It really pissed me off to hear people say things like, *"Hey, at least you're getting paid."* Most of the boys had tremendous egos. Not too many of them put much thought into what they could do for the company, or what would happen to their jobs if the company went out of business.

I didn't wrestle at all from December 20, 1999 through March 1, 2000, but that was due to me taking a few too many shots to the head. Prior to that, I was getting help from Danny Young, the trainer for WCW. Danny wasn't just my trainer. He was my friend and confidant. He would always get me through whatever problems I was facing … headaches, concussions, forgetfulness, and loss of eyesight … and keep me under the radar. In hindsight, the recreational drugs I was taking probably didn't help my judgment of pain or the seriousness of my problems. When we were in Baltimore, Danny went to Arn Anderson and told him I was in really bad shape. Being the professional he is, Arn asked me if I could work against Curt Hennig that night. Of course, I said I could. I wanted to wrestle, so it didn't matter what they wanted me to do, especially since the office kept telling Brian Knobs and me that we were going to be tag champs (once again, I believed their shit).

In the days that followed, the company sent me to a specialist in Atlanta. After running a number of tests over a three-day period, he suggested I quit wrestling. I had "clinical brain damage."

Hugh Morrus vs Scott Steiner

I went back to work in March after convincing Vince Russo and Ed Ferrara I was okay. I could have milked my problems because I was working on a guaranteed deal, but I wanted to work.

In early 2000, Time-Warner executives ousted Kevin Sullivan as booker and put Eric Bischoff and Vince Russo in charge of the creative end of the company. WCW would honor the two years Kevin had remaining on his contract, but he was released from any duties and sent home.

At the directive of Bischoff and Russo, the announcers, Mark Madden and Tony Schiavone, spent an entire show talking up the angle of whether or not Russo would agree to work with Bischoff. Neither man appeared on camera, but the "executives" were now the focus of the show.

One of their first decisions was to declare all WCW titles vacant and create a new stable of wrestlers called "The New Blood." New Blood, which consisted of younger talent, was booked in a feud with the "Millionaire's Club," which featured the older stars of WCW (Ric Flair, Hulk Hogan, Kevin Nash, and others).

Russo, who got more and more involved with the on-air details, as well as the running of the show, worked side by side with Bischoff. Their stated goal was to "move the company in a new direction." I fell "just short" of being involved in that "new direction." Once again, I didn't play politics well and I didn't travel and train with the guys who were getting a push. There were way too many cliques in the company and I wasn't a part of any of them. I was my own man and I had my own life to lead. On the other hand, there was a lot of talent standing in line waiting to kiss Bischoff and Russo's ass. Teddy, Johnny and Chris were all gone from the company by that time, so I decided to go my own way and deal with my situation accordingly.

Unfortunately, "accordingly" wasn't very healthy. I had no voices of reason (like Jimmy Hart) and I didn't have any boundaries. I was on a destructive path. I felt like I was in a rut and my home life was beginning to unfold. Trying to keep myself alive and in the mix at work was tough enough, but my life was made worse due to the fact that I didn't feel and comfortable in my own home. Rose and I were not on the same page. I often think that if I hadn't been gone as much as I was, we would have split up long before we did (or we would have killed each other). When I was at home with my head injuries, we were always at odds about something. Our biggest bone of contention when I was home was the chain of command would change. The girls loved me being home because they got a lot of attention and we did things differently from what they were used to. The only way I could find peace was to stay numb. In other words, take pills, drink, and get gooned out. In hindsight, I'm surprised I never drowned in our swimming pool.

During this same time, WCW helped produce a movie called *Ready to Rumble*, which was released to theaters on April 7, 2000. Some people were saying that it was the beginning of the end because the company had put so much money into the project. Diamond Dallas Page had a starring role in the movie and quite a few other WCW wrestlers had parts in the movie, including (to name just a few) Bill Goldberg, Sting, Bam Bam Bigelow, and Randy Savage.

Since I wasn't in "the clique," I wasn't invited. However, while they were shooting the movie, I was out in Los Angeles with the "no-clique clique — Jimmy Hart, Jim Duggan, Brian Knobbs, and Scotty Riggs — to shoot a week's worth of *Family Feud* with host Louie Anderson. Jimmy and Brian were actually a part of "the clique," but I seem to remember them telling me they chose not to be in the movie.

The best part of the *Family Feud* gig was that we were playing against the Playboy Playmates and the theme was *Beauty vs. The Beasts*. As you can imagine, it was every man for himself, and Knobbs was for everyone. I have to say, as many stories as there are about Brian Knobbs, until you spend a decent amount of time with him, you can't fully appreciate the things he's said and done.

When we arrived at the studio, we were treated like royalty and ushered to individual dressing rooms (like we were somebody important). After having our makeup applied, we met the girls in the "green room." The girls didn't know what to make of us at first, but they soon became very friendly. We reciprocated, of course, even though we were all naturally shy. Once the girls loosened up and realized we were good guys, we had a lot of fun in the green room, but whenever we made a little headway with one of the girls, Captain Obnoxious (Knobbs) would throw in a wrench. I really like Knobbs (in small doses), but when he gets going, he can be the world's biggest pain in the ass. He has to continually remind everyone that he's in the room. We shot all five episodes that one day and we took breaks in-between so they could switch audiences. It was a lot of fun, but it also was a lot harder than I ever would have imagined it being.

After the taping, Duggan, Knobbs and I went out on the town. Knobbs wanted to show us how he "rolls" when he hangs out with Hogan, so he took us to a famous cigar bar *"in his town, baby"* where we enjoyed drinks and a good smoke. All was well with the world until Knobbs spotted Peter Weller, the dude who played the title role in the 1987 movie *Robocop*. We listened to Knobbs bust Weller's balls about the movies in which he had appeared until it got embarrassing. When that happened, Duggan and I split because we had early flights home the next morning.

Things got interesting that night when my bed tilted to one side and I rolled out onto the floor. I immediately jumped up, ready to give Duggan and Knobbs a good cursing out, but after looking around, I realized that nobody else was there. I assumed I must have drunk more alcohol than I thought because I was swaying from side to side, only to become conscious of the fact that the room itself was moving. It was an earthquake! It was a beauty, too. The entire hotel was moving back and forth and people were running in the streets. When I called the front desk to find out what was happening, the lady laughed and said, *"You've never been here for one of these, have you?"*

I told her the truth. *"Hell, no, bitch! I'm from New Jersey."* The earthquake scared me so badly that I hurriedly packed my belongings and called for a taxi to take me to the airport. Before I left my room, though, I called my wife to tell her what was happening. I was touched by the note of concern I heard in her voice. *"Have you been drinking all night?"*

You would think that would have been the end of the *Family Feud* story, but no-oooo! The following month, a full-page picture of Jimmy, Duggan, Knobbs, Scotty, and I with Louie Anderson appeared in *US Magazine*. Great publicity, right? Not quite. The story was about Anderson soliciting acts of fellatio and sodomy from a "male" prostitute at a casino. The man extorted $100,000 from Anderson, but when his demands increased to $250,000, Anderson informed law-enforcement authorities and the man was sentenced to prison. How does that kind of stuff always happen to us? Here we were, thinking we got some good mainstream press, and there we were in a photo with "Gay" Louie Anderson. They couldn't have taken a picture of us when we had Playboy bunnies on our laps?

Don't get me wrong. Louie was tremendous and he loved wrestling, while I enjoyed meeting him and doing the show, but the only thing the rest of the country remembers is that we had our picture taken with him. One has nothing to do with the other, but that brings up a point I made earlier:

Perception is reality!

The upside is that I received checks from the show for quite a while. Love the Feud!

Another of Time-Warner's (WCW's parent company) ventures was to open a restaurant in Las Vegas' Excalibur Hotel Casino called WCW Nitro Grill. They opened in 1999, but closed less than a year later due to poor attendance and bad management. The company was constantly flying me to Vegas for appearances and signings. I enjoyed those times. They had my "Hugh Morrus" outfit on the wall of the restaurant, which I thought was cool. When they closed the restaurant, they gave me the plaque and outfit.

Chapter 10

Misfits in Action

On the April 17, 2000 episode of *WCW Monday Nitro*, which was held in Rockford, Illinois, we kicked off an angle featuring a group which would eventually be called "Misfits in Action" [M*I*A.]. During the show, Bischoff gave us hell (on air) for not helping the New Blood in their feud with the Millionaires Club. Two weeks later in Birmingham, Alabama, Bischoff called me and three other members of the group "misfits" and fired us (again, on *WCW Nitro*).

At that point, Russo sat down with us to discuss the Misfits gimmick and where he wanted it to go. That was when we came up with the name "Misfits in Action." We went to the meeting with high expectations of what he had to say. What we didn't see coming was the "bomb" which Van Hammer [Mark Hildreth] dropped on us. His great idea was for us to stay off TV and "starve the viewers." What? Arn Anderson almost gave birth to a cow when he heard about it. *"Nobody knows who the fuck you are to being with ... and you want to be kept off TV?"* I always (and still do) enjoyed the unique way in which Arn talked to people. To this day, there is still no one better at getting to the point than Arn Anderson. It was always somebody like Hammer who comes up with an idea that would hurt a guy's push (even his own) or screw up an angle which seemed to be going somewhere.

On May 7, we were in Kansas City for the *Slamboree* pay-per-view where I would be wrestling Scott Steiner for the U.S. title. Steiner was originally scheduled to defend the belt against Booker T [Booker Huffman], but "T" was injured the week before when his legs got caught in the ropes while he was taking a power bomb from Mike Awesome. Before my match, Russo and Ed Ferrara (one of the television writers) approached me with a piece of paper and verbiage for the show. Russo said that after that night, I would no longer be called Hugh Morrus. I would be appearing under a new name.

Hugh G. Rection.

Yes, you read that correctly. When I expressed my concerns about the name, I was told it was just a one-night thing. I knew it would be my big chance to prove I belonged in the mix, so I went to the ring in camouflage and told the crowd: *"From here on in, I never wanna be called Hugh Morrus again ... That name was given to me by Eric Bischoff and it was a brain fart. It was to make me look stupid. From now on, you address me by my real name: Hugh G. Rection. Captain Rection, for short."*

I didn't have a lot of time to really think about the name before I went out for my match with Rick Steiner, but afterwards, I gave it a lot of thought. The very next night after my big "introduction" as one of the "new stars of WCW," I (as Captain Rection) was asked to do a three-minute job for Shawn Stasiak on *WCW Nitro*. I never asked why I would be doing a job when I was just beginning to get a push, but they were kicking off a program between Curt "Mr. Perfect" Hennig and Shawn, so they thought I could help Shawn get over. I agreed to do what they asked without argument, but I was really beginning to doubt the new direction my career was taking. After climbing into the ring, I looked up at one of the two Jumbotron screens ... to see a caption that read "Hugh G. Rection" floating at the bottom of the screen. All I could do was stare slackjawed and think, *"Fuck!"* After my match, Russo told me that from that point on, I would be referred to as "Captain Rection, the leader of the Misfits in Action."

Bill makes his entrance on *NITRO*

In all, that was a very bad week in my career and my life. Everything I did in the ring as "Captain Rection" was the same as what I did as "Hugh Morrus," so I was a bit discouraged at the thought of changing my name. As Captain Rection, I lost my persona, my music, and everything I had built during the previous five years. I was excited about the new direction my career had taken, but I also was discouraged to see "Hugh Morrus" being tossed aside. No matter what name I used, my ring character was "me." Billy De Mott. I have a warped sense of humor and I tend to get a little zany. That didn't change when I became Captain Rection. I love to be physical and I'm not afraid to intimidate or be off the wall. That didn't change, either. I made a career and made a good living out of being ... Billy De Mott! Surprisingly, in the real world, I had a tough time separating Bill from Hugh. I felt like I had to be "on" all the time.

On May 15 in Biloxi, Mississippi, the Misfits were introduced on *WCW Nitro* under their new names. The original Misfits were comprised of me (as Captain Hugh G. Rection), Chavo Guerrero (as Lieutenant Loco), Lash LeRoux (as Corporal Cajun), and Van Hammer (as Private Stash). A former fitness model named Tylene Buck joined the group as our valet, Major Gunns.

We had all lost our identities to a man who had something bigger in mind. I'll be the first to admit I thought Vince Russo had come up with a terrible idea ... and the rest of the Misfits thought the same. We were probably at our lowest point at that time. However, none of us knew what was about to happen. We were about to begin a journey that would launch each of our careers to an all-time high ... and Russo was one of the few people who believed in us.

Tylene Buck had originally been hired by WCW to accompany the New World Order wrestlers to the ring. When she lost her job as an nWo girl not too long before that time, Chavo and I decided (with Russo's approval) she would make a great valet for the Misfits. From then on, she was called "Major Gunns," for obvious reasons. As Major Gunns, she would go to the ring wearing camouflaged shorts and a small, white t-shirt (which she would strip of after the match to reveal a camouflaged bikini top). Shortly after she joined us, the Misfits had a meeting with Russo to discuss the purpose of her character in the group. It was decided that when we got into trouble, she would give us mouth-to-mouth resuscitation in the middle of the ring. The fans always popped for the spot, so Tylene was a good fit.

A good fit for everyone but Van Hammer. Before the group ever had an opportunity to get over, Hammer was pushing for his wife to replace Tylene. He thought Tylene wasn't right for the group. In my opinion, I believe he was a little afraid of Tylene outshining him. He never voiced his disregard for Tylene when he was in her company, but he would complain to me, Chavo, whatever agent was in charge, Arn, or Vince Russo.

Hammer only had seven matches during his time with the Misfits. Off and on, Hammer had been with the company for almost seven years and he was doing well for himself, but he came into the program trying to "out-think" the people who were in control. He had problems from the very outset. First of all, he wasn't happy about his new name: Private Stash. It was a well-known fact among the boys that Hammer wouldn't share his "vitamins" with anyone,

Major Gunns, Bill and Leia Meow, 2000

and yet, he was always asking someone else to share with him. Some might say he was "frugal," but he was stingy and wanted to keep his stash private ... so, we thought the best name for him would be ... Private Stash. Hammer also was unhappy about being such a "low-ranking officer," especially since he had been with the company longer than any of the other Misfits. He saw that as a legitimate argument. *"Why is she a major and I'm just a private?"* He spent a long time in Bischoff's bus before a show in Biloxi, Mississippi, arguing his case. Well, he came out of the bus as the "low-ranking private" he was. He didn't have much to say during our on-air promo that night, either.

That was the beginning of the end for Hammer. He wouldn't be called "Private Stash" and have a girl rank higher than him. I know. This sounds like one of those "you had to be there" moments.

Booker T joined us as "G.I. Bro," a role he had played in 1989 when he was working with Ivan Putski's [now defunct] Western Wrestling Alliance promotion. I believe the company thought he would bring "believability" to the group and make us legitimate. When Booker left our group, he promoted me to General. I think the idea of Booker passing the torch to me made it more believable, or at least gave justification to me moving into the leadership position.

In time, we became a solid group ... but there was something missing. With Hammer and Booker T both (dishonorably) discharged from our group, we had an opportunity to bring someone into our ranks. Enter Jerry Tuite, a.k.a. "The Wall." Jerry joined our ranks as Sgt. A-Wall on August 8 in Colorado Spring, Colorado. Prior to the inception of the Misfits, Jerry was the bodyguard for Berlyn [Alex Wright]. He was big, strong, and intimidating, but he also was a sweetheart and not used to his potential. In my opinion, he was one of the best big men around, especially with WCW. When Ed Ferrara came to us with the suggestion of adding Jerry to our group, we instantly knew he would be a good fit. Since he was already known as "The Wall," we thought it only fit to rename him "A-Wall," thanks to Sugar Shane Helms, who came up the idea. We were shaving Jerry's hair into a Mohawk one night and throwing around ideas for a name. Shane walked by and, without missing a step, said, *"A-Wall."* Jerry was the final piece of the puzzle. We all were very comfortable with each other, both in and out of the ring. We looked out after each other and always did what was best for the Misfits, not the individual.

Every now and then, there would be tension between Lash and Chavo. We would just let them go at it verbally for a bit and then we would squash it before it got out of hand. They were two young studs who both had aspirations of going to the top, so when they had to work against each other, it would be easy for tempers to flare. It wasn't anything more than what you would see between two brothers, and by the end of each day, we were all traveling, laughing, and praying together.

Who would have guessed that after everything else I had done during the previous ten years, renaming me "Hugh G. Rection" would put me where I had been striving to be for so many years. Funny thing this sports entertainment.

At a time in WCW when all the "main event" talent believed their own publicity, the Misfits were a welcome change, and it pissed off a lot of the top guys when we were figured into storylines. I have to give Vince Russo credit. As discouraged as each of us was in the beginning, he groomed us into believing we could pull it off, and he convinced us that we could stand side by side with the "top guys." And that's exactly where he put us. Before we knew what was happening, we found ourselves involved in vignettes and doing run-ins with people like Hulk Hogan, Lex Luger, Sting, and Diamond Dallas Page. We proved each and every night that we could get the ratings and run with anybody in the company. I was fortunate to get the most exposure and I made the most of it, but I also made sure that everyone on the team was involved.

It was really weird. Nobody treated us the same again. It was like the company had hired us for the first time. Everybody looked at us like we were the new kids on the block. We took what we were told would be comic relief for the shows and made it bigger than what anyone expected.

When we became the Misfits, we were given a new look and outfits were created for us. On the day before the TV tapings, Ed Ferrara sent out a runner to purchase camouflage tights and boots. As time went on, we began frequenting Army-Navy type stores when we went to the various towns. We bought camp shirts and patches that represented all branches of the Armed Forces. There seems to be a sticking point for most wrestlers when it comes time to speak on-camera and be believable. When the company allowed us to dress in camo, we really began to get comfortable with our characters. The camo seemed to bring out the best in all of us. Lash and Chavo absolutely stole the show with their characters. We began to cut promos live on *Nitro* and did things "on the fly." I really settled in a groove and dubbed myself "one-shot De Mott" (for my promo skills, not my love life).

I was used very well on TV and I was one of the talents they used to promote towns and do autograph signings. Lash and I came up with an idea for a "Misfits in Action" t-shirt. Lash personally designed the shirt and we all pitched in and had them printed at our own expense. Originally, the shirts were produced strictly for the Misfits. Just like in the early days of my wrestling career, we made our own gimmicks which would sell our character. We wore those shirts everywhere and even gave them out to any of the wrestlers who would wear them. WCW eventually took the idea and sold them on their website.

A month into the program, I began producing my own F.U.B.A.R. shirts The FUBAR acronym was made famous in the 1986 Clint Eastwood film, *Heartbreak Ridge,* but the earliest reference dates back to 1940 when the magazine *Yank, the Army Weekly* used it to mean "Fruited Up Beyond All Recognition." Later that same year, military personnel had changed the meaning to "Fucked Up Beyond Any Repair. To the general public, that was the Misfits' definition of FUBAR, as well, but ranking members of the group knew what it really stood for: "Fuck you, Bischoff and Russo." It wasn't meant as a personal slur, but it fit in with the storylines.

Even when things were good, though, they were a struggle. It seemed that no matter how we played the game, the company would find a way to keep us just a little bit lower than we felt. Thank goodness I didn't bank my future on what I expected to receive in royalty checks. My total income from merchandise was in the low four figures (as in less than $100.00). By the way, I once received a check from WCW Merchandise for 43-cents! It cost the company more to print the check and mail it.

I don't think anyone could have picked a better group of people with whom to work. I truly loved them all. Every member of the team worked hard to get the gimmick over and I believe the fans felt our energy. At first, I believe our matches were viewed as "ha-ha" matches, but we gradually evolved and became one of the best factions in professional wrestling (at least, that's my opinion). The thing about the Misfits that impressed me the most was that no one member looked at himself as "above" anyone else. It was a true team effort and we all looked out after each other. We even said a prayer for each other every night, whether we were working as a team, in single matches, or not even working. Our enthusiasm became contagious and people wanted to hang around with us. Jimmy Duggan used to say, *"There goes Hugh, holding court in catering — again."* "Holding court in catering" was Jimmy's way of saying that every time we were in catering, I was talking to one or more of the guys about being positive. Strangely enough, the more destructive I became in my personal life, the more I tried to look out for everyone else. I wanted everyone to do well, especially the new guys coming into the company.

For some reason, the character of "General Rection" gave me the balls to speak up and become a mentor for many of the young guys. I gave them positive reinforcement about their matches and the direction of their careers. I encouraged them to work hard and stay focused. More than anything, I listened to what "they" had to say, and tried to guide them based on what they told me. I knew what they were going through and I thought my knowledge might help them avoid some of the pitfalls I had experienced when I first came to the company.

It was about that time that I began to "turn the corner" in my personal life. That is to say, I was feeling more positive about my future than I had in a long time.

I knew the Misfits might be my last opportunity to become part of the mainstream of the company, so I took full advantage of it. Nothing I did in the ring was any different from what I had done in the past. I just did more and tried to be as energetic as possible. In hindsight, my most successful run with WCW came during the time when I was one of the Misfits. It gave me a new sense of confidence, especially in front of the camera, and helped establish me in the eyes of my peers as a player.

On October 29 in Las Vegas at *Halloween Havoc 2000*, I won a handicap match against Lance Storm and Jim Duggan to become the new United States heavyweight champion. I was told to take the fall on Jimmy. All I could think was I didn't want to hurt him with the moonsault, so I hit him with my head, rather than landing directly on him. I was really battling my head problems that night and I didn't know where I was after the match. My vision would dim and I couldn't focus. Thanks goodness the boys were there to help me get to the airport and the hotel since we had to be in Irvine, California, the next night.

I didn't wrestle in Irvine, but Gene Okerlund called me out from the dressing room and I received a standing ovation from all the boys and the backstage crew. It came as a total surprise to me. It's one of my favorite memories and meant a lot to me, especially at the time. Bill Goldberg even stepped up and made speech, putting me over as the guy who kicked off his long win streak.

Being given the U.S. title meant a lot to me. I was a believer in wrestling and I took great pride in holding that title. That sounds ridiculous in a business that's worked, but it was important to me. Twelve days later, I dropped the title to Lance in London, England, and regained it on November 26 in Milwaukee. On January 14, 2001, my run as U.S. champion ended for good when I lost the belt to Shane Douglas in Indianapolis. The plan was to eventually put the belt on Rick Steiner, and I believe someone thought Steiner beating Shane for the belt meant more than Steiner beating me.

I was a little bit intimidated by Shane "The Franchise" Douglas. Not because of anything he said or did, but because I knew him before WCW and I respected his talent. Shane was down to earth and he had a good mind for the business. During the time I was wrestling Shane, my daughters hated him. Instead of "Franchise," they called him "French Fry."

The Misfits began to fracture in November 2000. During our promos on the November 15, 2000 episode of *Thunder,* we called each other by our regular names: Hugh, Chavo, Lash, and Jerry. It wasn't scripted. We wanted to let the viewers know that we were moving forward as "ourselves." Chavo was the first to leave because the company wanted him to branch out on his own. In December, the company once again began to bill him as Chavo Guerrero, Jr. Chavo never looked back. He took the ball and ran with it. He won the cruiserweight title from Mike Sanders and had a good run with WCW until WWF Entertainment, Inc. bought the company in March 2001.

I personally discharged (honorable, of course) Lieutenant Loco [Lash LeRoux] in January. Like Chavo, he began using his own name again and he returned to the cruiserweight division. He never again got the push for which he had worked so hard. He made a few appearances on TV, but didn't really seem to have his heart in it. When I was working as a trainer for Deep South, I brought him down a few times to work with the kids. He was very talented and he has a great mind for the business. He just never found the groove again.

In February 2001, Jerry and I were booked into a program against each other. We talked very little before our matches about what we were going to do. We simply went to the ring, hit hard, and did whatever we could to get the match over. One thing I learned when I began working with Jerry. I had to hit him *hard!* He was as strong and as tough as an ox, and he wouldn't register if I didn't lay them in. When the WWF bought WCW, Jerry was given a developmental contract, but was later given his release when they learned about his drug problems. The pressure of being on the road and dealing with a "make-believe life" took its toll on Jerry. He became very dependent on a lot of the drugs we all were taking. Don't get me wrong. I am not throwing stones. I'm the very last person who should be talking about drug abuse. I, too, fell into the habit of taking pills to ease my pain and to help me get through each day. From what I understand, Jerry went through rehab and cleaned up his act. He went to work for All Japan Pro Wrestling in 2003 and was doing well. Unfortunately, in what has become an all-too-familiar story in the wrestling business, Jerry was found unconscious in his hotel room in Narita, Japan on December 6, 2003. He was rushed to the hospital, but by the time they arrived 35 minutes later, he was dead. It's such a sad story because Jerry had turned his life around and was doing very well. He was only 36 years old.

Chavo and I always looked out for Tylene after she joined us. She had a "boyfriend" who was always suspicious about who she was with and where she was staying. She wasn't happy about it. She felt comfortable and safe with Chavo and me, so she confided in us. We were good listeners. When they switched her to Team Canada, she became more outspoken and wanted to be more involved. At that point, Lance Storm became her "big brother" and helped push her in storylines. Tylene was a good girl and I enjoyed working and traveling with her. After being released from WCW in February 2001, she worked for Xtreme Pro Wrestling in California and was featured in a wrestling documentary called *101 Reasons Not To Be A Pro Wrestler.* Since then, she has appeared in adult films and has her own adult-content website.

The Misfits were together for almost eight months. We successfully feuded with the other factions in the company, such as the Filthy Animals, Team Canada, and Natural Born Thrillers. We were sad to see it come to an end, but I believe we went as far as we could with the storyline. Wrestlers have a real need to feel important to the show and to the company, but the bottom line is that we are all expendable as soon as a "new flavor of ice cream" comes along. However, the upside was that the exposure and experience helped every one of us and I'm forever grateful for the time spent with the Misfits. Their influence in my life changed me in many ways.

By February 2001, we had all come full circle and were once again "who we started out as" when we were first presented with the Misfits program. However, the 2001 version of "Hugh Morrus" had a head of steam. Having been given the opportunity to be featured in storylines and programs with the company convinced me that I was doing what I was meant to do.

General Rection, Lash Larue and Chavo Guerrero in Australia

Chapter 11
The Invasion

Before I jump into my WWF run, I have to say that without Eric Bischoff and Vince Russo doing what they did to "repackage" me, I would never have been given an opportunity to cross over and become a WWF/WWE superstar. And as bad as things seemed to be in WCW at times, at the end of the day, I loved every minute of every day that I was in a WCW ring. I hated myself and the lifestyle I lived, but I had worked so hard to accomplish the things I did. For the longest time, I went to work every day with a lump in my stomach, dreading to hear what I was or wasn't going to be asked to do. I hated being around a lot of the people in WCW, but now that it's over, I realize I miss it very much. In every endeavor, there will always be something to bitch about, but at the end of the day, World Championship Wrestling was a trip I wouldn't trade for the world. I had an M*I*A t-shirt, trading cards, and I was featured in video games. I wasn't considered for action figures, videos, or TV roles, but I would like to think I played a small part in what made WCW tick.

Most importantly, WCW was the springboard for me going to work for Vince McMahon and the WWF. Thanks to them, I had made it to the top!

Or had I?

That's what we're going to discuss in the pages which follow.

I also have to mention the fact that I loved doing promotion work and making personal appearances. It gave me an opportunity to shoot the breeze with the fans and to tell them "thank you" for their support. I had so many opportunities to visit with sick kids in hospitals and get involved with charities and events. Doing those kind of things were, and still are, very rewarding to me. I really dug all the times I spent with kids and their families.

I was always in line for doing TV spots and commercials because I never complained about doing them. I never expected to be paid extra for doing promotional work on my days off, either.

The one thing I really enjoyed was spending time in the terminal wards at children's hospitals. I had to make a reality check after those visits (and there were many). Those visits never can be adequately described. The only thing those kids and their parents wanted was to say "hello." At least, the ones who were able to speak. The others would just look at me and smile.

Wrestling was the only thing those kids had on their minds. They didn't care whether you were a good guy or a bad guy. They just wanted to see the characters they had seen on TV and in the magazines. If you have never had the experience of spending 20 minutes with a child who only has a short time left to live, you're missing out on something wonderful. Just the opportunity to hold your hand and talk to you means everything to them. For those short minutes, the problems they face disappear from their minds. There are some who stayed in touch with me through the mail. Their parents were grateful, too, when I (we) took time to visit and write their children. The special children I met over the years have meant a lot to me, too. I don't think they ever realized how much they did for us, and what it meant to me to have been given the opportunity to see, talk, and just sit with them.

To see children who don't have long to live hooked up to dialysis machines does something to a person. When you get home, you hug your kids and thank God every day for giving them good health.

We were booked for appearances and media events by Alan Sharp, the "PR" media guy for the WCW. We were in Detroit when Alan booked us for our first appearance at a terminal childrens' ward. The nurses told us to not be shocked by what we saw, and that a lot of the kids wouldn't even know we were there. I was scared to death. All I could think was, *"How do I deal with these kids and their families? What do I do? What do I say? How do I act?"* I was very nervous and I couldn't hide it.

Jim Duggan and I split up and walked into different rooms. When I walked in, the little boys and girls looked at me with wide eyes. I put my fears aside and walked over to the closest bed. Holding out my hand, I said, *"Hi! I'm Hugh Morrus."* Those kids seemed so happy to see me. It was amazing to see their reaction. It did a lot for the parents and nurses, too. They didn't see the children smile very often. I thought, *"Hey, this isn't so hard, after all."*

A service of Pay-Per-View Network, Inc.
FAX 248 / 304-1839

VIEWER'S CHOICE

29000 Inkster Road, Suite 115, Southfield, MI 48034
248 / 354-3375

November 25, 1997

Dear Hugh,

I wanted to take a minute to say thank you for taking the time to meet with the kids at Children's Hospital in Detroit. I was very impressed with your ability to reach the kids in a friendly and non threatening way. I know that you must get constant requests for visits and for use of your time. I truly feel you made a difference in the lives of some kids who have seen far too much bad luck.

We wish you a happy Thanksgiving holiday. Pease give these "treat" bags to your little ones as a means of thank you from us.

Sincerely,

Your fiends at Viewer's Choice

Betsy Kellman, Jan Liddicoat and Tricia St. Andre.

Before Jimmy and I walked into the room of one little boy, the nurses told us, *"He doesn't talk, he doesn't smile, and he doesn't look up or acknowledge anyone."* When we walked in and stood close to his bed, he glanced up. Before you knew it, we were communicating. I began talking to him … and it was obvious he was listening. All of a sudden, he was smiling and doing his best to laugh with Jimmy and me. The nurses and parents couldn't believe it. Everyone was smiling, laughing, and crying all at the same time. That was one of the most unforgettable things I have ever been a part of. When I left the room, I was wiping tears from my cheeks.

Hugh Morrus

As wrestlers, we are truly blessed to be able to do what we do and get paid for it. We bitch and moan and demand more money, but we forget that "but for the grace of God" that could be us and our families. Realizing that, I have never turned down an appearance and I will never turn down anyone who wants to say hello or shake hands.

In 1994, years before my WWF run, Jerry Jarrett was booking for the WWF and called to schedule me for a series of tryouts. He simply told me where the tryout was to be and what time I was to be there. I went to that city, checked in, and wrestled. It didn't get much easier.

My first tryout match took place in Poughkeepsie, New York on February 21, 1994. I wrestled the following two nights, as well, in Bethlehem, Pennsylvania and Locksheldreke, New York. Each night, I wrestled a guy named John Paul, an asshole who did his best to squash me every night. I was trying to get a job, so I didn't do much to ruffle any feathers. I just put him over. In return, he refused to sell anything. Looking back, however, I made a name and a living in the wrestling business. He disappeared after making a few appearances. I'm not trying to rub it in, though. I'm just saying …

A little more than a year later, on March 24, 1995, I was called back. This time, I brought Chris Ford [aka Crowbar] with me as my opponent. He wrestled that night as Devon Storm. I trusted Chris and knew he would do his best to help me showcase my talent. We wrestled in a dark match that night on a card in Bushkill, Pennsylvania which featured Lex Luger and Tatanka in a "Lumberjack" match. Chris and I got a great response from the crowd and they went crazy for my moonsault finish. The result of my superb debut?

I never heard back from them.

Unfortunately, by the end of the tryouts, Jerry Jarrett was no longer with the company. My "in" was "out." Nothing ever came of any of them other than leaving me with a good feeling that perhaps, some day, I would be able to make the cut and be where I wanted to be (just like every other wrestler). After my final tryout, they decided to hire Duke "The Dumpster" Droese. I remember my good friend, Bam Bam Bigelow, telling me their decisions had nothing to do with "wrestling." If only I could have seen the writing on the wall of how things work. It wasn't about what a person could do or how he could do it. At the time, the WWF wanted big guys and they put a great deal of emphasis on characters.

Getting back to 2001, when I was working for WCW, I never thought about trying to leverage myself into the WWF, but in the back of my mind, I hoped I would one day be a part of the organization. Little did I know the buyout of WCW by the WWF would give me the opportunity to be one of the "original" guys who took part in the "WCW Invasion" of the WWF.

We had been hearing rumors for several months about Turner canceling WCW programming and taking us off the air. The Turner "suits" were stuck-up pricks who made no bones about saying wrestling didn't fit into the future of Turner. There was some concern, but at the time, most of the roster had guaranteed contracts, so they weren't too worried. Any worries they might have had weren't about wrestling. They were about money. They didn't want to see the gravy train roll to a stop. The rest of us were trying to plot out the next move of our career.

Nobody knew *anything* until the night of March 26 when we were booked to wrestle in Panama City, Florida.

Johnny Ace [John Laurinaitis], who was an agent with WCW at the time, called and told us to be there early for a pre-show meeting. As Chavo and I walked through the backstage area, we noticed some of the doors had WWF signs and WWF names on them. We didn't put it past WCW doing that to work us over, so we weren't sure what it all meant, but it sure started a buzz. The guys who normally talked and discussed things might have known something, but nobody was saying much of anything. Everybody simply went straight to catering and waited for the "meeting" to begin. The whole crew was there: workers, referees, and agents.

The funniest thing about the whole setup was that most of the guys came into the room with their typical "who cares" attitude ... until Pat Patterson, Shane McMahon, Jerry Brisco, Johnny Ace, and Bruce Prichard all walked into the room. All of a sudden, they were sitting up straight and paying attention. You could have heard a pin drop. Most of the guys sat there with a look of "What the fuck?" on their faces, and there wasn't a person in the room who didn't pay strict attention when the WWF brass began talking and explaining how things were going to work.

Everybody knew there was a chance they might be losing their jobs. The ones who sweated it out the most were the guys who had burned a bridge with Vince McMahon (especially when WCW was on top and they tried to shove it up Vince's ass). The guys with talent knew they would likely be hired by the WWF because they could be useful to the company, but for the most part, the guys who were "on top" were the most uncomfortable because they knew it was going to be almost impossible to topple people like Steve Austin, the Rock, Undertaker, Triple H, and Kurt Angle from their spots.

That night, I was asked to work the opening dark match. I liked the spot because I was nervous and wanted to get it over with. It felt really weird to be trying out for a company I had been with for 6½ years. My first official contact with someone from the WWF that night came after my match. Shane

McMahon thanked me and said he liked my work. Bruce Prichard and Jerry Brisco also stopped me in the back and paid me a compliment.

A lot of people did their normal "schmoozing" after the show, but most of us just went out and partied as usual. Nobody knew if they had a job and, for some, it just wasn't a good night.

It was a week or so before I heard anything else from the WWF. Johnny Ace called to tell me I was on board. I was shocked that out of all the people who were going to be approached, I was in the original ten. The other nine were Stacy Keibler, Sean O'Haire, Lance Storm, Chavo Guerrero Jr., Mark Jindrak, Mike Awesome, Chuck Palumbo, Mike Sanders, and last but ~~not~~ least ... Shawn Stasiak. I honestly hadn't expected to make the cut. I had been prepared to be passed up for the guys who "made WCW what it was," i.e. the main event wrestlers.

Jamie Noble and I drove to Tampa to meet with Johnny and J.R. [Jim Ross] (while he was on vacation). I never had much confidence when I went into meetings with executives and this one would be with "Jim Ross of the WWF." As we walked upstairs, Ace assured me that things would be okay. That was my first opportunity to sit down and talk with Jim Ross, and within seconds of meeting him, I knew without a doubt that I wanted to work there. He put me at ease by saying, *"Call me J.R."* He eased my fears even more when he told me he knew my history and knew what I could bring to the company. Within a few minutes of walking into his hotel room, he made me feel like I belonged there. From that day on, I would have done anything J.R. asked me to do. He was a straight shooter and knew exactly what to say to make people feel comfortable. He also made everyone aware of the fact that the "WWF company way" was the only way. I was shocked, however, when he said my contract was going to stay the way it was and would not be changed. I would be making $250,000 a year *and* working for the World Wrestling Federation. Things were going to be good.

That was misconception number one (on my part). As I said before, I'll get to the details as we go on.

The next time Johnny Ace called, he told me I would be making an appearance at *WrestleMania XVII* in Houston Texas. I came so close to blurting out, *"You have got to be fucking kidding me!"* Instead, in order to avoid any appearance of being a mark, I simply said, *"Okay."* The thoughts going through my head, however, were something like, *"Wow! Not only have I made the cut and kept my job, but I'm going to be a part of WrestleMania, the biggest and most high-profile wrestling event in the world."* I was being given a spot coveted by just about every wrestler in the world. I was headed to where every wrestler wanted to be. At least, that's what I thought. I would soon learn that I was headed towards a spot where most wrestlers on the WWF roster eventually wind up.

Each of the ten WCW wrestlers brought to *WrestleMania* was personally told to keep the details to themselves ... and that's exactly what nine of us did. On March 31, 2001, the night before *WrestleMania XVII*, we all met at a second-rate hotel on the outskirts of Houston, far away from the WWF wrestlers and their families. The company didn't want anyone to see us and even brought us to Houston on crazy, late-night flights so we wouldn't be seen at the airport.

I couldn't sleep that night. I had no idea what to expect and I am sure the others didn't, either. The next morning, as I got dressed to go to the lobby to meet everyone, my telephone rang. It was Johnny Ace. *"Who the fuck couldn't keep their big mouth shut? The angle and everybodys' names are all over the Internet."* I didn't know what to say. After our meeting at the hotel the night before, I had gone directly to my room and hadn't spoken to anybody. I didn't understand why Johnny was so pissed off, but I panicked when he told me that Vince McMahon and Kevin Dunn [an executive vice president with the company] wanted us fired and sent home. We hadn't been there for 24 hours and they already hated us.

Hugh Morrus and his sister, Debbie

We later learned that after our meeting the night before, Shawn Stasiak decided to get himself over by doing an interview. He gave the names of everybody involved and said we were going to be the surprise guests of WCW's new owner, Shane McMahon.

The company "suits" were so mad at us that our "guest appearance" went from being in the ring with Shane McMahon at *WrestleMania XVII* to being seen sitting in the shadows of the skybox for 30 seconds of the show! We were livid with Stasiak, but we became enraged when we found ourselves unable to make "Meat" understand what he had done wrong. We eventually came to realize Stasiak was on a collision course to end his career, anyway, so we left him alone and distanced ourselves from him.

What a great beginning to what should have been the most exciting time of my life. We had been with the company for one day and we had already been called "assholes" and "fuckups" by the company execs. It also sucked to be picked up and taken to the show on a bus in which Ernie "The Cat" Ladd was a passenger. He looked at us like we were marks and assholes. Man, that was the worst-best feeling in the world. I left that night thinking, *"Well, at least I met Ernie Ladd."* (insert humor)

During this time, I began making journal notes.

From Bill De Mott's personal journal

Sunday, May 20, 2001

Well, it's been a while, and I'm still sitting around waiting to get back to work, back to my world, and to what I do best (at least, in my mind).

The whole time I've been home, I have been fixing things, re-doing the house, and making it nice. Things that would make a normal man happy. That's my first mistake ... thinking I was normal. I have enjoyed my kids and, for the most part, being home with Rose, but this sudden and long change has taken its toll. For years, you could have kept me home and paid me and I would have been more than happy to do so. But I don't feel useful or good about being home this much. We have all become accustomed to our lives with me on the road and Rose in charge. Now, Dad's home and Mom has taken the back seat (as far as my girls are concerned). That's because, for the most part, I'm a pushover.

And now that everyone has adapted to me being home, I am getting ready to leave for Memphis for the WWF. This is the first time I'll be away from home in almost two months. I am very excited to get to my world, and now they are going to have to get back into another groove. It's funny how these things go.

Anyway, I did my first independent shot in six years for John Tenta. "Earthquake." It was an experience! In one aspect, it was great to be around "some" of those guys. Then you had the typical "been there done that" group and the guys who would just believe their own shit. Man, I don't remember acting like that, but I'm sure if you ask around, I was (and am) a bit of an asshole!

I get a kick out of sitting down and writing a little bit of what is going on. But then again, I start to think of things and I stop. My mind wanders from one story to the next. I just hope I remember them all and get them down on paper before the next great moment comes along. Right!

Two months later on the May 28, 2001 edition of *RAW,* Lance Storm made a "run-in" during a mixed match between the team of Steve Blackman and Trish Stratus and the team of Perry Saturn and Terri [Terri Runnels] to become the first WCW wrestler to "invade" the WWF. When he got into the ring, he "super-kicked" Perry, but he missed by a mile and it looked like hell.

The following week, I got a call from Johnny Ace and was told to be in Minneapolis, Minnesota on June 4. I was going to be the second man in on *The Invasion!* I was so freaking excited about going in by myself, but I also was nervous because I would be in a new locker room for the first time in a long time. The locker room was easy, though, and everyone there was very receptive. It really helped that I knew Eddie Guerrero, Chris Benoit, and Perry Saturn, Dean Malenko, and Chris Jericho, not to mention many others that I had met in previous years.

Jack Lanza and Shane McMahon took me down to the ring so the road agents could all see my "finish." I told them I was comfortable jumping from the mat to the top rope and then doing a moonsault, and I must have demonstrated that move about two dozen times, but none of the agents wanted to take the chance of me not making it on the first try, so I climbed up to do what I had been doing for the past ten years.

I was going to do my "run-in" during a match between Kane [Glenn Jacobs] and Christian [William Reso]. During the match, Edge [Adam Copeland] did a run-in to save Christian, only to be choke-slammed by Kane. When a siren sounded and the WCW logo appeared on the "TitanTron," I hit the ring and climbed to the top rope. In the dressing room before the match, I had told Adam not to move and to stay right where Kane dumped him. Unfortunately, for whatever reason, he turned into me while I was upside down, twelve feet in the air, and he was on his side when I landed. My knees landed squarely in his ribs. The crowd popped huge for my appearance and J.R. [Jim Ross] and the King [Jerry Lawler] put it over strongly. I thought things went very well ... until I got back to the dressing rooms. Edge was undergoing therapy in the trainer's room. When I walked in, Larry Heck, the trainer, lit into me and made a big deal about how I had hurt Edge with such "a dangerous maneuver."

That was the beginning of the end for the moonsault by Hugh Morrus (at least for awhile), and it was yet another reason for the WWF to question their decision to bring me in. In my defense, from the first day of my career, I had never been "accused" of hurting anyone. In this case, if you watch the video, you will clearly see Edge turn to his side and try to position himself where he thought he needed to be to protect himself. I watched it several times just to convince myself that it wasn't my fault.

In the weeks that followed, the company played out similar scenarios with other WCW talents who were originally signed. Dallas Page, Mike Awesome, and Booker T were signed, followed by Torrie Wilson, Billy Kidman, Shane Helms, Sean O'Haire, and Chris Kanyon.

Before you knew it, the guys who had previously been "running" the WCW locker room were now bringing that "loser" attitude to the WWF. It was horrible. As a group, we had ridiculous "heat" with just about everyone, and none of the so-called "stars of WCW" understood the reason why. The one thing I knew going in was that it was "their" locker room, and if we wanted to make it in the company, we had better adapt to the way they do things very quickly. Needless to say, most of the WCW guys didn't. As a result, the WCW storylines were awful and the "heat" in the locker room was terrible. If there had been as much heat in the ring as there was in the locker room, we would have been doing sellout business. Most of the WCW guys were welcomed, but the WWF hierarchy went out of their way to show certain guys they didn't belong there and were not wanted! Buff Bagwell was one of them. Buff had tremendous heat and wasn't liked at all.

Proper etiquette in the WWF locker room would be to be on time, shake hands, say hello, and watch all the matches. During the first month of being with the WWF, we appeared on a show in East Rutherford, New Jersey. A few of the WCW "superstars" waited until the very end of the night before they walked over to say hello to a few of the WWF guys. When they extended their hands, the Undertaker looked at them with disdain and said, *"Go fuck yourselves."* You see, in WCW locker rooms, there was no etiquette. Everybody thought they were somebody, so it was no big deal if they treated somebody else like shit. As long as they had the backing of the group they were loyal to, they were okay. I'm not saying that was the norm in WCW. For the most part, everybody got along, but it wasn't very professional or cordial. It was nothing like the time when I was brought up in the business. When we walked into the dressing room, the first thing we did was say hello to the people we knew and introduce ourselves to everyone we didn't. The problem was that many of the guys hadn't been brought into the business the right way. They were brought in before they were ready and never learned what it meant to be respectful of their peers.

I don't think the WWF talent looked at the WCW boys as being inferior to them, but I know for a fact they looked at us with the attitude of "don't think you're going to get away up here with the shit you did in WCW." As a whole, I believe the WWF guys took more pride in their association with their company than many of the guys did with WCW. They had heard the stories of guys who were sitting out their WCW contracts at home with the self-assurance of being hired by the WWF when those contracts expired. There was no hiding the fact that certain top guys in WCW thought they were going to walk into the same position in the WWF. That didn't sit well with the WWF talent, many of whom were worried about "keeping" their job from being taken by the jerks who were waiting to come in.

The attitude of the WCW talent didn't help matters, but I think there would have been problems no matter how we acted. Whenever 25 or more people are added to a roster of talent, all of whom are already competing for TV time, there will definitely be problems. Even with several hours of television programming, there just wasn't enough screen time for everyone.

At the house shows and TV tapings, the WWF boys used to have what they called "curtain calls." They would watch our matches from behind a curtain, or a spot where the audience couldn't see them, and then critique us when we came to the back. The WWF guys would laugh at how badly we were screwing things up and pissing off the other boys, agents, and whoever else might have been offended.

There were also many times in the early days of the WCW "invasion" where there was a call for the WWF talent to "put the boots" to certain WCW guys. Shawn O'Haire and Chuck Palumbo were the recipients of one of those beatings after their match in Madison Square Garden with the Acolytes.

Dallas Page had his own agenda. He was working with Undertaker at the time and, to put it mildly, things didn't go well. Mike Awesome had his own problems. A match on July 15 in New Haven, Connecticut, in which Taker and Kane tagged against Page and Awesome, didn't go very well. Actually, the match was awful. When they came back to the locker room, Taker was visibly upset and Kane had nothing to say at all. Mike walked in a few seconds later and said, *"That wasn't too bad."* Kane ripped off his mask and threw it across the room. He was really upset by Mike's statement and began reading him the riot act. I don't think he got through to Mike. Mike was on a different page ... no pun intended.

Buff Bagwell's problems began as soon as he began working for the company. When we first came over, several of us were sent to Traxx, the WWF training center in Connecticut. It would give us an opportunity to visit Titan Towers and meet many of the people who worked behind the scenes. We were there to train and workout, but there were some (like Bagwell) who didn't feel the need to "train." They thought it was beneath them to be asked to get ready for the WWF. One day, Buff and Shane Helms were arguing back and forth.

That happened from time to time. It wasn't anything unusual ... until Shane said something Buff didn't like. Buff slapped Helms across the face, which was something Buff did quite often to fans and those he looked at as underlings. Helms, who was nursing a sore shoulder, hit Buff over the head with a frozen water bottle and busted his head wide open.

Chris Kanyon and I left later that day to return to our homes for the remainder of the week. While we were driving to the airport, Johnny Ace called to ask how things went. When I told him, *"Fine,"* he loudly (Kanyon heard him from the passenger seat) said, *"You're full of shit! I heard about Helms and Bagwell."* When I tried to assure him everything was fine and no big deal, he laughed and said he had known I wouldn't tell him anything different.

Johnny and I had a great relationship. He knew I was just assuring him that whatever "happened" was done and over with. We had just joined WWE and we had enough ahead of us without acting like a bunch of douche bags who couldn't train together. It's comical to think of that story now, but at the time, they were looking for reasons to "thin us out."

Another incident took place on June 26 when Buff showed up at Madison Square Garden and walked around backstage like he was the star of the company. When the time rolled around for his match, nobody could find him. He had fallen asleep in one of the locker rooms.

During the *RAW Is War* taping in Tacoma, Washington, Buff and WCW world champion Booker T were scheduled to wrestle each other. Buff was the perfect example of someone who refused to take time during his matches to listen to the reaction from the crowd. It didn't matter what the people who bought the tickets wanted. He insisted on doing his own thing. To make matters worse, in the dressing room before his match in Tacoma, Buff refused to take direction from Pat Patterson. Pat was a legendary performer who had headlined territories from coast to coast. He also had the power in the WWF to give Buff the golden push. And yet, because of the things Buff got away with when he was with WCW, he didn't understand what Pat was trying to tell him (or worse, he didn't care enough to listen). When Pat laid out the ground work as to what he wanted to see to get Buff and Booker moving in their new directions, Buff told Pat it didn't matter what he (Pat) wanted. Buff said he was a babyface and the people were going to pop for him no matter what he did. He couldn't be a heel.

On July 7 and 8, I was supposed to work with Buff on house shows, but he didn't show up for either of them, so I worked with Mark Jindrak. The following night, July 9, Buff showed up in Atlanta as if everything was normal. He left his bag in the locker room and went to catering as if it was just another day. The guys there who had been on the road just couldn't believe it. We were told the excuse he gave was "mother thought I should see a surgeon about the stitches in my head."

That was the beginning of the end for Buff and, in many ways, his actions were the catalyst for the problems between the WWF and WCW guys. Buff was released from the WWF on July 9 following complaints about his attitude and the altercation with fellow WCW alumnus Shane Helms. He had been with the company a little more than a week and he only had two matches.

One week after Bagwell was fired, the WWF kicked off another "invasion" of talent ... this time, by the ECW guys. ECW and WCW, led by Stephanie McMahon, Shane McMahon, and Paul Heyman, merged to form *The Alliance.* The ECW talent that came on board understood they had a good job. They weren't as uptight about their positions in the company. They knew things would work out and we would all have an opportunity to shine.

The way in which we (both WCW and ECW) were programmed made it clear that we were not highly regarded as talent. I couldn't really complain, though. I was on the road again and booked on most of the television tapings. I was accepted by the boys and fit well into the locker room because I understood the chain of command and accepted the fact that I was going to have to earn my stripes (again) in the company. That was something most of the WCW talent never came to terms with or didn't understand. So many times, I wanted to scream, *"We're not in Atlanta anymore!"*

And so it went. One by one, the WCW and ECW guys were "weeded out" and the rest of us were corralled into a talent pool that was maxed out. The influx of talent was great for the wrestling fans, but internally, there was a constant struggle for power and airtime.

One of the things the boys seldom talk about is something known as "wrestlers' court." The first time I experienced wrestlers' court was during my time with the WWF/WWE. I had heard about it while I was working for WCW, but I had never witnessed it. I heard conversations and stories from guys who had been involved or taken part in one of them, but for the most part, wrestlers' court was a "don't ask, don't tell" type of thing.

The closest thing we had to wrestlers' court in WCW was when one of the boys had a legitimate beef with someone. They would bring their complaint to certain people and they would decide how to rectify the situation. Those remedies would come in the form of money, "chores," or public humiliation. It was all kept pretty hush-hush, but everyone knew they didn't want to be on either side of a disagreement. I did my best to avoid getting myself into one of those situations. I'm not saying I wasn't guilty of breaking the "rules" of the road or the locker room, but there were a whole lot more shit disturbers there than me. And besides, for whatever reason, I always seemed to have a good rapport with my peers.

When we came into WWE, it was hard enough to get to know and fit in with the guys we didn't know, but getting them to trust us (in and out of the ring) was no small task. As a group, we were simply labeled "schmucks."

One of the first rules of traveling is that even if you have a million miles on every airline and are able to upgrade, you must give your seat to the agents (at least, the respected ones who had made their bones), any of the boys who were the "main draw," or anyone who was too big to be sitting in the coach section of the plane. That wasn't a practice in WCW. Nobody cared who you were. If we got there early enough and could upgrade, we did, especially on the redeye, coast-to-coast flights. But in the WWF, we weren't in Kansas anymore. I gave up my seat a number of times. However, some people (like Torrie Wilson and Billy Silverman) would occasionally hide behind a newspaper and let the top-tier talent or agents make their way to the back.

Billy was a nice guy and a good referee. He had been with the WWF in 1997, signed with WCW a couple of years later, and returned to the WWF in 2001, so he knew how things worked. After being with the company for less than a year, Billy began sitting in first class. Some people thought he should have at least "asked" if they wanted his seat. That was the point. They wanted the courtesy of being asked. When that didn't happen over a period of time, he was brought to wrestlers' court.

Now, before I continue, wrestlers' court had nothing to do with the office or anyone involved with running WWE. It was strictly something conceived and handled by the boys. A judge, prosecutor, and witnesses align themselves against the accused, who has the option of either pleading out or standing trial and having one of the boys defend them.

With the evidence of his "crime" stacked against him, Billy decided to take a deal, rather than the consequences. It was decided that on the way to Toronto, Silverman would provide unlimited beer and booze for everyone on the plane. Not only did he have to provide it, but he had to serve everyone for the duration of the flight and be sure he had enough to last the entire trip. Silverman took his punishment like a man and his slate was "wiped clean." That should have been the end of it, but it escalated into something it shouldn't have.

When we arrived at the building the next morning, Billy was nowhere to be found, and was still missing when showtime began. J.R. [Jim Ross] and Johnny Ace made several phone calls and sent people to find him. They even questioned Nick Patrick, who frequently traveled and roomed with Silverman. We later learned Silverman went to the airport and took an early flight home. The rumor circulating during the next few days was that he had felt violated and humiliated when the boys patted him on the ass a few times while he was playing "stewardess." We began hearing talk in the locker room about a lawsuit, but we never knew if anything came of it.

At one time, Zack Gowen, the "one-legged" wrestler who appeared with WWE from May 2003 until February 2004, was headed to court for an infraction. He had become too full of himself, believing his own hype, and was being disrespectful to the boys. When the office caught wind of it, they pulled him off the road because they didn't want anything to happen to him. "Court" never took place, but he didn't return, either, which was probably better for him in the long run.

The rules are, (1) someone gives you a warning, (2) someone else tries to make you understand, and then, (3) if you're too thick to comprehend what you're being told or think you're untouchable, you will be brought into wrestlers' court.

I liked the idea of wrestlers' court and having the locker room police itself. In my opinion, there should have been more people brought up on charges. On the other hand, if someone was stupid enough to "drum-up" phony charges and ask for court, they could find themselves on the wrong end of judgment. Everyone knew that "court" was not something to be taken lightly, and anyone who treated it as such would feel the wrath of how it truly worked.

So, while the term "wrestlers' court" sounds funny and is rarely talked about, it's definitely for real.

One of the new talents the WWF tried to "groom" was a guy named Russ McCullough, a 6-foot-6, 300-pound, talentless goof. Russ was married to a different guy on every loop: me, Crash Holly [Mike Lockwood], and Tommy Dreamer. Russ came into the locker room one night and said he would have better matches with Tommy if Tommy would stop eating so many Twinkies. If Russ had any respect at all from anyone, he lost it all with that comment. You don't point fingers at others when your work sucks, especially guys like Tommy who are over with the boys. Russ sucked ice. They couldn't have made him a good worker if they had killed him and had his parents make a new one.

On August 28, 2001, we were wrestling in the Joe Louis Arena in Detroit. Billy Gunn and Bob Holly [Robert Howard] were notorious for competing against each other. Shane McMahon happened to be at the show, so when they began jawing about who could dropkick the highest, Shane fired them up by making a bet and upping the ante. Of course, that pissed off both Gunn and Holly, neither of whom would back down. They agreed to do a dropkick during their matches, with the one who had the best combination of height and technique declared the winner.

I was Bob's opponent, while Billy had Shawn Stasiak. To make a long story short, Shawn "fanned it," which is to say he put his hands up to protect his face and then took a lousy bump. I took great pride in taking shots and not "fanning," which was considered a big no-no in the WWF/WWE. When my turn came around, I planted my face solidly on the bottom of Bob's boots.

The funniest part was when Shane had the camera guys do a split screen on the JumboTron and show still photos of both dropkicks. Bob clearly won.

Referee Charles Robinson and Jerry "The Wall" Tuite help Hugh Morrus back to the dressing room at Starrcade 2000

Chapter 12

On the Sidelines (again)

On September 11, 2001, when the Muslims attacked our country and destroyed the Twin Towers, we were working in Texas. The day before, we had appeared on tapings of *Jakked* and *RAW is War* in the San Antonio Freeman Coliseum, with the taping of *Smackdown* scheduled for the following day [September 11] in Houston. Chavo Guerrero and I were staying at either the Fairfield Inn or the Hampton Inn. I can't remember which, but I know it was one of the two because we always stayed there when we were in Houston. Not only were they were clean and comfortable, but they were cheaper than most other hotels.

On the morning of the *Smackdown* tapings, I was awake and shaking off the effects of the night before. I usually kept the television on all night. As I got dressed, I looked at the TV screen and saw an airplane fly into the side of a building. I thought to myself, *"What movie is this?"* As I continued to watch, a similar scene played. I was shocked when I realized I was watching a live news feed. It was no movie. The scenes playing themselves out on the TV screen were all too real.

I could not believe our country was under attack and I was sitting helplessly in a hotel in Houston, Texas. I immediately called Chavo and told him to turn on his television. My next call was to my home in Florida to be sure my kids were okay. I also worried about my parents and my brother, Darryl. Darryl had a truck route in and around New York City and he was a fireman in New Jersey.

I had no idea whether or not we were supposed to report to work, but I assumed we were. When we were on the road, the company is our family, and more than likely, we would all gather in the arena to figure out what we were going to do. I later learned that all flights had been canceled, so it was a moot point. It's kind of funny to spend so much time with people and never know how they would react in a situation like the one in which we found ourselves. I have to say everyone was very concerned about each other's families and how they were doing.

In the end, WWE decided to go on with the show, telling us, *"Going on as scheduled is the best way to take the mind of the country off this terrible tragedy."* Given the fact we couldn't get out of Texas, anyway, the entire company showed up for the tapings three days later [September 14].

The two days we waited were the longest two days of my life. I remember Chavo and I going to the mall and just walking around aimlessly. We got drunk a couple of times and tried to stay positive (like the rest of the company and country). After the TV tapings, Chavo and I decided that since he couldn't get to California to be with his family, he and I would drive to my home in Florida where we could eat a home-cooked meal and sleep in a nice, comfortable bed. We left Houston and drove all night. Shortly after we arrived in Titusville, Chavo was able to book a flight home.

We were told we were expected to be in Nashville in two days [September 17] and that nothing was going to change. Once again, "the show must go on."

That incident is something that haunts with me to this day. I was on the road in a strange city with no idea about what was really happening in the rest of the country, and I wasn't at home to support and protect my family and friends. After that, travel was never the same, especially when we had to fly. I will say my surrogate family, the wrestling business, banded together to support each other during those uncertain days. I don't know if Chavo will ever realize the role he has played in my life, but it seemed like whenever I was going through a crucial period in my life, he was there to help me through it. He was my longest and best traveling partner. He was always honest and gave his opinion on anything I asked. Many times, he kept me from doing something stupid or making bad decisions.

I'm so proud to know my brother was heavily involved in the recovery and happenings in New York City. Things like that continued to impress the fact upon me that at the end of the day, what I was doing was just "wrestling." What we do for others is what's really important, and without all the people who gave their time and effort in the days following the 9-11 tragedy, we wouldn't be given an opportunity to "entertain" the world.

One of my favorite matches in the WWF took place in Valpariso, Indiana, on October 7, 2001. Hurricane [Gregory Helms] and I worked with Big Show and Spike Dudley with the great Mick Foley as the special guest referee. Valpariso wasn't a big venue, but it was a good, old-fashioned wrestling building with a crowd to match. At one point, Big Show told me to slam him. Paul and I have been friends for a long time and we worked together many times in both WCW and the WWF. When he told me to slam him, I took it as leading into a spot, so I went through the motions of slamming him. You can imagine my surprise when he went all the way up and I had no choice other than to ... slam him! The crowd went nuts. I couldn't believe what had happened because Big Show let very few people slam him. I fell to my knees and sold my back. Paul then said, *"Do it again."* I nodded. This was where he would stop me from slamming him and destroy me. But no-ooo. I picked him up again! I slammed Big Show twice in the same match in the same year in the same company. I later learned that it had been planned from the beginning. Taker, Kane, Billy Gunn [Monty Sopp], and several of the boys were watching and laughing behind the back curtain. The match ended with everyone throwing their socks and shoes into the ring and Foley giving everyone "el socko in the moutho." It was a great time for fun. It also was the most I was ever paid for one house show — $1,200 for that one match — but I didn't care about the payoff. I was just happy to be involved and accepted by the boys.

I worked with some great talent during my time with the WWE. One of the guys I worked with a lot during my early years with the company was Matt Bloom, who wrestled as "Albert." We wrestled each other a lot on live events and enjoyed beating the crap out of each other. Matt suffered a torn rotator cuff injury in June 2004 and was released from his contract before he could return to action. That was probably the best thing to ever happen to him because his career took off after that. Today, Matt is a big drawing-card for New Japan Pro Wrestling as Gigante Bernard.

Billy Gunn is, and was, one of the most talented names on the WWE roster. He had a great deal of respect from the guys. From time to time, he would lead little revolutions and get the guys worked up about certain issues ... and then he would quietly walk away. Some called him a shit-disturber, but he did it in a good, funny way. Billy took his job very seriously and knew how to get the most out of both his partners and his opponents. Whenever I see Billy at a show or an appearance today, we'll begin arguing in the locker room about "who was and is the stiffest." I say it's him and he says it's me. Then we go out, have a good match, and come back laughing.

Crash Holly [Mike Lockwood] was a funny bastard. One of the funniest stories I ever heard was about him applying for a job at Wal-Mart and using Vince McMahon and the WWE as references. When someone from the office approached him about it, he didn't deny it. He simply said he was looking for a job because he wasn't making enough money. I honestly believe he was looking for work to fill the time when he wasn't on the road.

Al Snow, aka Uncle Al, holds a special place in my heart. Working with and against Al was always fun, but it was the way he conducted himself and shared his knowledge of wrestling, with me and others, that drew me to him. Al was there for me during some of the toughest parts of this crazy life of mine. Together, we trained future talent, and no matter what he might say about me, *"Al was the bad cop."*

And then there was Tommy Dreamer. It didn't matter whether he was with ECW or the WWE. Tommy was a born leader who rallied the boys to positive thoughts. He let them know how important it was to do their job to the best of their abilities, even when they were unhappy and dissatisfied with their positions. He was honest and he had everyone's respect because he never blew smoke up anyone's ass. He made sure everyone knew where they stood — good, bad, or indifferent. In the ring, he always gave 100 percent, even when he knew what the company had him doing was bullshit. I love Tommy Laughlin and respect him in and out of the ring.

From Bill De Mott's personal journal

Wednesday, December 5, 2001

Since this is my story, I have decided to take time off. (Not really. I just can't find the time to keep going.)

I just got off the phone with one of my all-time-favorite people and someone who has gone thru a lot of shit with me: Lash LeRoux. (He) told me he was just let go from his WWF contract. This is something about the business I will never get used to. He has done everything asked of him and then some. Sure, we are not all made to become stars, or be involved in storylines, but this kid is talented and I am upset, mad, and disappointed to think that our paths may never cross again. He was there through the Misfits and then some. If you lose your feelings for people, even in this business, you're screwed. I know he will not be gone for long and I truly hope he shoves it up their ass!

There are a lot of people who play these games better than others — ones with no talent, no charisma, and no fucking idea of what this is all about. And those are the fuckers who make it. Maybe some people think I am one of those fuckers, but I haven't met any one man enough to say so. And this is the point where I stop again because it is too upsetting to think and then I drift to other stuff. So, for now, it could be months again before I come back. Let's hope it's with something good to write about.

From Bill De Mott's personal journal

Wednesday, January 9, 2002

Well, it's the beginning of my 12th year, or the end of my 11th (get it?).

Not much has gone on lately. I've been sitting home now for five weeks, with the exception of four of the coldest days I can remember being in. Where else? Lovely Canada. The saving grace there was I worked with the Big Show and traveled with him and (Billy) Kidman. Otherwise, that loop was the shits!

This sure brings back memories of when the old WCW sent us home for repackaging and [I] didn't get back on TV for a long haul. I got the call from Howard Finkel telling me I was taken off hosting *Sunday Night Heat* (big shock there). Instead, they added me to the Texas run to work with Brock Lesnar. I know I should be happy just being paid, but hell! I never much cared for that theory of who cares as long as I am getting a check.

Anyway, injury update: I have two fractured discs in my neck (C4 and C5). Big deal. Oh, yeah. I have torn apart my left shoulder, but decided not to get it fixed. I think it would be taboo now to start fixing things. I always thought "hurt" worked better for me. Too bad I'm the only one who thinks so.

I think Johnny Ace must have put in a good word about my matches last weekend [and] that's why I've been added. It's good news, but until I get back on the tube and in the swing of things, I will feel like a piece of shit. Besides, I make everyone crazy around the house. I am just a miserable bastard and my mood swings are ridiculous. Pain does that to people. Plus, I feel so useless.

Well, as I said, not much to write about. I know I need to catch up on some more of my "story," but maybe another time.

I was never a big fan of Canada. The payoffs sucked and the travel was terrible. It didn't take long to figure out that when we cashed our checks in the States, they were worth much less than what they would have in U.S. currency. I always seemed to be booked on the Canada runs because a lot of the guys weren't keen on going there for two or three days, especially in the winter.

From Bill De Mott's personal journal

Tuesday, January 29, 2002

Well, here I am sitting on my ass! I talked to Johnny Ace this past week and he said everything is fine. They are just trying to get guys ready for this so called "splitting of the roster." To me, it's just more bullshit. They are talking about sending some others and me to Puerto Rico or Cincinnati to help some guys out and stay in ring shape. What the fuck! You would think after almost twelve years you could stay in ring shape!

I've been home now almost three weeks straight. At least before they would send me on house shows, but now, I don't do shit. Since I have been home, I have refinanced my second mortgage and got the driveway done. Getting ready to do the kitchen. How come when I'm not working, all this shit comes into play. I want things to be nice, but it just never happens at the right time. I want my girls' house to be nice. Plus, I don't know what to do with myself. I have to keep busy.

This is when I get into a slump and no motivation. Everybody thinks it's great to be off, but it fucks with your head. You're new to the company, so you are starting from zero. You don't make any money to put towards your downside. How convenient for them. You have no respect for the guys who are out there busting their ass. And probably the biggest thing is, I have no direction, or wonder what they expect when you do go back. That whole "we will give you the opportunity thing" is the biggest bunch of bullshit I have ever heard!

Enough ranting and raving for now.

I just came back from getting more ink [tattoos]. It helps me feel better. I do this when I'm home and not feeling real good about myself. Maybe I think it changes me somehow, but this whole depression thing is getting bad. I feel bad almost all day long and then I can't sleep. It's getting brutal!

I'm not going to write about my past for a while because I can't deal with the present. After all, it's not like I'm busy, so I can get back to it ... later.

From my June 4, 2001, debut in the company until December 2, I worked pretty consistently. After that, my bookings all but dried up. Whenever I inquired about my status with the company, I was told they had some things coming up. In February 2001, I was sent to work for Les Thatcher's Heartland Wrestling Association [HWA]. I was told it would allow me to get back my ring legs and get me prepared for when they called me back. Shawn Stasiak, Tommy Dreamer, Raven, and Stevie Richards all went, as well. The HWA promoted a weekly show and we were expected to drive to the old Ohio Valley Wrestling [OVW] building in Louisville to work the TV taping. I had met Les Thatcher at the Brian Pillman and Brian Hildebrand benefit shows and he allowed me to work out every day with the kids. I spent a lot of time working with Eddie Fatu and Matt Onoa'i (who would later be known as Three-Minute Warning), Lance Cade, and Steve Bradley. I really enjoyed the time I spent wrestling and working out, but the rest of time was so boring.

From Bill De Mott's personal journal

Saturday, March 9, 2002

Well, I just thought I should get to this while I am still relatively sane! It seems that the WWF has come to the conclusion that they are paying me (as well as others) too much just to be sitting home. Oh, did I mention anywhere in this thing that they took me off the road. I know that doesn't matter. Just thought I would mention it.

Oh, did I also mention this is my second trip to Cincinnati (their developmental territory) so I could keep sharp and learn to improve my ring skills.

Can you sense the anger in this insert yet?

Anyway, back to the "story" [about] when I arrived in Cincinnati on the 6th of March after being home only two weeks after my last three-week stay here. They had Johnny Ace (whom I have the greatest respect for as a person and a boss) call me when I landed and notify me that they are going to re-negotiate my contract. Yeah, I know. It has been less than a year since I signed, but they feel I am making too much of a downside for a guy just "sitting home" (more sarcasm), so they have chosen to cut another $25,000 a year off my contract.

Sure, some of you might be thinking, "Hey, that's a lot of money you guys make, anyway," but this isn't the real world I live in, and in my world, I am lower than ant shit! So, within the past year, they took $125,000 off my contract initially, and now they need another $25,000 to let me have the "opportunity" to make more money and the second roster.

I guess if you look at it that way, it's fair.

Not a "reach around," a kiss, nothing! They have fucked me right to my face because after all — right now as I am venting — they are the only game in town.

Let me finish this little tantrum by quoting some "mark" you always seem to run into: "I wish I could do what you do. It must be great getting recognized and being famous." Don't judge us or tear us down, unless you know what you are talking about. After all, does this sound like a guy who has all the fame and money in the world? Be careful for what you ask for. You just might get it!

I am going to stop now because I am just going to get into frenzy, and everyone knows what a nice guy I am. I would hate to mislead all of you!

When I was first signed by the WWF, I was told my contract would remain as it was in WCW, but after a month or so, they told me it was too big of a "downside" and my guarantee would be cut in half. They did, however, say I would have the opportunity to make that money (and more) back when I became established with the company. My answer was as it had always been: *"I just want to be part of the company and to have the opportunity to better myself."* I guess that wasn't the best thing to say because they took me at my word and cut my pay a few more times.

From Bill De Mott's personal journal

Saturday, March 30, 2002

Here we go. I am going to keep it short and write just enough so I remember the last few weeks.

After spending three more weeks in Cincinnati, I was called back to the "show." Perry Saturn and I were getting a look as a tag team (or at least that's what they told us). We worked both shows in Pennsylvania [State College and Philadelphia, March 25-26, 2002] as dark matches, which went well. Oh, I forgot to mention that I was not "drafted." You know that whole split bullshit that was supposed to be a work, but is being treated as a shoot because they have no fucking idea what they are going to do with me. Which justifies them cutting my pay again, but I promise not to talk about that now!

Anyway, Perry and I worked on both Florida house shows [Gainesville and Jacksonville, March 27-28], as well. They were okay (worked with Stasiak and Hennig — 'nough said).

We were then informed by Dean Malenko that they are not even sure if they want us together as a tag. I don't get it! Besides that, Perry gets hurt and it turns out that he has torn the ACL in his right knee. He is out for six months and now, for sure, the team is dead — all because Stasiak is a clumsy bastard and over-thinks everything he ever did. It made him dangerous in the ring!

As well as any hope of me getting going, Johnny seems to think there is still a chance of Chavo and myself tagging. That would be great, but I refuse to keep believing anymore shit that is said.

Besides all this drama, all is well. "Professionally," my life just keeps getting more interesting (hint-hint).

Started taking steroids again for the first time in a while, and while I can see some changes in my body, things are happening on the inside that I don't think can be good. I have pulled out all the stops now. I have to get noticed ... if not for ability, then for appearance. Sucks, but this is the life I choose. Once again, I am going to stop here because I would probably spend all day writing and drifting from one thing to another. So much more to write about — drugs, women, my kids, Rose, work. This sure will be interesting reading when I am gone later.

The WWF's 2002 "draft" was held in March, but it wasn't just for the fans. The boys would actually jockey for position. The backstage politics and ass-kissing during those weeks always rose to an all-time high. Nobody wanted to be on the show that was considered to be the "B" show. Everybody wanted to be on *Monday Night RAW* where the "big stars" were. Except for the "chosen few," the boys weren't told ahead of time where they would be going. People like me sat through the entire draft, and when it was over and we hadn't been "drafted," we knew once again we weren't figured into anything.

On March 28 in Jacksonville, Perry Saturn and I teamed up against Shawn Stasiak and Mr. Perfect [Curt Hennig]. We were known as the "New Eliminators," a reprise of the role played by Perry Saturn and John Kronus in the original ECW promotion. The four of us had done the same match the night before in Gainesville. It was easy working with Curt, even though he wasn't happy about his partner or having to put us over. During the match in Jacksonville, Stasiak rolled over Perry's knee, whose ACL popped so loudly that every one of us heard it. Perry was out of work for the remainder of the year and was released by the company in November. Perry was one of the funniest, and yet, most miserable bastards, there ever was. I enjoyed his humor and I liked his work ethic. If he had just lightened up, he could have done so much more.

From Bill De Mott's personal journal

Thursday, April 25, 2002

Well, I am sitting here trying to figure out where to go with this next. Not because I have a lack of material, but because now it's going to get personal on a lot of levels!

While I was working in HWA, my contract was downgraded by several thousand dollars. We worked under what was called a "downside guarantee." I never understood all the details, but to the best of my knowledge, we were paid a certain amount per year. Let's say it was $250,000. We were paid an amount of money each week based on the number of times we worked. If we don't work a lot in a 12-month time period, we are paid the difference at the end of the year. If we made more than our contract amount before the end of the year, we got a check for anything we made over our contract. If you made too much early on, you don't get paid anything at the end of the year and you may be taken off the road the closer you get to making your downside. I never understood it. It felt like I was paying off a never-ending student loan. When they explained it to me, I just said, *"Oh, okay. I understand."* But I didn't. And it didn't matter.. All I knew was I was working a getting paid ... something.

One day, while I was hanging out in my hotel room with Stevie and Crash, Crash's phone rang. He left the room and came back less than a minute later. The call had been from Johnny Ace. As soon as Crash finished telling us what Johnny said, my phone rang. I was given the same "rah-rah" speech. I told Johnny I would do whatever they wanted and that I appreciated the opportunity to work for them. I'm sure he was thinking I was stupid, but he thanked me and I thanked him in return. After I hung up, the three of us sat looking at each other, proud of the fact that we were important pieces in the company puzzle (again, insert humor).

In May 2002, due to a lawsuit by the World Wide Fund for Nature [also WWF], the World Wrestling Federation changed their name to World Wrestling Entertainment, Inc., and subsequently, changed their initials from WWF to WWE.

Bill hosts *Smackdown* at New York restaurant, "The World," May 23, 2002

Chapter 13

Tough Enough

From Bill De Mott's personal journal

Tuesday, June 25, 2002

Well, it's been a while since I've come back to this thing. And wouldn't you know it just gets "better" (that is, for the one who reads this). As for me, work has not changed much. They (creative team) still have no idea what to do with me, but "good ol' J.R. has taken it upon himself to put me into the *Tough Enough* scene. Yeah. I will be the only male trainer (besides Al Snow) at the newest *Tough Enough*.

A lot of people are telling me this is the best thing to happen to me. I say "bullshit." Whether or not you do well in this business, they [the company] hold your fate! And now I will be out of the public eye for another three months. Realistically, this should be the platform that puts me on top of my game and in the show where, at least, I should have a shot.

I don't know how it works, and quite honestly, I am as skeptical as ever! We will have to wait and see.

I will be keeping a daily journal of the experience! You should enjoy this!

From Bill De Mott's personal journal

Monday, July 22, 2002

The funny thing about this journal is that I thought I would be able to tell you the ins and outs of my life in wrestling. What has happened is that this fucking business has taken over my life.

Kind of strange.

I am on a plane headed to Los Angeles to start the third series of *Tough Enough*. While this has been a great thing for MTV and the WWE, it has been a roller coaster for the trainers involved. Almost a "make you or break you" kind of thing.

I should be ready for this, but instead, I am wondering what is going to happen at home! Rose and I are not getting along and I have told her I don't know if I am coming back to the house.

Bold statement? Yes! Confusing? Yes!

I am not sure what lies ahead for the De Mott family or where I will wind up, but I just thought there would be an interest in letting you know. We don't just get to see the world and meet interesting people. We get to ruin our lives and the lives of those around us!

I will be keeping you updated and still try to remember why I was writing this in the first place.

Sometime in early 2002, I was approached by Al Snow. He told me my name had been brought up in meetings by John "Big" Gaburick and Kevin Dunn as a potential instructor for the third season of the WWF's reality-based television show, *Tough Enough* [TE]. Al said they liked the way I handled myself and how I was working out in the ring every day with the younger guys. Believe it or not, I had a great work ethic. It was the rest of my life that sucked.

During seasons one and two of *TE*, they used Tazz and Hardcore Holly, respectively, as their "tough-guy" trainers. I don't know if they considered me to be a tough guy, but they knew I had a passion for the business and for doing things the "right way."

The premise of the show was for twelve athletes to undergo professional wrestling training and compete for a contract with the WWF. It was the WWF's version of the hit reality show, *Survivor*. The kids who went through the program all wanted to become "the next WWF superstar." And let's face it. Spending fourteen grueling weeks as part of a reality show was a lot easier than what most of us had to do to get into the business.

Big [John Gaburick], one of Kevin Dunn's right-hand men, also was one of the producers of *Tough Enough*. When he called to tell me I would be a trainer with Al Snow and Ivory [Lisa Moretti], I was very excited. I thought *Tough Enough* would be my opportunity to show the company who I was and what I could offer the company and the business. As time would tell, it was exactly that.

Right around this time (actually, for a long time before I began working for the WWF), I was going through some very "interesting times" in my marriage. I wasn't happy in my relationship and I was only going through the motions because of my kids. It wasn't hard to do because I was on the road a lot and I didn't have to be at home with my kids' mother. I couldn't really talk to anyone about my problems. Wrestling was my "out" and my saving grace at the time. The only thing Rose was interested in was how it benefited her and the "things" she could buy. She was in a very "me-me-me" stage and didn't really take care of the house, the kids, or anything else. She was all about taking and not giving. The thing she took full advantage of was being the wife of Bill De Mott — Hugh Morrus — because without that, she was nothing.

Al Snow, Ivory, Bill, and "Big" clown around at *Tough Enough 3*

Being a part of *Tough Enough* seemed very fitting based on my own personal and professional struggles. During the course of the show, I not only learned a lot of things about the students who were trying to get to where I wanted to be, but I also learned a lot about myself.

During the first week of taping for the show, "Big" called me into his office and told me he had just talked to Vince McMahon and Kevin Dunn. They had decided that Hugh Morrus had no place in WWE and they were letting him go! *"What the fuck?"* I thought. *"I've been in California for a week and I've done everything possible to do my job and get the best kids possible ... and I'm being released?"* "Big" went on to tell me they had "fired" Hugh Morrus, but they were bringing in a guy named Bill De Mott. For a moment, I was totally confused, but the meaning of what he had said slowly dawned on me. Apparently, they liked what they saw in the *Tough Enough* footage and had decided it was ME they were looking for.

Me. As in Bill De Mott. Not Hugh Morrus.

"Big" explained that Bill De Mott was believable and that was what they wanted to see from now on. From that point on, I was able to be exactly who I was and I would be accepted for it. I was on cloud nine. The vote of confidence from Vince and Kevin made me even more determined to do what I did best, which was to train and teach people to be the best they could be. I was going to give it my all, but on the other hand, I was going to expect my students to give their best, in return. If they weren't willing to work hard and listen to what I had to say, they could step aside and make room for those who really wanted to be there.

When Big and I returned to the gym, he went out in front of the kids (on camera because that makes great TV) and let them know that Hugh Morrus was no longer going to be their trainer and would be leaving. Several of the kids had big smirks on their faces, obviously relieved to know they would no longer have to deal with me. I smiled along with them. What they didn't expect was Big's next statement: *"Hugh Morrus is being replaced by Bill De Mott ... and he is going to get serious about your training."* The smiles left everybody's face ... except mine. *"Okay, you hoodlums,"* I said cheerfully, *"Let's get back to work."*

We had a lot of fun during the filming of *TE*. I wasn't quite sure what to expect because I was on the road during the first two seasons and had only seen a few episodes.

A few of the producers would stop by the studio from time to time, but other than Al, Ivory, Big and I, the only people there on a regular basis were the kids and the camera crew. I didn't have to answer to anyone other than at our daily meetings at the end of each day when I gave my reports. The MTV people were in awe of what we were doing and I think they were a bit scared of me, which may be why they didn't interfere with anything we did. They let us know they were there simply to watch and learn how we did things. Our job was to teach the kids about our business and give MTV enough stuff to work with, while theirs was to take what we gave them and turn it into a presentable format for television. They never stepped in and suggested (or demanded) anything of us or our process. They did tell us they wanted "drama," but there was enough of that without us having to make it up, so that was never a concern. If they had any problem at all with what we were doing, it was the repetitive nature of our training because they couldn't wait for us to finish our sessions so they could do interviews with the kids.

There were a few times when MTV interrupted us during a training session because someone's mic pack broke, or because they wanted to try a different camera angle. Once, when we were doing "drills," they asked us to stop so they could reload the cameras and get better angles. Sometimes it was frustrating, but I understood. That's show biz.

The trainers didn't often go to the house where the contestants lived in the mountains near Calabasas, California (which was where they filmed the TV series M*A*S*H). They had us over a few times for a barbeque and some dinners, and Al and I made a few unannounced stops to "raid" it and scare the hell out of them.

The "confrontation" between Bob Holly and Matt Cappotelli wasn't as big as it appeared on TV, but it turned into one of the most talked-about incidents of the *TE3* season. I'm not sure if MTV or the WWE was in charge of the editing, but whoever it was did major edits to the tape to make it look like Matt took a serious ass-kicking ... but he didn't. The editing process is a beautiful thing and, without a doubt, made that incident look more sensational than it actually was. The fact that Matt was a good-looking kid just enhanced the drama. The sponsors and the ladies all loved Matt

As a whole, there must have been miles of unused footage left on the cutting room floor. There were so many things that were never touched on, including a major part of the training and trials. Since *Tough Enough* was a reality show, the producers wanted as much drama as possible to draw the viewers, but a lot of what those kids did and went through wasn't touched on.

What should have been the biggest story of *TE3* was the meltdown of a contestant named Lisa. When it came to training, Lisa was the biggest screwup of the season. She would miss moves and laugh about it, which didn't sit well with the trainers or her fellow contestants. During the second week of training, she lost her mind. I mean, she literally lost her mind. One afternoon, Big received a phone call from the production crew who were working the night shift. They said Lisa was wearing a dress and jumping on the roof of the house. The biggest problem with that was, the side of the house on which she was jumping was a one-way ticket to the bottom of a canyon. She had blown a circuit and nobody knew what to do. By the time Big arrived at the house, the producers had talked her down. When John walked over to her, she pushed him against the wall and said something like, *"They are going to get you, too ... he is going to get you."*

While I was driving to the studio the next morning, Big called to tell me what happened. What he told me was so crazy that I had to pull over to the side of the road so I could concentrate. Lisa was diagnosed with having suffered a psychotic breakdown and was to the "rubber room" at UCLA (I think) for her own safety. She was held there for three days before being released to her parents, who had flown in from New Mexico to take her home. When she saw them, she physically attacked them and claimed they weren't her parents. After they arrived at Los Angeles International Airport, she escaped custody and a wing of the airport was shut down until she was located and subdued. She was again hospitalized, only to check herself out a short time afterwards, whereupon she contacted the *Tough Enough* producers to tell them she was ready to return to the show.

None of this information was released to the general public and the *TE* contestants (and, subsequently, the audience) were told she had decided wrestling "wasn't the right career for her."

The next time anyone heard from Lisa, she appeared at the OVW training center and said Al Snow and Big had sent her for additional training. During the week of September 21-24, she talked her way backstage at a series of WWE house shows in California, and was even allowed to assist with pyro for the wrestlers' entrances at the TV taping. Someone said she had a face-to-face conversation with Vince McMahon, who was unaware of her situation with the *Tough Enough* program. Her photo was later circulated to security personnel and she was barred from backstage areas. Her picture also hung in the MTV studios with a note that said, *"Do not give this person access to any part of the studio."*

It was said I was pretty hard on her, and to this day, Al often speaks of how I "drove that poor girl crazy." I just look at it as one of those incidents that enhanced my reputation, and apparently, she just wasn't "tough enough." Bad humor, I know.

One of the other girls, Rebekah, touted herself as a Christian who turned to her Bible for support. At one point, she said she had hoped to have more Christian fellowship during her stay in the house. Well, after two beers and a cigarette (one of my favorite sayings), she turned into a wild child, dancing like a stripper on the top of a bar. Sometime during her stay, we discovered she was a former Hooter's girl, so Al and I gave her the nickname "Hooters." Rebekah was a good-looking girl with some ability, but I don't think she had what it took to be a wrestler. She finally made the decision to go home after hearing her mother was going to lose their trailer due to foreclosure and would have no place to live.

Speaking of nicknames, Al and I gave names to most of the contestants. We named Jamie "plumber" because her butt crack would often be showing.

Surprisingly enough, there were no real "lovey-dovey" moments during *TE3*. There were a few "Romeo and Juliet" encounters, but nothing that lasted. The closest anyone came to that was Jonah teasing and leading Jill along, without telling her he had a girlfriend back home, and then talking smack in his interviews. Of course, the producers loved it because it made for great television.

Jill and Jonah should have been on a reality show like *Big Brother*. Jill made the cut through the original selection process. There were a few good kids who got cut because she was selected ... and then she quit after the first day of training. Jonah had a lot to do with it, but I think Jill thought it was another kind of reality show. In favor of Jill, we actually cut Melina Perez in the final cut of the first episode. Two years later, Melina would later sign with the WWE and, as "Melina," would become one of the best all-time Divas in the business.

The guys were ridiculous when Trish Stratus made a visit to the house. Every one of them acted like "little boys," giggling and turning red as they all tried to curry her favor.

Most of the contestants worked hard, but one of the guys, Nick, went to see a doctor when his arm began hurting and was diagnosed with tendonitis in his elbow. Nick told us he had to follow the doctor's orders and rest for a week. Strangely enough, though, he was well enough to play volleyball at the beach and fool around. His lack of desire to work through the pain resulted in him being cut from the show.

One of the contestants, Jonah, was sent to the hospital after he took a bad bump and injured his neck. When he came back to the house, he was wearing a neck brace and had bandages wrapped around his head. After asking everyone to sit down with him, he began to cry and told everyone he had to leave the competition because of his injury. Of course, when Jonah began to cry, everyone else did, too. It was really an emotional time. Jonah then proceeded to ask everyone to say something nice about him before he had to leave. Choking back tears as they spoke, everyone shared something about Jonah they liked. Matt, who was blubbering like a baby, walked over and gave Jonah a hug. Jonah then said something along the lines of, *"I want everybody to remember this moment,"* ripped off his neck brace, and said, *"when I'm kicking your ass in the ring."* That was one of the funniest ribs I've ever seen, in or out of the business. While Jonah was giving everyone his song-and-dance act, Al, Ivory, Big and I were all behind the curtain, trying hard not to laugh out loud.

The following week, the kids got back at Jonah by putting a laxative in his protein shake. While everyone was waiting for the laxative to kick in, Al and I decided to teach "roll-ups." If you ever have to shit uncontrollably, the last thing you want is people squeezing your legs to your stomach. When Jonah finally made a mad dash to the bathroom, he discovered there was no toilet paper. Al took "pity" on him and gave him three sheets. Of course, that wasn't enough, so Jonah used his clothes to wipe his ass. Ivory was so disgusted over the fact that he left them in the bathroom that she made him walk them out to the dumpster.

After the series aired, people told me they thought I was acting, or going over the top to enhance the drama of the training, but that isn't true. Everything you saw on the program was "me" being "me." I didn't have time for acting. I believe in training and repetition. I also was being paid by the WWE to get the kids ready for professional careers, so my goal was to train those kids and give each one of them an equal opportunity to win the prize. There is no greater feeling than to succeed and know you did it by busting your ass. If there *was* a problem with "acting," I believe it was the talent thinking they were "acting" on a reality show.

When I would go to one of the WWE shows, I would hear the younger guys in the locker room talking about how "unfair" it was for the *TE* guys to be getting such a big break without having pay their dues. I had to remind them that many of them didn't have to go through what guy during my time had, and I didn't have to go through what the guys from the past did. Like anything else, it was simply jealousy. I can say without hesitation that more than half of the locker room would have "taken advantage" of the situation in the same way the *TE* contenders had. I also believe a lot of those negative opinions changed when they met the contestants and got to know them, especially the WWE superstars who came onto the show as guest trainers and speakers. The contestants went through a hell of a lot to get involved and proved themselves to be worthy of the title "WWE Superstars." The perfect examples of that would be Maven [Maven Huffman] [season 1], The Miz [Michael Mizanin] [season 4], and John Morrison [John Hennigan] [season 3], each of whom went on to have great careers with the company.

I still hear from some of the kids who didn't make it in *TE3*, like Justin and Kelly, but I've lost touch with Matt Cappotelli since he had his surgery for brain cancer. One of the kids I stay in touch with is Scott. He wasn't as good as some of the other hopefuls who had been sent home, but Scott was good for TV purposes. He was very immature and naive, so he was a target for abuse by the other kids. It was all in good fun, though. Scott was well liked by the others and they wanted him to do well. Everywhere we went, he took samples of dirt back with him because he had never ventured far from his home in Harrisonburg, Virginia. When we went to the beach, he said he had never been in the ocean and couldn't swim, so (of course) we threw him in the water. I still get e-mail from Scott from time to time. The last I heard, he landed a job with VH1 doing production work. When all was said and done, Scott was a good kid.

Al and I became very close friends during our time with *TE3* and we have maintained our relationship through the years. I miss the "hijinks" that Al and I shared. He's good people and one helluva man. He also gave the funniest toast at my wedding to Lacey Storey. I can't remember most of it because I was drunk like everyone else, but it ended with something like, *"... it took her long enough to fucking die."* It caught us so off guard that everyone laughed for a long time. Nobody tells a joke or story like Al Snow.

Chapter 14

Lacey

I met Lacey Storey at a bar in California after the WCW SuperBrawl IX pay-per-view on February 21, 1999 in Oakland, California. She had been a wrestling fan for a long time before we met. In fact, she was probably the biggest Hulk Hogan fan there was. Even today, she has more Hogan memorabilia than I care to admit. The only person she knew connected to wrestling was Dave Penzer, the ring announcer. Dave left her at the bar to go meet up with some other friends and asked me to keep an eye on her. She looked young and I didn't like the fact that she was alone, especially since so many "wolves" were hovering around. I reluctantly agreed. Okay, that's a lie. It didn't take much persuasion. She was, after all, the hottest lady in the room. She was only 22 years old at the time and looked even younger.

When we left that night, we exchanged phone numbers, and during the next few months, we would talk from time to time. I was going through a lot of crap in my marriage and she was a good listener. We didn't date or hang out together for a long time. Part of the reason was I knew she was a lot younger than me. The other reason (okay, and this is probably the real reason) was she lived in Iowa and I was in Florida. Oh, yes. I was married at the time, too.

In high school, Lacey had been an honor student, a member of student council and dance committees, and was very active in school activities. She was only 17 years old when she lost her mother and was left alone to take care of her younger brother. That forced her to grow up really fast and deal with the responsibilities she inherited. Lacey attended community college for three semesters before realizing it wasn't for her, opting instead to attend cosmetology school in Des Moines.

The thing that really attracted me to Lacey was she was never interested in "who I was." She just wanted to talk at a time when I needed a friend. Not a "female friend," but someone to whom I could actually talk and vent about everyday stuff. When I was on the road, we talked almost every night. If the Wicked Witch of the West (do I really have to explain who that was) happened to be around when Lacey and I were talking, she would ask me who I was talking with. I would say, *"Someone in Iowa."*

"Who? A girl?" I had nothing to hide. I admitted it and said she was just a friend ... and that was the truth.

Lacey and I stayed in contact for a long time. It wasn't until I was in California for *Tough Enough 3*, and going through a separation, that we would begin to become more than friends. During some of the toughest days of my life, when I was being bombarded with details about the divorce and not being around my girls, Lacey was there to keep me sane. We spent a lot of time together talking about things going on in both of our lives and how things might someday work out between us.

Lacey Storey and Bill on the night they met, 1999

It was during *Tough Enough* that I found out how tough I was and how much that girl wanted to be a part of my life. Nothing was left untouched. We discussed my girls, my marriage, her plans and dreams for the future ... and if we would have a future together.

As it turned out, Lacey would become the most important person in the world to me (along with Casey, Keri, and later, our son Billy). We began dating in June 2000, we moved in together three years later, and we got married on December 18, 2004.

From Bill De Mott's personal journal

August 26, 2002

When I come back to writing in this thing again, it will be about the most damaging parts of my life. I write it like this (1) to remind me where I was and (2) because if I don't leave little notes like this to myself, I forget a lot. Blame it on the somas.

And the fact that I am completely fucking every aspect of my life up!

Later.

In early September 2002, the cast and crew of *Tough Enough* were preparing to leave for Iceland. Knowing my marriage was all but over, Lacey and I went to a theater and sat through a terrible movie called *Serving Sara*. As we pulled away from the theater in my Ford Mustang convertible, an old truck veered into our lane and hit us head on. The collision pushed the front of the car into the back of the car, while the rest blew out in all four directions into the intersection. The air bags inflated and kept me from suffering any serious injury, but Lacey was caught between the dashboard and the trunk. After I pulled her out of the car and laid her on the grass, I tried to catch the bastard who hit us. He left his truck and took off, running down the street. I didn't catch him, but he appeared back at the scene after the cleanup had begun and the cops were writing reports.

When the paramedics arrived, they took one look at the car and said, *"You guys are lucky you're not dead."* We were shaken and bruised up, but they made us comfortable as possible. Big showed up and took us to the hospital. Lacey's leg was bruised and swollen. I didn't want to miss the trip to Iceland, so I lied to the doctors and we were cleared to leave. I didn't like hospitals ... never have, never will. Lacey walked away with just a bruised leg and a sore neck. I, on the other hand, had a lot of pain in my shoulders, knees, and back. I didn't let on that anything was wrong, though. I wanted to stay and work with the kids, so the filming of *Tough Enough* continued as scheduled.

From Bill De Mott's personal journal

Monday, November 4, 2002

Yeah, I know it's been a while since I wrote in this thing. (I was) in LA shooting *Tough Enough*. And just for the record: "I am not tough enough."

This begins the writing of Bill De Mott. I tried to tell everyone that being Bill De Mott was going to be bad for everyone involved. And it has been.

I am now writing from my new home, this little shit apartment on the other side of town. I want to be close to my kids ... and Rose, too, I suppose. Right now, I don't know what the fuck I am doing. My family is having their own thoughts on this. Casey and Keri are dealing the best they can, and as for Rose, I'm not sure what she is thinking or doing now that I am out.

My girls are hurt. I'm sure of it, and at the same time, they don't know what's going on (as do Rose and myself). It breaks my heart to see the confusion in their eyes. I can't think about it too much or I break down (which is happening a lot lately). I need my kids around me-it. It's not the same life I lead anymore. I am as alone as one guy can get.

Lacey is caught in the middle. She is great. She honestly cares for me and tries very hard to understand all this while getting blamed for all that has happened. Totally not her fault, and it is hard to make others (family) believe she did not do this. She doesn't deserve this and I'm not sure if she will stick it out.

Back to my girls. They've come to the apartment and helped in moving stuff. I thought if I got them involved, they would feel better about the whole thing. I don't know how they feel. I hope in the upcoming weeks they will open up a little more. I know they are confused when they see me and their mom laughing and sitting next to each other, then I say good night. If you think it doesn't make sense, come take my place!

I hate this fucking apartment and sitting is the last thing I need to do. When I am by myself, I have a tendency to overmedicate and fall into deep sleeps. What the fuck, right? Some people would probably say I deserve it.

I will start to write more again since I'm by myself. I know Lacey is going to be coming down soon and wants to move in. But, right now, everyone needs to get used to this before any more "bombs" are dropped. I told you this was going to get good ... good for the ones reading this shit, not for the ones living it!

While I was in California filming *TE*, I told Rose about Lacey. Her retort was, *"Why would anyone want you? You don't have two dimes to rub together?"* I really didn't understand that statement and it was a long time before I knew what she was talking about. That was her way of telling me she was about to fuck up my whole world. What I didn't know what she had already set the wheels in motion to take everything I had ever worked for.

I was the one who had to sit down with my girls and tell them, *"Mommy and Daddy won't be living together anymore,"* and I had to explain that it was the best for everyone. Of course, that's not true. Divorce is never, in any way, manner, or fashion, "the best" for children. After having the toughest conversation I would ever have with anyone, I had to move out of the house I had built and into a two-room apartment on the other side of town. I stayed in town so I could spend time with my kids when I wasn't traveling. I also gave $3,000 a month to Rose long before she filed for divorce. That gave her more than enough to pay the mortgage, make payments on her brand, new car, and continue to live the lifestyle to which she had become accustomed. I did that without question because I didn't want my girls taken out of their comfort zone.

Bill, Matt Cappotelli and Justin in Iceland during *Tough Enough 3*

Al Snow, Bill, and the kids in Iceland during *Tough Enough 3*

From Bill De Mott's personal journal

Friday, November 22, 2002

Well, again, it's been a while. Not like I have much to do where I can't write a little. After all, I am in a shitty little apartment by myself and sit here taking somas and going crazy, but I would be doing that wherever I was.

I turned 37 years old two weeks ago and it just seems like my life is going backwards. I can't catch up to all the bills, and at the same time, I can't make Rose realize this is a problem. I know I have been in this situation before, but not at this fucking level. I am making better than a decent living and I can't get this shit paid-. I feel like saying "fuck it." I mean, what are they going to take from me. I don't have anything anymore!

The girls "seem" to be adjusting to the situation (probably better than me). I'm not sure how much they understand. I haven't been able to spend as much time with Casey as I have Keri. Casey is dancing three to four days a week, so her time is very scarce. Keri is doing great! A little crazy at times and full of energy, but okay. I wonder what goes on in their heads? Same with Rose. I wouldn't mind going over to the house more, but it is more uncomfortable now than ever.

I told Rose yesterday that Lacey was coming down the weekend of the 13th (December) and this went over like a "fart in church." As I knew it would, but how else are things going to go. I don't know what's right and wrong with this whole thing.

Lacey is a good girl and caught up in this mess. I really enjoy being with her and spending as much time as possible with her as I can. I guess that makes me a bigger asshole for involving her in this, especially when everyone is looking at her for being the reason I left (she is not the reason I left).

Anyway, I'm sure it's taking its toll on Lacey, too. I've tried to tell her that maybe we should take a little break from each other until this all works out, but she wants to hear none of that. She is looking forward to coming here and eventually staying! I know that's another fucked-up issue, but we will talk about that when the time comes.

As far as work, I have been traveling to the TV tapings (*Smackdown*) and been doing nothing! Then I got a phone call from Kevin Dunn (actually I called Big after a *Tough Enough 3* episode and Kevin was there). He put me over huge and mentioned that I should start thinking about TE 4! I was honored and said I am in. He also said he had a new vignette of me and that they will air it soon. Well, true to his word, I got to Stamford, Connecticut, and there it was for me to work on *Velocity* (as a heel), and they would show the first of three vignettes that night on *Smackdown*. So, it looks as though Bill De Mott is on his way to becoming a player in this company. You know me though. After all these years, I will need more than just one week to see if they give me shot.

It was good to see it, though, on *Smackdown*. Makes me look like a bad ass!

Enough for now. I get to the point where my thoughts go a million different ways and I start to get worked up. This is supposed to be relaxing and therapeutic, but I get worked up. I will go pace for a bit and try to figure out how to spend my day before I pick the girls up at school later!

From Bill De Mott's personal journal

Tuesday, December 31, 2002

Well, I don't know how to start this little episode of mine. It is the end of what will prove to be the hardest year of my life. Hard because of a lot of things. I lost $150,000, I've lost my self-esteem, and most importantly, I have lost my family.

Make no mistake about it. Right or wrong thing to do, I have lost my family!

Let's start with the positives:

I have a new-found career with *Tough Enough* and the success I had coming off that series. I would do it all over again. The downside is no one knows me other than as "that guy" from MTV. It sucks, no matter how successful I become. I have given everything, as well as the people who stayed with me. To be known after all this time as the *Tough Enough* bad ass. But that's the business I chose and love!

The next positive is that I found Lacey! She is nothing short of great. She has walked into a situation a kid her age doesn't need to be in and has faced everything very well so far.

Which leads me to the negatives:

I have left my home and the three people who mean the most to me. Well, at least two out of three: Rose (not so much), Casey and Keri. I didn't leave for hate. I left because I am unhappy. So many things have taken over and played a part. That I don't think I could ever explain. I loved Rose, I did. I just don't think we can go on like this. We have our moments of happiness, but they are just that: moments.

The whole time I am out there making a living and providing for my family, she is and was just worried about her and what she wanted to do for herself. I love my daughters with all my heart, and the things I have had to explain to them are killing me, but no one sees that side because all I do now is hide. I don't have everything under control, but how am I supposed to let everyone know that. My folks are different and that just adds to the pain of all this. I don't care how Rose's folks feel because, to them, I was never good enough, anyway, so fuck them. They got what they wanted!

Right now, I am so unsure about what I am doing and how I am doing it that I almost don't care. Everyone thinks I say that to say it, but it's the truth. I am not out to hurt anyone. I just don't know happiness anymore. I'm sure the pills and booze don't help, but I can't sleep or relax any other way. I try talking to God and I know he is watching right now. I know my thinking has been clouded for a long time, but what am I supposed to do?

This year has been very rough. No spotlights, no fame ... just drama. This is what has become my life. No, this is not a pity party. This is that same kid who didn't know who he was in his teens, and I turned out to be no better than when I grew to hate my old man. I'm more like the kid who struggled in New Jersey than the man who is typing this shit!

I don't know how to get close to my family anymore. I know they are all disappointed and my mom tries real hard to get it, but nothing will ever be the same again. Right and wrong don't fit in anymore. I go day to day trying to figure it out.

I don't know what this next year holds for me, my family, or my girls, but I do know it can't get much worse. I think I said it somewhere in this journal. "Be careful what you ask for. You just might get it." No one said at what cost.

Being Bill De Mott is nothing to be proud of, and believe me when I say, I am not proud of anything I have done (except my two girls).

This is a helluva way to end the year. God only knows what's next, but I really am not looking forward to it.

For those who read this when it's done. I love my family. That's my girls! My mom, John, and Pop.

I'm sorry for the setbacks and letting everyone down. I can't fix it. I can only try to make it up to you. And I know I can never do that, either.

As for Lacey, I am sorry to you, too. You didn't ask for all this and don't deserve it. I love you for sticking with me. Who knows where you will be when this is read.

I never, ever claimed to be anything special. I just didn't think I would have proved it!

I have been blessed with a lot of things in my life and, somehow, looked past it all. I know this and I am sure, somewhere down the line, it will come back to haunt me. I am haunted enough now, but I am sure there will be more to come.

I am not proud of myself, and don't know where I will be this time next year ... but I did make it interesting.

You didn't think I would end this entry without some kind of sarcasm, did you?

From Bill De Mott's personal journal

Wednesday, January 1, 2003

Well, here it is a day later, and what do you know? I made to the next year! Yep, it's 2003 and everything changes from here on out. How about the fact that I have actually written two days in a row (there's that sarcasm again).

Rose called this morning to say "Happy New Year." We are both going to start new lives now. Don't know where it is going to end up or how we will get along.

I will start this year by going to work. I leave for New Mexico and an eight-day run, then I am going to go see Lacey in Des Moines. It looks like she will be down here around the end of the month. I'm not sure how this will turn out, either... for the girls, Rose, or Lacey, for that matter.

I guess if you are going to do something, you might as well go "balls out." My only hope is that I find whatever it is I am looking for ... if I am looking at all! Starting over at the age of 37 is scary. It's not like I'm the most secure mother fucker in the world.

Anyway, I am not sure why I write this thing or call it a book. All I know is I started it to help remember, but now I would rather forget everything that is going on. Maybe it is just another thing I will leave my kids. The sad part is, they will find out a lot about their dad. Somebody, someday, will have the great privilege of putting this all in order and making it into something.

I wish my family and loved ones a Happy New Year and hope that this somehow becomes more civilized down the road. I truly never meant to hurt or destroy anyone's feelings about me or anyone else.

It should be an interesting year!

From Bill De Mott's personal journal

Sunday, March 9, 2003

Well, it has been a while again since I wrote in this thing. I have just returned from a trip in South Africa with the *Smackdown* crew. Yeah! South Africa. Where else could a schmuk like me keep seeing the world and doing things he never dreamed of?

Anyway, where to begin this entry:

Lacey and the girls (Casey and Keri) have finally met. Yep, Keri was first and then Casey followed. They have since become friends and are getting along very well. Rose, as well as me, have been quite shocked. Not for any other reason than my girls are so grown up and can be with the both of us. It's not hard to get to like Lacey and she has really been great with the girls. I am sure that they will become very good friends in the future. It is very important to me that all the people in my life can get along (as for Rose and Lacey, it will have to take its own course).

As of late, I have become very bad with the pills and drinking ... again! I am afraid this is going to hurt my relationship with Lacey. I don't think she knows how to handle me when I get like this. I don't expect her to, but at the same time, I know I have a problem with this. And as things go on with the girls and their mom, I get into weird thought patterns and shit. Last night, while we were in bed, I started mumbling and talking about stupid shit while we were making love. It scared me and I know it scared Lacey. I have been telling her for a while I have these problems with my head, and when I get "gooned" out, I can't control my thoughts. There is so much going on it's like a circus in my head. I don't want to lose her or make her sorry she is down here.

It has been very hard for her since moving in with me. One, she has moved away from home for the first time; two, she doesn't know anyone here yet, and three, work is too far away and stressing her out. And the biggest thing is this is the busiest I have been in a long time and haven't been home much. She has not had it easy since coming here. I want her here and I'm afraid she will crack!

> The company has been behind on paying the boys, so there is no money for bills and no time for us to get to be together as much as we would like. I know how this is and it is easier for me to deal with, but right now, it is very hard for her, and I know I am not helping with my pills and shit. Maybe this is what I do to everyone. Maybe I am that Jekyll and Hyde guy.
>
> All I know is Lacey means a lot to me and I don't want to lose her. I have lost enough things in the past year and she is so good for me and to me. I want to make her happy and give her the things she deserves and needs. Me, I am starting all over again and am kind of set in my ways. We are learning a lot about each other. I'm afraid she is learning more than she wanted to. Hell. I don't even want to be with me lately.
>
> This is where I stop again. The brain starts to think of a million things and it is too much to try to put together. I will try to stay on one subject at a time from now on. No promises, though!

Lacey never looked back or reconsidered entering the crazy, mixed-up world of Bill De Mott. She was only 22 years old, but she was enthusiastic about helping raise my girls, even when she encountered the raft of shit that came with being "the new girl in town." You never know how things will work out or how people will react to change, especially when there's a mix of divorce, kids, parents, friends, and anyone else who will stick their nose into your business. As it turned out, she got grief from everybody I knew in Titusville. Even the cats who were supposed to be my friends were told by their wives that they couldn't "play with Bill anymore." Jim Duggan's wife actually "banned" him from being around me. That was a shame because I could have used a friend at the time, and it hurt when Jimmy turned his back on me.

The girls took their time in making their decisions to meet Lacey. I didn't force or even encourage a meeting. I didn't ask them to be nice or treat her in any certain way, either. During the first few days of Lacey and me living together in Florida, Keri decided she wanted to meet her. Casey was at dance class when the meeting took place. A few days later, Casey followed. Both meetings were civil and quiet. It was like "the first day of school." Everyone was nervous and took their time feeling each other out.

Lacey, Casey and Keri became friends, and then good friends, and if you saw them together today, you would think they were her kids. Actually, when you get right down to it, they are! They have grown to be as close as any three could be. To the outside world, they are mother and daughters. I'm happy to say Lacey takes great pride and responsibility in the raising of our girls, and has been a major influence on shaping them into beautiful, responsible, caring, young women. They are inseparable. They do everything and go everywhere together — shopping, hair and makeup, the movies, shopping, vacations, lunch dates, and in their spare time, they go shopping. The most important thing is they communicate and tell each other everything. They go to Lacey when they want to talk about "girlie" things, their personal lives, and everything in-between. Lacey knows their lives inside and out. The older they get, the more they rely on Lacey, and I know Lacey relies on them, as well. It's so awesome to sit back and watch them interact with each other. I often tease the three of them, saying, *"Don't worry about me. You guys go ahead. I'm fine over here by myself."*

Lacey has never complained about the baggage that came along with me. She went through a lot to be with me. She never blinked when she moved from Iowa to Florida, even though she spent a lot of time alone while I was on the road. She didn't know anyone and my family didn't want to know her (at least, in the beginning). Lacey was excited about meeting my family, but it didn't happen right away because my mother and father didn't want to meet her. In fact, they refused to talk to her for a long time. Alice (my mother) had known Rose for a long time and they had a good relationship, so she didn't want anything to do with Lacey. I had tried to explain the problems Rose and I were having, but Alice didn't seem to hear what I was saying. It was tough on Lacey, but she understood. I had enough drama in my life, so I chose the woman who stood by me and we went for a time without seeing my parents.

(l to r.) Casey, Bill, Keri, Lacey

The 16-hour trip to South Africa was grueling, but I was excited about going because I had never been there. I looked at it as another chance to "shine" and stay in the loop. I wrestled all three nights of the tour. On the first night in, February 27, we wrestled in Cape Town. Edge had suffered a neck injury during a match with Kurt Angle on January 27, but he was a trooper and made the trip. He wasn't going to wrestle the first night in, but with the crowd being so big (I think it was a sellout), he made an attempt to work. I did a run-in during his match. On the two nights that followed, we wrestled in Durban and Johannesburg.

Back in the States, the night of April 13 stands out in my mind because it was one of the few nights in my long career when I completely lost my temper, both in and out of the ring. We were taping *Smackdown* in Montgomery, Alabama, and I was wrestling Nathan Jones. Nathan was getting the WWE rocket shoved up his ass and they were building him to work with Taker. The office wanted me to help get him ready for the big push, so they booked us together on three consecutive house shows. We wrestled in Chicago and Daytona Beach before we appeared together in Montgomery.

The company laid out a spot for our match during which time he would "take over" on me. During our first two matches, he hit me in the back of the head during that spot. Before our match in Montgomery, I told him, *"Don't hit me in the back of my fucking head or I'm going to get pissed off."* He was very careless and didn't take care of the guys who were putting him over. Sure enough, when the spot came around, he hit me in the back of the head. I refused to sell it. I stood up and acted as if nothing had happened.

After he "beat" me with the spectacular "kick to the chest" move, we went to the locker room. I was hot! I couldn't wait for him to walk through the door so I could let him have it. Big Show, Bob Holly, and Taker knew I was upset and tried to calm me down, but I was past all reasoning. When Jones walked through the curtain, I went for him. The other guys were waiting for that to happen and stepped between us before I could get to him. Jones was so thick-headed. He couldn't understand what he had done wrong. I eventually gave up trying to explain and told him, *"Go fuck yourself and stay away from me."* If someone else had acted like I did, I would have said they were acting like an asshole ... and perhaps that's what I was ... but Jones was greener than goose shit and we weren't there for him to step on and disrespect. Jones lasted less than a year, but for the short time he was in the business, he took away a lot of spots from guys who knew how to work and who would have relished the opportunity he had been given.

I can only remember losing my temper in the ring one other time. It was during my "First Family" run in WCW when I was getting a series of wins on the Saturday night program. We were somewhere in the northwest and I was going to be working with Bart Sawyer, who was booked as enhancement talent. Arn Anderson sat us both down and told the kid what was expected of him. He said I was gaining some steam with the company, so they needed him to "do the right thing." He shook his head up and down, indicating we were all on the same page.

When the opening bell rang, the kid went to the top rope and clotheslined me in the jaw as I turned into the ring. When I didn't move and didn't sell it, he tried it again. I got so pissed off, I shot a clothesline from a standing position and all but took off his head. I wasn't happy about him taking liberties and I spent the rest of the match manhandling him until I was ready to go for the "No Laughing Matter." When I did, I placed him far out into the center of the ring and landed as hard as I could. After the referee made the count, I pulled him to a seated position and began to wail away at him. Jerry Flynn, Brian Knobbs, and referee Johnny Boone bum rushed me out of the ring and back to the dressing room, where Jimmy Hart stepped up to help calm me down.

There have been many times when one of my opponents has been stiff, or tried to impose their will on me. I never had a problem with that because I had been taught to "give it as hard as you get it," but nobody was going to make me look foolish or abuse me when they didn't have the right to do so.

From Bill De Mott's personal journal

Friday, June 6, 2003

I don't know how long it's been since I wrote last. I guess I should have looked. Anyway, the divorce papers are done and I was just served with them. Who knows if it was supposed to get this complicated, but it has. I'm trying to work through a lot of things. None of it has come to surface yet.

I have had battles with Alice. We yelled, screamed, and said things that should have never been said. We talk now, but things will never be the same because, like I have said before, I have changed everyone's life … except I'm the only one going through the changes.

Casey received a scholarship for all of next year's dancing and competitions. I am so proud of her. I am equally as proud of Keri. She has really been coming out of her shell. They are dealing with all of this well (as far as I know). They get along great with Lacey, and from what I understand, they now see Joe a lot more, as well.

Although I see them when I am home, they are getting distant (at least it seems) towards me. I think now that their mother has her boyfriend in the house (my fucking house), the more they get the "whole family" thing over there. So, I kind of get the feeling that dad isn't needed much anymore. I'm sure they are still confused and working through it, but I am not doing well with not being with them as much. And I don't think Rose could give a shit either way. She doesn't go out of her way to make sure they call when I'm gone. She picks the times to remind them they have a dad and I think she will be fine with someone else filling my shoes.

I've said it before. Rose learned a lot in sixteen years (and had some pretty good teaching from some of the other boys' wives), and being hurtful without feeling was something that worked well for her. She holds on to her stories and brings them across to others. Her faith and her thinking are a whole different matter. She has become one of those, *"I believe it to be this way, so it is this way,"* and, *"I cannot be wrong as long as I believe what I say"* kind of people.

I don't have much feeling for her, not even as my kids' mother. She has turned this into a battle, a battle that she is winning in every way. Rose can convince my kids of anything. Financially, she has the means to treat them to things when I am the one providing the money. Yet, I can't do things the way I want because she is taking all the money and leaving me to fend on what's left.

I guess what's right and wrong doesn't really come into play here. You either have to fight or live with it. I guess for right now I will live with it, but they are all bringing me to the point were I want to fight. Win, lose, or draw … I will not lose the next battle. Someone will be hurt emotionally or otherwise. I will probably wind up hurting myself first.

I think a lot of people will be relieved when I am not around. Everyone but my Lacey. I love her. She is a good woman and I am glad she is in my life.

No more now. This writing thing gets me worked up.

Have I already said that?

Even though our divorce proceedings were coming to a conclusion, my arguments with Rose soared to new heights. What bothered me the most, though, was the fact that Alice (my mother) still refused to accept Lacey. Alice and I weren't seeing eye to eye and that bothered me because we had always been so close. The one saving grace was to see my daughters slowly begin to warm up to her. Keri, who was very quiet around everyone, even family, found a friend in Lacey. They began talking and Keri slowly came out of her shell. It was really awesome to see because Keri came out of her shell and opened up with us. She got more involved with dancing and socializing.

"Joe" was the guy Rose was seeing during the time she was claiming to be so upset and distraught over me serving her with divorce papers. Apparently, she was "dating" Joe while I was in California filming *Tough Enough 3*. I was later told Joe didn't know what he was getting into with Rose and, after a while, realized it "wasn't for him." I never had words with him and didn't really care who she was seeing as long as my girls were okay. I did think it was weird how a guy looking to buy a house in the area wound up "dating" the real-estate agent (Rose). It's not what I would call good work practice, but I thought it was funny at the time.

From Bill De Mott's personal journal

Monday, July 7, 2003

The real "First Family"

Casey and Keri

Today is Casey's tenth birthday. Yep, I said ten years old. Unbelievable to think that it has been that long already. To this day, I still don't know what I did before my kids were born.

On the 4th of July, the kids spent the whole weekend with Lacey and me. It was great having them back with me for that time. It almost felt like a family again. I know it must have been weird for them, but you would have never known it. They have accepted Lacey and get along great with her, and she absolutely loves them. She told me last night she is in "awe" of my girls ... that they are teaching her so much. Not sure I understand that, but I am grateful for the way the three of them are getting along and getting to know one another. You would think their mother and I would learn from the example, but that's a whole new discussion.

I'm trying to keep this "episode" on a good note, so there are a lot of things I will not write because of this. There are things going on that would push normal people to do drastic things, but as we all know by now, "I'm not normal people."

Just very happy for my "bear" to be ten today.

Sometimes I have to sit myself down and talk to myself, and try to remember that every time I get to look in their eyes, happy or sad, they are the best things that have ever happened to me! I love Casey and Keri with all my heart, and someday I hope they will understand all that has gone on in their lives so far. And I hope they come out of it better than I did or will. They are good girls and I just want them to know how much I love and need them. A lot has changed in the past year, but I never want them away from me.

This was the best weekend I have had in a very long time, and watching them get picked up yesterday was very hard for me. As I am sure it was for them. Anyway ...

Happy Birthday, Casey Lea De Mott!

From Bill De Mott's personal journal

Thursday, July 24, 2003

Well, still dealing with the whole "broken neck" thing. If you are not caught up to speed, here we go. Update: thought it was only two discs. Not! It's the whole neck!

My last match was in Corpus Christi, Texas against Sean O'Haire. I was paralyzed for a while and really scared, but Larry [Heck], Jamie [Noble], and Crash (might have been the last time I saw Crash before he died) got me to the next town (pilled up and drinking, of course). I went to TV and that would be the end of that. I flew home from San Antonio and never went back to work as a wrestler.

I was taken off the road the middle or end of June (I can't remember). It's been a long time. I have been to too many doctors, but every one of these fuckers has a different story. Staying in contact with Bob Clark (shithead in charge of me making a living). That's my official title for the guy who doesn't know shit about you, but can keep you off the road until you are medically cleared. Or by his work title: Head of Talent Relations/Medical.

Long story short: My neck is in pain all day and night. I have relied on pills (Valium, somas, Xanax, and two different antidepressants) to make it through the day and put me too sleep at night. The funny thing is, if I was anyone else but Bill De Mott, I would have been fixed or cleared back to work by now. Not to mention all the bullshit with this divorce still going on. It's taking a toll on my and Lacey's relationship!

The days get longer, and without money and wheels, and the freedom to be where I want and see my kids without a schedule, this could definitely bring some bad things ahead. I don't know how to stay busy, so I do what I do best ... get numb and watch the day go by. Just not in front of the babies. They just walked in, so am done for now.

I feel bad for the poor bastard who has the job of making sense of this when I'm gone.

I guess by now we all know that Scott Teal is the "poor bastard" who got saddled with the task of making sense of my ramblings. LOL.

June 16, 2003 was the date of my last match with the WWF. I had suffered several injuries and my neck was really hurting. The pain had spread down into my shoulder, so it was tough to use my right arm. The match with Sean was no different from what we had done any other time, but during the course of the match, I took a bad bump and I couldn't get up.

My neck injury was just the result of years of abuse I had suffered in the ring. Needless to say, I had my fair share of injuries: three knee operations, torn ACLs in each knee (that I never had repaired), broken ribs on my left side, a torn AC joint in my right shoulder, a torn groin (both sides, never repaired), torn hamstrings (both), dislocated jaw (several times), torn right bicep (never repaired), torn right pectoral muscle (never repaired), growth plates removed from both big toes (from landing the moonsault so often), torn right calf muscle, and countless concussions.

During my eighteen years in the business, I worked through every one of my injuries and never asked for a night off. I actually had to beg and plead with Vince Russo one night to allow me back in the ring. During that time with WCW, I had a lot of problems with my balance and eyesight. There was one particular night when we were working with Lance Storm and the Filthy Animals. When I told Lance about my problem, he was very gracious and made sure he stayed close by my side when my sight went.

I was booked to wrestle on *Smackdown* the following day in San Antonio. When I got to the building, I was ushered into the office and told to go home. After the scare I gave them the night before, they didn't want to take any chances of me suffering a permanent injury.

Over the next few weeks, I called Bob Clark, who was head of developmental at the time. Part of his job was to deal with injuries and schedule appointments with doctors. For some reason, Bob was too busy to get medical treatment for me. Instead, he sent me to rehab, which did absolutely no good. When Bob finally granted me an audience with his royal self, he told me I could get my neck operated on, but if I did, I could be out for as long as six months, and if that happened, I would lose my job. Bob Clark was a non-knowing, non-caring douche bag who was a big mark for having control.

At the time, a lot of the guys were getting treatment for injuries as an excuse to get off the road, or to justify why they weren't working, and certain "superstars" had been out for long periods of time after having neck surgery. They knew good and well that I wasn't looking to take advantage of them because I bitched all the time about wanting to work more than I was. I was legitimately hurt, too. It all came down to who you were or who they thought "deserved" medical treatment. I didn't fall into either category and the company didn't want to spend the money on someone who wasn't a top draw ... or, at least, that was the way Bob Clark put it. If you weren't a top guy you didn't get top guy treatment. I never knew they had that attitude until that time. I couldn't believe how many different doctors they sent me to in the hopes one of them would give them the diagnosis they wanted, or how many times they told me my neck injury probably wasn't as serious as I thought.

From Bill De Mott's personal journal

Thursday, August 7, 2003

Hey! Today's the girls' first day of school. Casey is now in fifth grade and Keri in third. They are getting so big!

Things have been very heated between their mother and me. I have been hearing from everyone about how bad she has it. I had to find out from my folks that "my house" is in jeopardy of foreclosure. Why? Because the kids' mother has been getting $3,000 a month and not paying the fucking bills. I left so the kids could stay in the house. I made so nice and this douche bag is letting everything go into foreclosure: house, car, trucks.

This stupid bitch doesn't even have the common sense to fill me in on shit like this. I have been threatened with repossession of the car "she owns" (my name and my responsibility). She is fucking me over and over, but as long as she doesn't look bad and can make everyone feel sorry for "poor Rose," she sleeps well.

Two days ago, they stole Lacey's bicycle from in front of the apartment. Never ending!

I have been getting the big yank from work and every doctor involved to date. I have a broken neck that can cause me to become a quadriplegic, but they don't feel I need to fix it. Instead, they feel I should work out! If this is a test, I don't think I'm going to pass it.

On the lighter side, I have been "pill free," except for the antidepressant the doctor has me on, and I have not been drinking. It has made me crazier, but hopefully, I will make it over the hump and start to feel better about myself and not need to numb-up so much. I doubt it, though, judging by the way things are going and the direction they are heading in.

Enough for now. I'm going to watch my motorcycle get soaked in the rain. Just for the record, it's the only thing I still have besides my Elvis collection.

When I called Rose about the possibility that my house might be foreclosed, she told me that wasn't the case. By the time the mortgage company finally contacted me at my apartment address, Rose had done enough damage that I couldn't fix things and keep the house. When she realized things had reached that point, she gave them my new address. It was plotted well and timed perfectly. I was strung along until she had rented a new house and I couldn't move back into my old house.

From Bill De Mott's personal journal

Thursday, August 14, 2003

Well, this is going to be a short entry. Its starts off like this: Yesterday, I went to see a "bankruptcy lawyer." Yeah, that's right! I am filing for bankruptcy. And if that is not enough for you to read ...

The "office" called, not to see if I am feeling okay, or to come right back to work, or worried about how I am. Those fucking assholes who hide behind their bullshit speeches about team and caring have told me that I am being sent to Louisville, Kentucky. Yep! I get to see if I still have it and can take being in the ring. Not me seeing the right doctor to specify why I am in pain, and why its "not necessary right now" to fix me. But while I am there for at least a month, I can help train the other guys and work on my tremendous weight problem. Yeah! They are setting me up for the "axe," just like they do to everyone else. We are truly a dime a dozen. I'm not going into this with a good attitude. After all, I get to pay my ex-wife (she shouldn't be responsible for anything). I have to pay all these other bills. Never mind the rent here, and now I need a car and room in Kentucky for at least a month. Yeah, if I live through this and "bankruptcy," it will be a miracle. This one is the straw.

I was so excited because Lacey and I have pulled the strings tighter and can afford to take the girls to "Sea World," and I had enough Marriott points left to get a really good room for the four of us to stay. I should have known there is no bottom for me to hit!

This fucking fall will be never ending, but "at least I have my health." Sense the sarcasm in that sentence? Good!

From Bill De Mott's personal journal

Friday, August 22, 2003

Well, this will be the last entry for at least a month. I am heading to OVW [Ohio Valley Wrestling]. That is where the developmental facility is. The office is sending me there for a month to get "my legs" back.

Also, Bob Clark said they are concerned about my weight. It's funny how a guy with a broken neck can be sent to four different doctors, be told he could become paralyzed, and there is no need to operate "right now," but there is a problem and I should learn how to fall and work in a different manner. Whatever!

Anyway, when I get back, I will start to focus on my career and the places and things I was blessed to do and have accomplished. I really have to try to get back to what this book was about. Me, wrestling, and some of how it affects your life.

I look forward to seeing John [Hennigan] and Matt [Cappotelli] from Tough Enough. It will be good to see and get in the ring again ... I think. I have mixed feelings about all of this. The feelings aren't there that once inspired me, but it's a pay check, right? I will stick to "whatever is whatever" for now. I will miss my daughters and my girl Lacey very much while I am gone. I haven't been alone in a while and should play a big part in my "come back."

However this works out, no more injuries and no more comebacks! One last time for the sake of trying. It is time for this clown to take off the paint.

From Bill De Mott's personal journal

Tuesday, October 21, 2003

Well, to catch up to what happened in Louisville ... I went to OVW, and right from the first day it was a "cluster fuck." That is to say, I was told to be there first thing on Monday, and wouldn't you know, they only have class for three to four hours a day for four days a week. This [is a] far cry from the boys who would spend nine to ten hours a day for the week and in-between jobs, but "this business is ever evolving," to quote some douche bag [who] makes six figures doing nothing or never took a bump.

I spent most of my time in a lonely room and working out, then the second week I was there (for TV on Tuesday), Arn Anderson was the traveling agent that week. He had asked how I have been feeling and when I got down, and if I was fixed and ready to go.

This opened a big can of worms. Danny Davis was under the impression I was there rehabbing from surgery, along with Jimmy Cornette. When everyone was informed I was not, and was still in pain, down there bumping and teaching, they used their pull. This is one of those times where the boys look out for one another. It doesn't happen too much anymore, but every now and then. Dr. Tom [Prichard] got involved, and then Johnny Ace and I had multiple discussions that day, and I was sent home until I would see Dr. Jho in Pittsburgh.

The bottom line with Jho was, he would fix me when I couldn't take the pain any more, and he wanted to know "why hasn't Steve Austin come to see me?"

Didn't much care for that guy.

Now I would be sent to Dr. Youngblood in San Antonio (where I was four months ago when I originally went down, get the picture?).

Youngblood was very through and laid it all out. He would be the guy to go to when this all comes to [a] head. Now the reports and everything will go back to Bob Clark and the rest of "talent relations" to decide my future ... if I had one at all.

So now I am doing more therapy to try to take the pressure off this old neck. And pretty much going crazy. Johnny called me last week (off the record) and informed me I should get the surgery because he doesn't see Stephanie and the "creative team" investing any time in me. They don't want to take a chance of starting something I can't finish, unlike Benoit, Edge, Holly, Austin, Angle, Rhyno, Scotty, who have all come back from broken necks and got taken care of the right way! More sarcasm.

This is where I kept getting the "Quality of Life" speech from all of them. What they forgot to say was this is how they thought the "quality" of my life should go. I wasn't considered a big star and didn't require a lot of attention. If you are not worth a lot to the company, then that's what determines your "quality of life." The worst part is they still use that line of bullshit, and what's even worse is, I think they actually believe it.

(Not they I ever had a chance to begin with) He [Johnny Ace] said they were looking to get me to be the *Velocity* announcer (since that was the only way I would keep my job —- not many options there?), which I was flown up to the studio in Connecticut to audition for a few weeks ago (it went well).

Or, they would like to see me down in OVW, instructing there for them. Now that means I would have to move there, away from my daughters, and they would have to take $50,000.00 away from me a year. The money is understandable and I would like to think I would be a good instructor, but at what price now? And before I forget, I wasn't worthy of getting back in the ring and wrestling full time, but I was more than capable of getting in the ring with "green" kids and teaching them how to bump and work (mm-hmmm).

Do Lacey and I just pack up and move, hoping the girls will understand? And Lacey can find work after all she has been through to finish school and just start working? Do I stay here and hope I can still make a living doing something else? It going to be a long, hard decision and it all lies in the hands of the WWE right now.

Oh, by the way. With all this other shit going on, I forgot to mention that Lacey and I got engaged on September 13, 2003. Everyone was very happy, especially my girls!

Chapter 15

The Doody Man

Johnny Ace told me they thought my personality would bring something to the *WWE Velocity* show. They weren't happy with the job Ernest Miller was doing with the commentating. I wasn't prepped or coached before my first appearance [October 28, 2003 in Atlanta, Georgia], but my co-host, Josh Mathews [Josh Lomberger], gave me all the insight I needed to get into the groove. Josh was awesome and a lot of fun to be around.

From Bill De Mott's personal journal

Thursday, November 6, 2003

Today, I was going to write about my "new job" with "World Wrestling Entertainment" as the new *Velocity* announcer, but instead, I am writing about the death of my friend, Mike Lockwood (Crash Holly). Mike was found dead in the home of Michael Manna (Stevie Richards). He leaves behind his daughter, Patty, and mom.

I don't have much to write, although I have a lot to say. Just two weeks ago, we lost "Hawk" of the "Road Warriors," another brother of mine, but this is different in "some" ways. I love my job and all the boys I work with, but some of us become so close that we "live" each other's life. Hawk took me under his wing while we were in WCW. I think because I loved to party and wrestle. Mike was a good guy, and as most of the guys I know, had his own demons.

Crash was my friend and my brother. I understood him and he me. All the things that could be said right now don't matter because no matter how I write, you and anyone who reads this won't get it.

We are different, but we are human.

No one person deserves to be found dead on the kitchen floor. No one! Especially my friend, Mike Lockwood. I love you. I am glad that you knew this and am fucking mad you left your friends, your brothers, the ones who really loved you!

You look after us now and make sure we don't fuck up. Mike, what the hell happened? You were doing well. What happened?

Every time I lost a friend, it was within days of when I had seen or spoken with them, and we always seemed to have the same conversation:

"Are you okay?"

"Don't take any more shit."

"We'll work it out tomorrow."

"Remember, it's just wrestling."

"I love you, man!"

And that would be the last time I would talk to those cats.

Eddie Gilbert — I was devastated when I got the phone call about Eddie Gilbert. I had just returned from Puerto Rico and had been with Eddie when he was "fighting for his life." It was ugly to see how the pills had taken him over and he was making a valiant effort to kick the habit. I had just walked through the front door of my house when the phone rang. It was Louis Fabiano, who did a Sheik-type gimmick in Puerto Rico. He simply said, *"Eddie was found in his room. Talk to you later."*

Crash Holly [Mike Lockwood] — I talked to Crash one night and he seemed to be in decent spirits. He was going through a bad split/divorce from his wife (as many of us were at that time). I told him I loved him and to be safe. The next day, I got the call from Stevie Richards: *"They found Crash dead on my kitchen floor."*

Jerry "The Wall" Tuite — Jerry was doing well in Japan and hoped to get back with us in WWE. He looked great, he was working hard, and he was sober. During a flight back to Stamford, Connecticut, I got a call. Once again, it was Stevie. *"They found Jerry in his room. I'm sorry."*

General Rection (Bill), Lash Larue and The Wall as the Misfits

Eddie Guerrero — Chris Benoit called me while we were training in Deep South Wrestling. *"Billy, they found Eddie in his room."*

Hawk [Mike Hegstrand] — Dave Penzer called while I was in Deep South Wrestling. *"They found Mike alone in the trailer."*

Chris and Nancy Benoit — Scott Norton called me at home after I got back from a show. *"Hughie, they found Chris, Nancy and Daniel in the house. They're all gone."*

Every one of those deaths could have been avoided … maybe. But it seems like no matter how close to home they are, we always fool ourselves into thinking "it will never happen to me."

From Bill De Mott's personal journal

Monday, November 10, 2003

Well, today was my 38th birthday and the beginning of my second life!

How does it start? With the loss of Crash Holly. This has hit me hard. In spurts, it has been very upsetting. I don't know if I am more scared the closer these deaths get to me or what. All I know is, I will miss Michael Lockwood. He was a good man and an even better buddy.

Now, onto what is in store for the next 38 years (ha fuckin' ha!).

This commentating thing seems to have some legs to it. I might have found another notch in this business. I am comfortable doing it and seem to have a knack for the bullshit involved. They shaved my head and cut my beard. Kevin Dunn seems to think I should look along the lines of "Howie Long." I don't see it, but if it works for Kevin and I can get away with the look, we will try it for a while.

As far as my neck situation is coming along, the company seems to think that Dr. Jho from Pittsburgh would be the best bet (especially where they are concerned). It would be a quick recovery and I wouldn't miss any TV time. That's right. I said I wouldn't miss any TV time. Bob Clark called and said Jho would review the films again, but doesn't see a reason to fix me "in his professional opinion."

Which makes me lean toward Dr. Youngblood even more. Fuck the company! I will get fixed and they will do what they have to do. That's where this one ends. I'm wrong. I got my final divorce papers in the mail today! You would think this would be a big relief, but along with them, she sent a foreclosure notice. She will never quit!

My head wasn't really "shaved." It was cut high and tight, but my hair had been long for so many years that I felt like I was bald.

The week always began on Tuesday by going to wherever the *WWE Smackdown* and *WWE Velocity* tapings were being held. Unless the tapings were held on the west coast, I would leave on the morning of the show. I would arrive as early as possible so I could spend some time sitting around and talking with the guys. We would then attend the production meetings, which were led by Vince and Stephanie [McMahon]. After that, we could do what we wanted until an hour or so before the tapings were scheduled to begin. During that time, I would study the match lineups and talk to the guys about what they were going to do and the direction in which their character was moving. I wanted to get as much information about them as possible so I could really put over what they were trying to get across to the audience.

When Josh and I heard our names announced to the live crowd, we would make our way to the commentating table (which was the same one used for *Smackdown*). During the taping of the show, we had two scheduled "on-camera" appearances. I used my time on air to "put the boys over," rather than talking about things that had nothing to do with business. Too many of the commentators wasted time talking about everything but what the guys and girls were doing in the ring. I wanted to make them matter, so I put the emphasis on their abilities and characters.

They would fly Josh and me to Connecticut on Fridays to do the voiceovers. I would leave home around five in the morning. When we arrived at Titan Towers, we would order lunch and get to work selling the next big show. When we finished, I would be taken back to the airport in a limo or town car and fly home or to Louisville for Ohio Valley Wrestling, depending on what I had on my schedule. That was my life every week from October 28, 2003 until December 7, 2004. I had surgery after my first week of tapings and missed one week of doing voiceovers, but other than that, I never missed a show. I was at every *WWE Smackdown/Velocity* taping and in the studio every Friday morning.

One of the differences between being in-ring talent and a commentator was how the company handled expenses. They paid for all my expenses — rental car, airline tickets, and hotel. I didn't even have to make any calls. Everything was taken care of by the office.

On December 14, they replaced me with a guy named Steve Romero [real name Todd Romero], the sports director for KSHB-TV in Kansas City. He didn't know wrestling and he didn't respect the guys. He was always making stupid comments about the guys and was disrespectful. I remember him saying things like, *"Why the hell are we watching Billy Gunn again? He does the same thing all the time!"* and *"Why don't they use the stars instead of guys no one know?"* He was constantly making comments about people like Mark Jindrak, Chuck Palumbo, and Shoichi Funaki, who were waiting for the "turn" on the main roster. When I was there, I put guys like them over as much as possible because they needed the push. That's the problem they face when the bring in guys like Romero, who aren't fans and don't appreciate what the enhancement guys bring to the table.

From Bill De Mott's personal journal

Sunday, December 28, 2003

This will be my final piece of writing for the year 2003. Although this year has held a lot of drama, it has also given me a lot to be thankful for. I have a beautiful fiancé and two wonderful daughters. My parents and I are all getting along again and I am trying to get myself back to normal (whatever that is).

I have lost two very good friends of mine, Mike "Crash" Lockwood, whom we discussed earlier, and Jerry "The Wall" Tuite. Jerry was found in Japan dead in his hotel room. Not knowing what the real cause was, it is a safe bet that Jerry had been back to the "old tricks." Jerry played a huge part in my career and became one of my close friends. I love him and he will be missed. I talk about Jerry in the "Misfits" and WCW, but he was more than just a "wrestler." He was a man who was doing the best he could. And like so many of us, dealt with things the only way we feel comfortable. But again, when is enough?

There is no way to tell all of this year's problems, drama, and other bullshit. The bottom line to this one is "I fucking survived it!" And although I know it is not over as far as [Rose] is concerned, Lacey and I are looking forward to what our future holds for us and the girls.

The commentating thing with WWE will work out … or not. I am getting ready to finally get my neck fixed and call it a career (?), and I want to get healthy, mentally and physically. Emotionally, I guess I will do the best I can. I have two daughters to worry about and Lacey. We will be okay. I know this. Struggling has become my calling card and I am getting good at it. Funny to think you had nothing and how will you survive? Maybe this "big fucking mess" was my wakeup call … again!

In case I have not mentioned it so far, Bob Clark was the biggest asshole I have ever run in to, and had no business guiding or dealing with anyone's careers. This jerkoff hurt the WWE more than they know. He was underhanded and learned to cover his ass very well. The WWE should have been sued by many people during Bob Clark's time as an employee. He was a no-good bastard who had people's futures in his hand and could spin it any way he wanted. I may not have ever wrestled again, but to have that dipshit give me the "Quality of Life" speech and tell me "how I would lose my job if I got my neck completely fixed" was beyond me. That was his claim to fame , telling all the talent who didn't call him an "asshole" to his face that the company would have to let you go if you were out with an injury. Not very good publicity for a "publicly-traded company."

I don't think I am going to write so much about events of everyday life anymore. I want to get back to the wrestling aspect and my family as a whole. After all, who would believe half the shit that has gone on in my world, anyway? You can't make this shit up. No one is that good.

I am hoping that as this year closes out, there will be light at the end of the tunnel. And no matter what comes in front of us, we can get through it. For you poor bastards who actually read all this. what can I say?

From Bill De Mott's personal journal

Friday, January 30, 2004

Well, here we are in the New Year! For this first installment, I am going to tell you about my neck surgery.

Yeah! I finally got my neck fixed. It was a three-hour operation (they thought would only take 1½ hours), but there was so much more wrong than what showed on the MRIs. This made me feel better because I knew I had some serious issues going on in there. It didn't make me feel good there was so much wrong, but just to know I am not as big a "pussy" as I have felt like, ya know?

Anyway, there were two ruptures along with the hernia ions. Also, there were a bunch of bone spurs and calcium deposits. I have bone chips in my spinal canal that are cutting off the fluids needed to feel normal. This was a bigger deal than expected. Dr. Jho said afterward it was the smartest thing I did, getting this done.

The recovery will be a while, but I am going right back to work and entertaining the thought of getting in the ring again (in a couple of months). I have the feeling in my right arm and hand and I feel pretty good as a whole.

Darryl (my younger brother) went in for back surgery. It took nine long hours and he will have a long road to recovery. He went in the day before me. I sure hope he finds some relief and gets that famous "quality of life" back.

As for the other drama: They are foreclosing on the house, although I have a great realtor trying to sell it. I have found a lawyer and I am petitioning the whole divorce decree. Rose has not paid anything in seven months and I am losing almost $200,000 on the house, if not more. I bought that house for $150,000.00 and it was a steal. At the time I was trying to sell it, it should have sold for over $400,000.00, but that inconsiderate bitch kept the money and let things get foreclosed and repossessed. It is time I start fighting back and get my life back. Too bad for her she doesn't seem to think she has to answer for all this shit. My daughters are going to smarten up soon and start questioning their mother's methods and responsibilities.

Pop got a good bill of health from his doctor, told him to get off his ass and do something. You're getting older, so what?

That's all. When something good comes up, I will be back. Like I said, I will "try" to keep the drama to a minimum.

The WWE flew both Lacey and me to Pittsburgh and put us up in a hotel near the hospital where I had my neck surgery. They paid for everything, including therapy. After the surgery, I had no pain whatsoever, but within a month or so, the pain returned. I still have the pain today and the muscles my right arm seem to be deteriorating, so I guess you never really recover fully from a serious spinal injury. Kurt Angle also went to Dr. Jho and had to have the procedure done two or three times. I'm no Kurt Angle. I'm not going through that again. I'll just do things my own way, which is living with the pain and discomfort, only now I'm doing it without the drugs, but I'm cool with that.

What a surprise I got when I was served with divorce papers. That bitch either pocketed or spent every cent and paid nothing on the mortgage, car loan, or utility bills. Her theory was, *"Who gives a shit what happens to him. I deserve this."* She gave no thought to the problems my daughters would face if they were evicted from their home. She let the house go unpaid for thirteen months and it would have gone into foreclosure if I hadn't sold it (a $400,000 house) for a little more than $200,000.

It gets better. That sneaky bitch convinced the other real-estate agent to give her a commission. That's right. She made money on the sale of the house she hadn't been paying for in the first place. And it gets better than that. She made sure I didn't get a dime because she contacted the IRS and told them I had sold our house. During all those years while I was on the road (and sending my family most of what I earned), not only was she not paying the bills, but she wasn't paying the taxes. When the time came for her to bail out on everything, I was left holding more than $100,000 in debt to the IRS. I thought she had taken a little pity on me when she left the new car in the driveway ... until the repo man showed up and repossessed the car. I didn't find out until later that she had already convinced her father to help her buy another car.

I also discovered she had been moving my personal things out of our house with her boyfriend (one of her clients) long before we began talking about divorce. The divorce had been in the works before I knew anything about it.

After the divorce was final, people began to tell me that she had been singing the song "Bill is an asshole and has a girlfriend" all around town to anyone who would listen. The fact of the matter is that for a long time, Lacey and I were nothing more than friends. She was always willing to listen and encourage me when I was feeling low. However, on my wife's side of the equation, isn't it unethical to be boning one of your clients, as she was?

I also heard Rose consulted with Jimmy Duggan's wife, Debra, and got some great advice on how to put the screws to me. It's ironic that we moved to Titusville, the same town in which Jim and his family lived. Little did I know that after all the good times, long talks, and partying together, when the shit hit the fan, Debra wouldn't allow Jim to "play" with me anymore. Jim never told me he couldn't associate with me, but he suddenly got "busy" and fell out of touch. I held it against Jim for awhile because I thought the Duggans were my friends, but then again, Jimmy probably had to agree with his woman so he didn't wind up like I did.

You would have thought that after Rose took everything I had and did all the cruel things one so-called "human being" could do to another, the terror would have stopped. But no-oooooo! That fucking bitch of a woman went out of her way to keep me going back to court, until she finally forced me into bankruptcy. She accused me of all kinds of things, and even tried to turn my girls against me, especially since they were becoming very close to Lacey. You would have thought that if she was really that unhappy, she would have changed her last name. Then again, if she had done that, she would have just been some sour, old bitch who lived in Titusville, Florida and the "former Mrs. De Mott." She couldn't let that happen, so she made sure to get personalized magnetic signs to put on her car so people would remember who she thought she was. But they didn't ... and she got more frustrated. Even after we made the move to Georgia when I helped start Deep South Wrestling, she was still dragging me back to court, making me prove I was no longer making big money and couldn't afford to compensate her for what she thought was hers. I jotted down my thoughts for this chapter while I was working at FedEx. I was putting in twenty hours a week, making $12.23 an hour, and she was getting sixty percent of my paycheck ... and still claimed she was owed more.

Things worked out better than I could have hoped as, in later years, when Lacey and I got married and bought a house in town, my daughters wanted to spend as much time with us as they could. Our house was where they felt the most comfortable and was where they wanted to be.

One day, I got a letter from the Roman Catholic Archdiocese of Atlanta. It was a letter she had sent to the church asking for an annulment from her marriage on many different levels, mostly adultery and stuff like that. She justified it to my girls by saying if she ever wanted to get married in a Catholic church, it had to be done.

First of all, nobody is going to marry that bitch, especially if they knew her and saw what she was doing to me. That's why the guy she was seeing left her. He thought it was cool at first to see her make me squirm, but when he realized she might do that to him in the future, he hit the road. She also tried as hard as she could to make me look bad in front of my girls. That takes a special kind of evil because one parent denigrating the other does nothing but tear down the psyche of children.

I *never* talked badly about Rose to or in front of my daughters. I did, on occasion, keep them informed about court dates and things their mother was saying about me. I never crossed the line and denigrated their mother, but I wasn't going to stand idly by and not defend myself against the accusations she was making and lies she was telling. In fact, I actually told them time and time again that, whatever their feelings, they shouldn't be disrespectful to their mother. I didn't tell them they needed to treat her nicely, but as a parent, she should be respected and spoken to properly. Every once in awhile, I would get pissed about something Rose did and Lacey would have to calm me down. Now, the roles are reversed. Lacey has so much love for my daughters that she gets mad about something Rose did or said against them and I have to settle her down. Rose has been saved more times than she knows, but she continues to live in a world where everything is hers and fuck everyone else. She doesn't take the cares, needs, or feelings of anyone into consideration ... not even those of her children.

Unfortunately, being mean hasn't done much for Rose, and as badly as I wanted to let the church know who and what they were dealing with, I didn't. I received a long letter from the church which told the story about a good Catholic girl who wanted her marriage annulled so she could lead a productive Catholic lifestyle and get remarried. I sat down and began to respond with a letter of my own, telling them about all the things I knew about Saint Rose, but

I realized a letter from me wouldn't change anything, so I didn't reply and let events take their own course. It was sad to see her pull the religious card when we were going through our divorce. The girls had to leave my house and be home every Sunday, and on all religious holidays, so she could take them to church. When everything was said and done, the only time they darkened the church doors was (some) holidays and when my girls were confirmed (which Lacey and I were present for).

No matter what she has done or will do in the future, I still get "the last laugh." I came into this world with nothing and I'm sure I'll leave the same way, but I have what's most important — the love of my wife, my kids, my friends, and my family.

When my parents began to realize the things Rose was doing and saying were false, they came to the conclusion that Lacey wasn't the problem. It took a while for all my family and friends to come around, but when they finally got to know Lacey, they realized she was one of the best things that had ever happened to me because she was saving me from myself. It took time, but as with anyone who meets Lacey, you can't help but love her.

Lacey and I got married on December 18, 2004. We had the ceremony at the beach and a party in town. It was great. Stevie Richards, Al Snow and Doug Basham were there. More of the boys would have attended, but they were in Iraq supporting the troops. Casey and Keri were bridesmaids and they looked beautiful. And words can't describe how radiant Lacey looked. Both sides of the family were there: Alice, John, Pop, Darryl and his daughter Nicole (and one of my goddaughters), Larry and Ruth (Lacey's dad and stepmother), Lucas (Lacey's younger brother) and his future wife (bitch), and Grandma Bonnie. Bonnie is Lacey's grandmother and one of the nicest people you would ever want to meet. Man, can that lady drink! All kidding aside, Bonnie loves Lacey and it was an honor to have her there. I have grown close to all of Lacey's family. They're good people.

In case you wonder about my comment about Lucas' future wife, at the time, Lucas was engaged to marry her. She was all about herself and really shit on everyone in Lucas' family when she didn't come to our reception. Instead, she hooked up with a girlfriend who "just happened" to be visiting Florida at the same time. That really embarrassed Lucas and pissed off Bonnie. Hey, what's a wedding without drama, right? It's not like we didn't have more than enough of it surrounding us, anyway. Nobody liked her, but they wouldn't tell him that because they didn't want to offend him. They got married shortly after we did. It didn't take him long to realize he wasn't in a good relationship and they went through a nasty divorce.

From Bill De Mott's personal journal

Monday, December 27, 2004

Well, according to where I left off, it has been awhile, so I will do a brief catchup of the events since last writing.

Al Snow and I just finished the "$1,000,000" *Tough Enough*. It was a lot different and had nothing to do with wrestling (except that Al and I went at it like we would any other time). We only had eight weeks with these kids and every week someone got voted off. It was like the fucking "diva search." All bullshit. We met some good kids, and just like anything else, no matter what our opinion was, everyone (just about) will be offered a job. But one kid, Daniel Puder, will now have the chance to make $250,000 a year for the next four years.

Definitely more on this later.

During the last two months I was hosting *Velocity*, I also flew back and forth to California to film *Tough Enough 4*, better known as the *$1,000,000 Tough Enough*. The prize was a $1,000,000 contract with the money split evenly over four years "with only the first year guaranteed." The reaction from the boys was as expected: *"Why in the hell is the company doing this?"* From the beginning of the season, I said it didn't matter who won. They wouldn't see the first year of the contract ... and I was right. He might have been paid the first installment of $250,000, but they released him less than a year after he was announced as the winner. Daniel didn't win any points with the boys, either. He had a problem with a little thing called "humility," often reminding people that he was "the real deal." Daniel has done well since then, however, competing in MMA competitions (and doing really well), launching his own MMA company, producing two MMA pay-per-view events, and launching a gym in Hollywood.

Although he didn't win the competition, Michael "The Miz" Mizanin joined the WWE in April 2006 and, since then, has held WWE titles on several occasions.

From Bill De Mott's personal journal

May 30, 2005

Let's see. Where to begin. Lacey and I have sold the house in Florida! Yep! The company has decided that the place for me is in Atlanta (McDonough). We are trying real hard to make the best of it. We have a new home there and the kids will be with us all summer. That's right. It is part of the "latest court battles." I will have them all summer, half the winter break, and half the spring break. I can come to Florida whenever I want and they will be made "available" to me.

The only up-side is the girls love Lacey and me and Casey doesn't want to leave us. It will be very fucking hard to do at the end of this month. I have been away before, sometimes for weeks, but never "lived" away from the girls. Am not sure how it will turn out.

The company has graciously kept me on with them, but now I work for "Deep South Wrestling." I have taken another $25,000 pay cut, but they did give me a $5,000 bonus for leaving my kids. They are good to you that way. (That's more fucking sarcasm).

Things are going to be new to us up there and I'm sure we will have our ups and downs, but I have to tell you. Lacey is the best thing that ever happened to me. It's not about money, fame, or who you are. This girl loves me for being the miserable bastard I am.

I'm really not, but you know.

She is the best. No questions asked. If this is what we have to do, then that's what we do. I probably would have "jumped" by now.

I have been going stir crazy at home. I haven't worked but ten days since December 14th. I had some issues with a no-good liar named Marty Wright. He was the piece of crap we cut on the beach on the last Tough Enough and then bull-shitted his way to getting a deal in OVW. Long story short, he claimed I threatened him and was the cause of him not doing well.

See, if you cry "wolf" loud enough with the WWE, they think you will sue and they give you the world, so they kept me home and he kept his job. (Later on, he would become the Boogie Man. Go figure. Still worthless, but now he is "FAMOUS").

Before I move on, I have to tell the story about the "Doody Man." Actually, that's a name I made up for Marty Wright, whose claim to fame was a run with the WWE as the "Boogeyman." Marty was a *$1,000,000 Tough Enough* contestant who was kicked out of the competition because he lied about his age (he was forty, not thirty) during the auditions. After getting kicked out, we left him on the beach. A few months later, he cried his way into the OVW developmental camp. They thought he was crying because wrestling was his "passion," but he was only being a baby.

Marty was a nightmare from the first day he came to OVW. Lance Storm and I both tried to teach Marty the basics of wrestling. As always, I spent my time with people who actually wanted to put in some time in the ring. While demonstrating a series of "hold and moves" with some of the other students, I put Marty in a headlock ... and he shit his pants. That's the God's truth. Marty was so worried about getting "roughed up" by me that he shit his pants and ran out of the building. He came back later to explain himself, admitting he had shit his pants and had to go change. How do you respond to something like that? I didn't know then, and, if faced with the same situation, wouldn't know how to respond now.

That night, the OVW crew performed at a live event in Indiana. I made the trip with Al Snow, Matt Morgan, and Kevin Fertig. The next day, Marty called corporate and cooked up a story of how I called him on his cell phone and left a message saying he would never make it in the business because he was "black" and "too old." When Johnny Ace and Tommy Dreamer called (conference call), I had no idea about what they were talking about. In fact, I was so surprised that I didn't even know how to react. When I asked to hear the "so-called" message I was supposed to have left on his answering machine, Johnny said Marty told them he "must have accidentally erased it." On the other hand, I had the drunken message he left for me! I didn't think anything about that and I didn't mind. I had a lot of the young guys call and leave me goofy messages when they were drunk. I had a good relationship with most of the kids in OVW and enjoyed the camaraderie.

Al Snow had been with me in the car the night before and he would have known if I had said anything like that, so John and Dreamer called him to see if it was true. (You would think they would have done that *before* they jumped on me) Even after talking to Al, I was told the WWE was worried that a racial lawsuit would be issued, and with no proof of any kind, they decided to send me home until things cooled off. Even though Marty couldn't prove his allegation, the office thought it would be best for me to stay home for the next couple of months while they sorted things out. They knew it was bullshit, but they didn't want bad publicity of Marty pulling the "race card." I still received my guarantee, which would have been fine with most people, but as I've said several times, I like getting paid to work, not sit around.

There are times when things have a way of coming back to haunt bad people. The very next day, Marty had nine teeth knocked out by Danny Inferno [Danny Gimondo] during training. The Dudley Boyz [Brother Ray and Brother Devon] were there and told me Marty didn't duck when Danny was "throwing" a clothesline. The next thing Marty knew ... new bridge work. Marty told Danny he'd get even with him, but that never happened. It didn't take long for the stories to get back to me. Marty claimed that Danny was one of my headhunters and had told him to *"do something to Marty."* It was merely a coincidence, so I cannot take credit for setting it up, but I couldn't have been happier to hear the news that Marty had been taught to "keep his head up and his mouth shut." He also lost a lot of respect (or, at least, any respect he might have had). Could it have been Marty was no good and got hurt because he didn't (or couldn't) do what he was being asked to do? And could it be that Bill De Mott was right when he said Marty had no business in the ring?

After just six months at OVW, the WWE brought Marty up and began to promote his character ... the Boogeyman. Based on his impromptu bowel movement at OVW, I always called him the "Doody Man." He made a living for a few years by eating worms and banging clocks on his head (not to mention having one of the worst matches in the history of *WrestleMania*).

Two contestants from season four — Ryan Reeves, who wrestles in the WWE as Skip Sheffield, and Luke Gallows [Andrew Hankinson] — both keep in touch and have done well in the business.

Between *Velocity, Million Dollar Tough Enough,* and OVW, I was on the road more than when I was a full-time, active performer. I was traveling to the shows on Tuesday, flying to Connecticut to do voiceovers on Friday, training the kids in the *Million Dollar Tough Enough* competition at Traxx, and spending the rest of my time in Louisville at OVW. It was a brutal schedule. At best, I was home one or two days a month.

Neither Lacey or I knew how much time I would be gone. Lacey knew that no matter how hectic things were, I wanted to be a part of the company and the business. She never once complained about my schedule. She gave me 100 percent of her support and took what time with me she could. I'm blessed to have a woman like that.

When they took me off *Velocity*, they told me Al Snow and I were being sent to Louisville as the full-time trainer for Ohio Valley Wrestling. A few days later, they called to tell me I would be going to Atlanta. A few days later ... well, suffice it to say that over the course of the next few weeks, they changed their minds several times. I wound up going to the new training school in Atlanta, while Al would move to Louisville.

Bill at the Ribera Steakhouse in Tokyo, Japan

Chapter 16

Jackass of all Trades

Long before Al Snow and I were finished with our commentary gigs, the company had been discussing the likelihood of having me move to Louisville, where I would work with Ohio Valley Wrestling. I hated to break the news to Lacey. However, like everything else we had been through, Lacey embraced it and said, *"Then let's make the most of it."* Lacey never made waves or let negative thinking control her life.

Our first and biggest concern with moving was being so far away from our girls, who were living with their mother in Titusville. We had just bought our first house together. It was about a mile from Rose's new house because we wanted to be as close as possible to them. Lacey and the girls had grown very close and she was just getting settled into the routine of being married and living in Florida. After all, it hadn't been that long since she had made the move from Iowa. Lacey also had a good job at an upscale spa as a hair stylist. She had a great client list and she was making pretty good money.

As soon as the holidays were over, Lacey and I began traveling back and forth to Louisville to find a place to live. While we were there, Johnny Ace called to tell me they had changed their minds. They wanted me in Atlanta (actually McDonough) to run Deep South Wrestling [DSW], the newest addition to the WWE developmental system. I'll never forget what Lacey did when she heard the news. She laughed and told Johnny, *"Thanks for the wedding present."* She had developed a sense of "humor." Over the next couple of weeks, we made quite a few 460-mile trips from Titusville to Atlanta to look for housing. As time passed, we couldn't find anything that Lacey really liked. We finally stumbled across a new development in Hampton, Georgia, which was located about 12 miles from the training center in McDonough and 30 miles south of Atlanta.

Looking back, I should have done things the way Al did — rent and travel back and forth on weekends — but the company had assured me that my future was with WWE, so we "went for it." We also wanted a house that would be big enough for four of us — Lacey, the girls, and me. Actually, that was what *Lacey* wanted, but her desire for a house was not self-serving. She wanted the girls to have a house like the one in which they lived before their mother allowed it to be taken from them.

I would be making less than I had before ($75,000 a year), but I never discussed or asked about money. As always, with everything else I did in wrestling, I figured if I was doing my job, everything would work out. After we moved, Lacey took a test that would allow her to practice cosmetology in the state of Georgia. She opened her own business and built up quite a large clientele.

Before the move, I met with Johnny Ace and Tommy Dreamer at Titan Towers in Stamford. Joe "Jody" Hamilton and Bill Behrens, who also would be working with me at Deep South, were also at the meeting. I had heard of Bill, but we had never met before the meeting. I knew Joe from my days with WCW when he ran the backstage for the TV shows.

Unfortunately, the meeting didn't begin too well.

The first words out of Johnny's mouth were, *"Who the fuck is on the Internet telling everyone we're having a meeting about opening a new system."* He was really mad. I think it's safe to say everyone in the room thought it was Bill, especially given the fact that Joe and I were both computer-illiterate at the time. Joe could find the power switch by himself, but I didn't know if it was on the front or the back of the computer. Apparently, whoever posted the information on the Internet named each of us and said we would be having a meeting in Stamford.

The troubles between Joe and Bill began there — and it all boiled down to control. Bill thought he was going to run the show and Joe ... well, Joe *was* Deep South Wrestling and nobody tells Joe what to do. It's possible those early problems could have been avoided if Johnny had just laid all his cards on the table when he first talked to us individually. John told us Joe was going to run the building, I would be in charge of the training, and Bill would be in charge of the TV and help with the shows.

Joe and I had discussions about DSW when Joe was brought to Louisville to watch how Danny Davis ran the OVW training school and to get an idea of what WWE was looking for, but at that time, I never suspected I would be going there. After our meeting in Stamford, Joe, Bill, Johnny, and I had dinner and threw around ideas and thoughts about how we would run the operation. At first, I don't think Joe was comfortable with me being the trainer, but after we got started, I think I surprised him because he later said he liked the way I was doing things.

I received my pay each and every week from Joe. I was never paid by WWE during my time in Deep South. Knowing Joe as well as I do, I think he hated writing those checks. Joe had always been known for being tight with a dollar, and, even though he was being reimbursed by WWE, he didn't like the fact that he was spending money.

On the other hand, the talent was getting their checks directly from WWE. However, there were times when people were sent to us for a week, just to have a workout and get evaluated, and we were asked to pay them $500. Joe refused to do it. He said his money shouldn't be used to pay people they sent to be evaluated. Many times, I paid the talent out of my pocket and was reimbursed by WWE. After awhile, Johnny or Dreamer would call or e-mail me directly and ask me to pay them. I didn't ask questions. I just did it. As far as I was concerned, it was just a part of my job. Joe didn't like me doing that.

In his opinion, WWE knew they were sending people to us, so they should have paid them before they got there. I could see both sides, but I never worried about getting reimbursed.

During the course of writing this chapter, my editor posed a good question: "*How did you keep the money they sent as reimbursement from looking like income?*" You know, I never thought about that. I probably got screwed and was paying taxes again on money I had already paid for. Damn!

To the best of my knowledge, Joe was being paid by WWE, and then Deep South (Joe, wink-wink) also was being paid by WWE. Joe was hired to provide a training center and oversee all aspects of training, to secure TV slots and venues, and to get the talent wrestling and in front of the cameras as much as possible. When we began running shows, he did the writing of the shows and timing them out. At the end of the week, and later, after the shows, he would take the "lead" in critiquing the talent. During the week, Joe didn't come out of his office very often, but we had set up a TV in his office so he could keep his eye on the training.

Tommy Dreamer and Bill at the Deep South training center

I felt comfortable working with Joe from the very first day. I never felt like I had to "report" to Joe, but we would talk about everything at the end of every day and bounce ideas off each other. On the other hand, I did report to Johnny Ace on a regular basis, and Tommy Dreamer and I had daily, and sometimes nightly, conversations. My concerns were all about dealing with Joe and Johnny at the same time. I knew from the start that I was going to be in the middle of everything because one of my responsibilities was to be sure things went the way WWE wanted them. Johnny made it clear on the night we had dinner in Stamford that I was there to make sure things went the way he wanted them to go. Knowing that, I knew I would be taking a lot of heat from both sides, but I was okay with it. When I first met with Johnny in Louisville, he made two things very clear to me: I would be taking "heat" for some decisions, whether or not I was responsible, and I would be taking a load of shit from some of the trainees (which is exactly what happened). I told him then, *"I'm your man."* When I was still working as talent for WWE, I once heard J.J. Dillon say, *"I'm just the heat man."* I didn't get it at the time, but when I began working for Deep South and found myself sandwiched between the immovable force and a hard place, I suddenly realized why everyone used to blame JJ for everything. That's exactly what I was … the heat man. I took more heat for things I had nothing to do with, and took more shots to the chin for things Johnny, Tommy, and others knew were wrong, but it was part of my "job description."

I would also report to several of the company agents about talent. Once a month, I delivered a detailed evaluation of all talent in Deep South to both Creative and the agents.

Joe's attitude was one of the major differences between the operations of Deep South and Ohio Valley Wrestling [OVW]. Danny Davis [Daniel Briley], the owner of OVW, had a comfortable working relationship with WWE. He did what they asked and didn't rock the boat. Joe, on the other hand, didn't like being a "yes man" and would usually voice his opinion on whatever it was WWE asked him to do. Joe used to say *"Danny cowers down whenever the word WWE is mentioned."* I don't know if that's true or not, but OVW operated as the WWE developmental program for more than a decade. Read into that whatever you want.

While I was with DSW, Danny and I had conference calls with Johnny, Tommy and Al Snow. We had some good conversations, as well as some bitch fests. Either way, I got along well with Danny.

In my opinion, there shouldn't have been any problems between Joe and WWE. It was a simple formula: we were getting paid to prepare the kids for whatever character the company wanted and to develop a territory. Again, any problems we had were due to Joe wanting to do things his way. The company would tell him the way they wanted things done, but he would always resist. As a result, everything we did became a non-stop pissing contest between Joe and the company. I have to say I was amazed that Joe was able to talk to people the way he did and get away with it. Joe would holler and tell WWE personnel (Johnny, Tommy, Paul Heyman, Greg Gagne, and whoever else rubbed him the wrong way) what he was and wasn't going to do, and if they didn't like it, he would "shut the whole thing down!" I believe the first time Joe made that statement, our fate was sealed, and they began looking for someone else to run things. The company stayed with Joe for two years, but in early 2007, WWE took their ball and moved their developmental territory to Florida. But I'm getting ahead of myself.

As many times as Joe got into heated arguments with WWE personnel, the two of us never had words or a heated argument. Like I said, Joe and I had a good working and personal relationship. In my opinion, Joe knew what he was doing, but WWE didn't always like the way he did things. I went out of my way to protect Joe from WWE bullshit, while at the same time, I tried to do what I could to please WWE. It was an all-but-impossible task.

People use the term "developmental" for OVW and DSW, but I don't think that's what they were. They were places to send young kids who already (most of them, anyway) had a background in wrestling and to groom them so they were ready for the road. I called DSW a "holding pen," as in a place in which to send people and more or less forget about them. We were supposed to keep the kids for up to six months, evaluate them, and either get them on the road with the major brands or decide if they had "it." It's amazing to think some people spent up to five years in "developmental." A person can only learn so much and do a certain amount of training before they become soured on the process and give up.

From Bill De Mott's personal journal

(late April 2005, no date recorded)

At the time I'm writing this part, the building is not done. The students haven't all gotten to Atlanta and I hate this Bill Behrens that will be "helping" with the TV in Deep South. Not a strong start to this life-altering move, but what did you expect in this story ... a happy ending?

The upside since the last time is Pop went to therapy for awhile and was doing good, but as soon as he stopped, he went backwards again. I think he is just giving up, and then sometimes, he just wants to be babied. I don't mean that disrespectfully, but he has gotten used to doing nothing for himself and is lazy and dependent on Alice, when for most of the time, he doesn't need to be.

John has had surgery on his knees and shoulder and is driving my mother the rest of the way to "crazy world." Hopefully, I can convince them to come to Georgia with us. We will see.

When the kids first got there, we trained at Gold's Gym for four hours a day, mostly doing cardio. The Deep South building, which was located in a strip mall, was one to two months from being completed, so I struck a deal at Gold's to use their cardio room. Since we were all getting paid, I thought we might as well get to know each other and begin to get in shape. Besides getting them into shape, my goal was to get to know each of the kids on a personal level. I wanted to develop a rapport so when we began doing actual ring training, they would both respect and trust me.

When everyone first got there, they seemed to be under the illusion they wouldn't be there long and they weren't very keen on doing cardio. It became a good bonding time, though, and they became a tight-knit group. Johnny Swinger [Joseph Dorgan] didn't think he should have to be there, so he didn't show up until the building was ready, even though we made several phone calls to him. I can't blame him for not wanting to train because he was a "veteran superstar" by that time (sarcasm intended). When we finally got into the building and into the ring, he realized most of the other students could outwork him and drill better. Swinger hated the training. Not only did it show in his performance, but he had no problem expressing it. He thought he was above it.

When we moved into our building, it had everything we could ever dream of having in a training center ... except for water, electricity, lights, air conditioning (we were looking at summer in Atlanta where the heat could be brutal), bathrooms, floors (dirt since they hadn't been poured), and a ring. The guys would go behind the building to piss and Angel Williams (the only girl at the time) would go to the convenience store next door to use their restroom. Since we still didn't have a ring, we did conditioning, stretching, and the "dreaded" squats. I put them through the workout I had developed for myself (and which I use to this day every time I train).

Joe shopped around in various markets for local television stations. Somehow, he stumbled onto Comcast Sports South. Their people fell in love with the program.

After Joe put the shows together, we would meet and he would go over them with me. He would ask my opinion and I would make any suggestions that came to mind. Usually, they were based on what I thought (or knew) WWE would want. They wanted certain talent to do certain things, and in ways they preferred, so at times, I would be trying to make both sides happy. In Joe's mind, he had free rein to do what he wanted to do with the shows, but the shit hit the fan when Dreamer (and Mike Bucci when Dreamer left) wanted a "proof-read" of the show sent to them on the Wednesday before we did our tapings.

We did all the DSW tapings/shows on Thursday nights. It became a weekly occurrence for someone (usually Dreamer) to call me on "show-day Thursday," usually in the morning, to tell me Joe had to rewrite his TV. Not because it was wrong, but because it wasn't punctuated the right way, or the bullet points and breaks weren't typed in correctly! It became an every week thing between Joe and the office. It had *nothing* to do with me, but for some reason, they always dragged me into the middle of their arguments. Joe would get the TV to them as early as two and three days before the taping and nothing would be said ... until show day. The phone and bullshit wouldn't stop all day. They had nothing better to do than to complain about the smallest details: *"Stephanie can't read it this way," "We don't do our shows in this format,"* and *"This isn't correct."* It got so bad they were threatening weekly that they were going to write Joe's TV for him and have Paul Heyman come down to take care of the taping. Of course, Joe went ballistic when they said things like that. It seemed like every Friday, Johnny would call and try to calm Joe down. After that, everything would be fine ... until the following Thursday morning when it would all begin again. That went on for the entire eighteen months we were open for business.

I don't remember Bill Behrens being there more than a month or so after we moved into the building. Joe didn't want him there. Joe hated to spend money and didn't like it when Bill turned in receipts for light bulbs, extension cords, and other small items. He didn't want to reimburse Bill for things like that, which was ridiculous. It wasn't Bill's responsibility to pay for those things, but Joe thought that was a part of what each of us should do to make things work.

We all had a good laugh at Bill's expense when we first set up the cameras. Bill couldn't get them to work or focus properly. Whenever he tried to get a shot, the display screen was bubbled and distorted. Bill had talked Joe into buying those specific cameras, so Joe was really pissed about it. Joe's wife came in one day, studied the camera manual, and told us how to make it work properly. The next day, we had a perfect picture. It was funny, but it was just more drama to add to Joe wanting to get Bill out.

My only problem with Bill was due to the fact he wasn't very positive when he tried to help the kids with their promos. The kids all hated his attitude, both towards the company and themselves. He did have an interest in some of the guys and took time to work with them. He was high on Johnny Swinger and everything he did. If others did promos he didn't like, he would just tell them, *"That sucked."* Bill had his own way of doing things (like Joe and I) and it just didn't click with some of the people there. They didn't understand and weren't comfortable with the direction he wanted them to go.

My understanding was Bill was supposed to be there every day. In my opinion, if he wasn't there to watch talent during their training, he couldn't get a feel for who they were when it came time to direct their on-screen characters. On the one day a week he did come in, he was there to critique (criticize) the promos, and that didn't sit well with the talent. It was like an outsider coming in just long enough to tell everyone what they wree doing wrong.

Joe also let everyone know that while he was in the DSW training center, Bill spent the majority of his time on the company computer "booking" his own promotion and handling other business. When Bill came to work for DSW, he shut down his *Wildside* promotion. At least, that's what he said he did. What he really did was just change the name to *NWA Anarchy*.

Bill had been around the business long enough to know how to get along with people, but he and Joe just didn't click. The company sent Bill there to produce the TV show and Joe wasn't going to take direction from him or anyone else. It was a no-win situation for Bill.

Tommy Dreamer came to the building one time after Bill took all his things and snuck out the back door. Tommy wanted to see if we could work things out, but Joe was happy Bill had quit and didn't want to pursue it. When Tommy contacted Bill, he insisted we pushed him out. According to Bill, he had produced more than 80 million hours of wrestling for TV and he should be the final authority on how things should be done. Actually, I was under the impression that, in regards to the television, he was the final authority. To Joe, however, it always went back to, *"We'll run this company my way or I'll shut this fucking place down."*

Regardless of who was right and who was wrong, we must have looked like a trio of idiots to the students. We were supposed to be the leaders, but we couldn't get along or work together.

A few weeks after Bill left, Neal Pruitt came in to take his place. I believe Joe had Neal in mind from the start, but to get Neal on the payroll, it had to be cleared with WWE. He was the cameraman, the producer, and did the editing. He also filmed all the promos and created the openings and closings for the weekly show and the live events. Neal became a full-fledged member of DSW. He loved it there and gave his whole being to the operation. He did a lot for the kids and hung out with them. The best part about the addition of Neal to DSW was that he knew how to work with and get along with Joe. He knew his stuff, like how to get the shots we needed, and how to get our points across to the viewing audience. He directed the kids in their vignettes and made them feel comfortable whenever they worried about their part.

Neal Pruitt and I were like Oscar and Felix from the TV show, *The Odd Couple*. We were complete opposites, but we worked so well together. Neal was so creative and good at his job. His one failing was that he was never in a hurry and procrastinated, which caused him problems when it came to meeting deadlines. Okay, he had another failing. He was a pig, and I say that with the utmost affection. In no time at all, he had turned my office and promo room into a flea market. He had stuff everywhere, most of which we didn't need and/or couldn't use. I was very organized (yes, me) and I had a place for everything. If it wasn't necessary, I didn't want to see it. I remember walking in one morning to find a futon in my promo room. It turns out Neal didn't always go home at night and just slept in the building. I spent a lot of time making sure the wiring to the TVs and recording systems were neatly arranged and hidden. Neal, on the other hand, flew by the seat of his pants. He would rummage through stuff, and in the process, scatter things everywhere. I loved working with Neal, though. Yes, we were Oscar and Felix, and the end result was we produced a quality show each and every week.

Once the company was up and running, I did the grunt work of setting up the arenas and making sure everything worked, from the cameras to the toilets. I suppose you might say I was a "jackass" of all trades. I made sure everybody had copies of the show lineup and knew when they were scheduled to do promos. I sat down with the talent and walked them through their finishes. I made sure the camera shots were good and the music was ready to play at the appropriate times. After the first few weeks, Joe asked me to do commentary with Nigel Sherrod. Joe said I had a way of sounding excited and getting the points across to the viewers. That task also allowed me to sit at ringside and use a series of hand signals to communicate things with the talent, like "get more heat," or "fire up and fight." I had done the same thing at ringside during *Velocity*. When one of the guys would look over, I would give them signs on what was working and where they could switch gears.

On the day following a show, I had to be there early in the morning to type up the results for the [WWE] office and package the DVD copies that would be sent to them in the mail. When everybody showed up around ten o'clock, we would all sit down, watch the show, and critique it. After that, we would do our training. When everybody left, Bill the Janitor would clock in and clean the building.

To sum it up, working for Deep South Wrestling was nothing out of the ordinary ... just your normal, typical, average, standard, ordinary, common 15 to 16 hour days.

WWE wanted to be sure the talents were working on their characters, or that they were being given opportunities to do promos on the show. They issued directives on who they wanted to have more air time, or how they wanted them portrayed. Most of the time, the changes they made would send Joe into orbit. Later, when they began sending guys like Paul Heyman and Michael Hayes down to either watch or run some of the matches, Joe would get so mad that he wouldn't come out of his office. From time to time, others would stop by to watch the tapings: Dusty Rhodes, Greg Gagne, Steve Keirn, Arn Anderson, Dean Malenko. Johnny Ace, Tommy Dreamer, and Mike Bucci [who wrestled for WWE as Simon Dean] were there the most often.

We had a good following for our TV show, which aired in nine states, and we taped TV every Thursday to a full house of "paying customers," something OVW never did. We experimented and charged three bucks, and we had no complaints. We even had weeks when we had to turn people away!

We also presented 10 shows a year at the Six Flags Over Georgia theme park. For some reason, though, WWE told us we weren't working often enough. I think one of the things that set them off was Joe refusing to do shows in locations where there wasn't any money to be made. WWE told us to run everywhere and anywhere, but Joe didn't like that idea ... and since Joe *was* Deep South, we did things his way.

For awhile, our show was being aired on a TV station in Tallahassee, which gave us some good visibility. WWE thought it was in conflict to what they were doing because they were going to be using Deep South talent on their TV under different names and characters at the same time. I'm sure that was, in part, a valid reason for not wanting us on the station, but I believe they thought Joe was in business for himself and they didn't like him making money off their talent and product. That's just my theory (although several people said the same thing to me on more than one occasion).

In October 2006, MavTV decided to add Deep South Wrestling to their network lineup. MavTV, billed as *"TV Created by Men for Men"* had been around since 2002 and had distribution through both cable and satellite distributors. I don't know how they came into play, but their plan was to air footage of our training process. That's right ... another *Tough Enough* series. They called it "Learning the Ropes." Everyone was on board at first. The MavTV people came in and taped the workouts and conversations, and then edited the footage for TV. Joe had the say-so of what they could and couldn't use. It was really good, but the kids got the idea that it was their own private TV show and began acting like idiots. Instead of taking it for what it was, they took it as a chance to "act," rather than be normal and go about their business. I hate to criticize them because they were young and wanted to get as much camera time as possible, but the [WWE] didn't like it and told MavTV they were no longer welcome at the Deep South facility. Ed (the guy responsible for directing and producing the show) and the crew from MavTV were good people and I enjoyed my association with them. The MavTV show was successful, but it just wasn't what WWE wanted.

Wednesday at Deep South was known as "promo day." Every week, we had to submit tapes of the talent doing promos to show their growth and to give the company an idea of who could talk and how their characters were coming along. The promos were then edited into the TV program the following day.

From the day of our meeting about me going to work for Deep South, Johnny Ace told me that within a few years, he envisioned me taking control of the company. That doesn't mean I was going to screw Joe out of his position, but quite the opposite. I would learn as much as I could from Joe, and when Joe's deal with WWE expired, I would be in place to run things. Joe would retain ownership of Deep South, but the territory and developmental center would be mine to run. Johnny wanted me to feel as if I had a vested interest in the success or failure of the company. I was told that by Tommy Dreamer, as well. Joe and I actually had a few conversations about that, as well. He said that when he was "done," he would like to see me take it over. Whether or not I ever took control never changed my way of thinking. I was there to do one thing: to help those kids to reach their goals of becoming WWE superstars. To reach that end, I was going to do what I knew best and everything that was asked of me.

DSW was a new concept for WWE and, before we were even in our building, WWE seemed to think we should be pushing out talent and be up and running with TV and house shows. Johnny wanted everything done "yesterday." During the two years I was with the company, we never seemed to get up to speed with them.

I lived in the Deep South building. My primary job was to keep an eye on 35 "adults," keep them healthy, and prepare them for the phone call they wanted to get. I wanted them to be successful as people. Even if they never got to the level they wanted, it wouldn't be because they didn't work, fight, and play hard. I constantly told them, "At the end of the day, it's just wrestling." I wanted them to be prepared for life before, during, and after the road finished with them and spit them out.

In addition to taking care of talent, I prepared schedules and made sure travel arrangements got to the right talent. I answered phone calls and e-mails from every agent, coordinator, boss, creative member, and writer. I was called on to train certain guys at night when the building was closed, or to stay late with some guys so they wouldn't feel "stupid" in front of the others.

Lacey played a big role at Deep South, as well. She heard Johnny talking about how much they counted on me, so she gave a lot of herself to help me. The kids would talk to her about things, or she would cook for them so they would have something nutritious to eat. It was awesome to watch her become such a big part of what I was doing. It was a 24/7 job and we treated it as such. We were trainers, counselors, babysitters, big brothers/sisters, and mentors. Sadly, nobody ever talked about those things. They just painted me as a wild man who tortured everyone.

Deep South trainees — (l to r.) Derrick Neikirk, Mike Knox, Eric Perez, Mike Taylor, Ryan O'Reilly, Tony Santarelli, and Freakin' Deacon

Chapter 17

The Heat Guy

During a typical training week, we spent an equal amount of time doing ring work and talking about the psychology of the business. We wanted to prepare them for any situation they might encounter. We didn't hesitate to stop in the middle of a training session to talk about our reasons for doing what we were doing. When the talent seemed to be getting hurt, we would spend more time walking through things, and talking about the "whys" and the "why nots" of what we were trying to teach. We found our best method of teaching psychology was to first allow the talent to come to their own conclusions. When they "got it," we encouraged them to apply those ideas to every situation or "spot" they might be using. After we spent several months together and I offered my personal thoughts, the students began calling them "Bill-isms."

We covered everything from making their beds to making the people believe what they were watching. When Joe was really involved, we had a few kids who really fit together well and made good tag teams, so he spent a lot of time talking about tagging and the thought behind it. We talked about the role referees and commentators play in their matches. We showed them how to tie their boots and discussed outside-the-ring activities like "passing the piss test." I know a common saying in the wrestling business is that the kids today *"don't even know how to lace up their boots,"* but we did have a few who didn't have a clue about how to do that. We spent most of our time helping them with promos and developing their characters.

We really put those cats through the paces. We pushed them hard. Some of them would blow up so badly they would pray for an injury so they could take a rest. We didn't treat the girls any differently. If we thought someone was dragging their ass around the ring, we would pick up the pace and work them until they dropped.

Since my days with DSW, whenever I hear someone talk about pussy, the female anatomy is no longer what comes to mind. The first thing I think about is Mikey Batts [Michael Altieri]. Mikey was trained by his cousin, Billy Kidman (which is probably how he got his deal with the company). From his first day with us, that lazy bastard did nothing but puke, whine, and cry. I mean, literally cry. After his first two-hour workout, he dropped to the floor and began puking and crying: *"Wa-aaah! I can't do this!"* While he was with us, he never completed a workout and he never had a match. He called the office and complained about how badly he was being treated and, a little more than a month after he came to DSW, he got shipped off to OVW. Six months later, he was given his release (fired). That kid was as useless as tits on a bull. There were many others like him who came from independent promotions, each thinking they were "the bomb" and could handle anything thrown at them. The students who were serious about their training took pride in the fact that they could hang with anyone and quickly showed the "newbies" how out of shape they really were.

There wasn't any teasing or hazing in DSW, but there was a healthy, competitive spirit between students who took their opportunity seriously. On their first day in DSW, Johnny, Dreamer and I challenged them to be leaders and to set examples. The guys and girls who were the best at what they did were constantly "challenging" each other. They encouraged each other to execute and be more entertaining. One of the things I drilled into their heads was that one of the jobs of being a "worker" was "to make the other guy look better than he really is," and they did that. When someone called someone out and that person "bettered them," they had to prove themselves all over again. Nobody did anything to push another student out, but we had a phrase we liked to use (actually, we had many, but this one was used more than most): "Shit or get off the pot." The kids weren't afraid to call someone out, or to pull someone aside and tell them to get their head out of their ass. That was one of the best things about the training. The students (at least, the good ones) had a healthy take on the students who were dragging their ass, and conversely, who the leaders were. They all wanted to be the best and become the leader who would police the DSW locker room. They were proud of how they trained and who they trained with. There was a pride about being a Deep South trainee, and among the good students, there was a silent code about weeding out the never-would-bes from the wannabes. The same held true in OVW and HWA. As a result, we knew who the athletes and wrestlers were and we let them run their own locker room (to an extent).

From the very beginning, we told each kid that they needed to police themselves so the office didn't bring heat on everyone, and they needed to keep each other in check to protect the locker room and the business. They realized the bullshit being said and reported was making them all look like a bunch of jackasses, and they didn't want that, so they went out of their way to make sure stories stayed "in house" and didn't make their way to the office.

I also held extra training sessions on Saturday mornings. It wasn't anything I was told, or even asked to do. I just enjoyed working with the kids, so I gave them the option of getting extra time in the ring. It was always the same group of kids that showed up: Angel Williams, Brett and Brian Majors, Derrick Neikirk, Eric Perez, Freakin' Deacon, Mike Knox, Mike Taylor, MVP Striker, Palmer Canon, and Shantelle Taylor. The kids learned more on Saturday mornings than they did the entire rest of the week because everyone there was focused and there for one thing ... to become the best they could be. I was so proud of those kids. There were times when I wouldn't call a session for a particular Saturday and they would call to see if I would come down and open the doors so they could work. There were other times when a group of the kids would call and ask if they could come to the house to watch tapes or just talk.

On the other hand, the students who couldn't hang with the best spent their time stirring the pot.

When we all trained together at Gold's Gym, nobody complained about anything. We worked those kids for two to three hours a day and nobody grumbled or whined. However, on our first day in the new building, those problems began ... in spades. When we were working at Gold's Gym, everyone was blowing up, but that was a good thing because nobody was really in great cardio shape. When the time came for everyone to show what they could do in the ring, the kids were quickly separated into two groups: "those who could" and "those who couldn't." As soon as the dead weight began to realize they weren't as good as they thought, and they couldn't hang with some of the others, they began making phone calls and sending e-mails to WWE to complain about their "mistreatment." In most cases, they blamed me for asking them to do things they shouldn't have to do.

The intensity of the workouts dictated how the "problem children" handled themselves. Whenever we had a particularly grueling workout, I knew I would be getting a call from the office asking me to explain why I was doing something or another. It became absolutely ridiculous to have a really good day of training, only to get a phone call at the end of the day with someone telling me so-and-so was complaining about being thrown out of the ring. Other complaints ran the gamut:

"We're expected to do too much each day." (we trained four days a week for "maybe" three hours a day)

"The conditioning is too much for us to handle."

"We have to begin training too early in the morning." (eight o'clock)

"Bill plays favorites and doesn't push them as hard as he does the rest of us."

"Bill brought in some of his friends to intentionally hurt the people he doesn't like."

"Bill talks nice to some people and treats others like dirt."

"Bill took so-and-so out for a drink, but didn't invite me."

"Bill invited a group out to his house for dinner, but didn't invite me."

Bill gets in the ring and stretches the guys he doesn't like."

The list of complaints was endless. At one time, we had too many kids in the building at the same time, so we had to split the training into two sessions (that was about the time Dave Taylor was brought onboard as the second trainer) so everyone could get more training and ring time. One group was "rewarded" and called the "A Team," while the others, the "B Team," had to train with me as "punishment." It was simply a rib. One of the guys in my group came up with the idea for a t-shirt and we asked everyone (from both sessions) if they wanted to participate and order a shirt. The response from both groups was unanimous: "Yes." Printed on the front of the shirts was — I'm just happy to "B" — and on the back was — HERE! It was just a play on words about the "A" and "B" team bullshit.

Even that warranted a call to Talent Relations. Someone called to say they hadn't been asked to participate and they didn't get a shirt. I got a call from Dreamer that night and was told we were no longer allowed to wear the shirts because it offended some of the trainees. I was told if they did, they would be fined. When I hung up the phone, I said to myself, *"Fuck that,"* and I continued to wear it. The students continued to wear them every chance they got — to the gym, to Saturday workouts, and out on the town. They were proud to be known as the "B Team."

It was ridiculous on all levels because the students themselves were the ones who came up with the idea to call Dave's group the "A" team and mine the "B" team, and before we ever came up with the idea of t-shirts, I had switched the schedule every so often so everyone would have an opportunity to train with different people. During one of these transitions, the talent came up with the idea for t-shirts as a rib on those who had been placed in Dave's group *for the week!* It was absurd to think either Dave or I would label any of them. Of course, after I got the call from Dreamer, I didn't make any bones about who was or wasn't ready for the main roster, or for that matter, who really belonged in Deep South. They opened up a can of worms and I began to vent.

Some of them even called the office to complain about one group of students getting special treatment. They said, *"Bill's giving them extra training on Saturday mornings and that isn't fair."* What they didn't tell the office was that I extended the invitation to our Saturday morning sessions to *everyone*, and the students they were complaining about were the ones who took me up on my offer. The complainers couldn't get out of bed before the crack of noon to take advantage of the "extra training," and yet, it was my fault they were excluded from the sessions. They knew we were there every week. If I had gone with my gut, I shouldn't have asked the crybabies in the first place because it was my day off, and why should I have to ask them to train when they didn't give me their attention during the week?

My sole purpose in being there was to help everyone get to where they wanted to be (WWE), so I treated everyone the same as everybody else when they walked through the door ... but so many of them didn't see it that way. If I left them alone, they said they were being neglected. When I asked more of them, they said I was picking on them. When they couldn't do something or keep up with everyone else, the fell into the selfish mode of "It's everyone's fault but mine." Their only recourse was to complain because they were the ones who weren't up to speed with the rest, were threatened because they didn't stand out, and couldn't account for their lack of talent. And when the complainers made their calls to the office, one of the things they didn't mention was that they sat on their ass outside the building while the others trained. They just painted a picture of abuse and being treated like animals.

If those crybabies tried that stuff on the road with WWE talent, every one of them would have suffered a far worse fate than me getting in their ear. "Back in the day," the guys left the assholes naked on the side of the road in the middle of the night, shit in their gym bags, padlocked their gym bags shut, or tied their bootlaces together. You know, the "fun things" the guys did to let people know it's time to grow up.

One of the things I did with the kids was to have "Make-a-Deal Friday," during which time they would be allowed to replace my regular workout with something of their own choosing. I either agreed to their deal or held out for more. It's funny, but nine out of ten times, the things they decided to do were far worse than any workout I was going to have, but they thought they had an "out" from training and would get to leave early. One week, Mike "The Miz" Mizanin came up with a bright idea. *"How about if we do 2,500 squats and then we can leave?"*

I immediately said, *"Deal."*

I have to give them credit. They did it. On Fridays, they worked harder and trained more than they ever would have. I wanted them to have the opportunity to do something that would make them feel good about themselves, and still allow them to leave earlier than usual so they could get out and begin their weekend. The important thing was, "they" made the deal.

On Monday, I got a phone call from Johnny asking why I was beating up the kids and making them squat all day. Most of the kids were okay with what we had done because most of them took it for what it was … a bonding experience and an opportunity for everyone to get away from wrestling for a day and just screw around. But just like always, the shit-disturbers had to make sure they were going to survive and keep getting paid. They called the office and painted a picture of something it wasn't. *"Bill made us squat all day."*

The complainers would say their heels were sore, their thigh muscles ached, or they had strained a finger or a toe. I can't understand how they could justify sitting out when guys like Bradshaw [John Layfield] was working while he was having treatment on his back. Triple H was itching to come back to work early after an injury. Many of the guys put off having surgeries so they could continue doing what they loved — wrestling. The company didn't help matters. During the last few months Deep South was in business, everyone was sent home when they discovered one of the trainees had a cold. They were afraid the rest of the class would catch it!

On the flip side, some of the kids had legit injuries, but they refused to sit out. There were even times when I had to order them to take a break. Like professionals in any other sport, those kids knew there were times when you had to work through an injury. They were there to prove they had what it took to be a "superstar" in the wrestling business. The pussies (that's the best description I can come up with for them), on the other hand, just wanted the weekly paycheck and to wrestle on our show so they could call themselves superstars. They didn't understand the difference between being "hurt" or "injured," as opposed to being sore and achy. The funny thing was, whenever company execs or the creative team showed up to watch the training, they always seemed to be able to work through whatever aches or pains they had.

I take that back. Everyone *except* … Kevin Matthews. He's the only guy I remember sitting in the bleachers when we had visitors from the office.

Tommy was constantly getting phone calls, text messages, and e-mails about how unfairly certain people were being treated, how they weren't being welcomed, and how their feelings were being hurt. The next day, I would get a phone call from Tommy who would give me one of the "who didn't fit in" and "no one likes them" talks. Man, it was Babysitting 101.

We had kids who were signed to make anywhere from $500 to $1,500 and more a week. A few kids were paid $500 just to come in for a week to be evaluated. Not only that, but their hotel and trans expenses were covered.

None of them were signed or proven talent, but the company was paying them what I considered to be a ridiculous amount of money. I can't begin to tell you how many times I walked into the room to hear someone bragging about how much they were making, and as a rule, the ones shooting off their mouths were the ones who complained the most. It reached a point where the kids who were there for the right reasons got pissed off because the trainees making the most money were the ones with the least ability. We actually had guys there who had been in the business for seven years, but couldn't do a headlock takeover.

Not only were those kids being paid $100 and more a day just to train, the company also paid their airfare, their hotel bill, and sometimes furnished them with a rental car. And then, when they came to train, they complained because they were tired, or they had a bruise that hurt, or they blew up. Well, wake up and smell the coffee! That's what developmental is all about. If you can't run with the big dogs, get out and get a job in the real world. Where can anyone work three hours a day, four days a week, and make $500 a week? Nowhere! And that isn't even a true picture of the schedule. Wednesday was cut short because it was "promo day." We didn't train on Thursday because that was the day we taped the TV show, and Friday was "Make-a-Deal."

One complaint that really stirred the pot was, *"Bill De Mott told me to get the fuck out of his ring."* I love humor, and that was one of my humorous ways of getting a point across. Whenever someone would blow up, fall down, screw up a spot, get hurt, trip over their own feet, or fart in my ring, I would point at them and yell, *"Get the fuck out!"* It was meant to be humorous, and everyone in the room knew it. Everybody always laughed, even the person who was being evicted. Of course, there were some people who didn't like it, and they were the students who were inept and clumsy with no hope of improving. The next thing I know, I'm getting another phone call from Johnny. *"What the fuck are you doing?"*

I never knew who would be calling the company next, or what they would be calling to complain about. It all depended on who felt the most insecure at the time, and the intensity of the workouts usually dictated the frequency of those complaints. The funny thing was, 97 percent of the time, Johnny let me know who was bitching. Most of the time, I would let them know I knew without coming right out and saying it, but it was always interesting when I told someone that Johnny told me they had complained. They would *always* deny it, of course, even though I had heard it from the horse's (sorry Johnny) mouth. At other times, I would just throw out one of my little "one-liners" to let them know I knew what was going on. *I don't want anyone to be tired today, so you guys just stretch and we'll see where it leads."* There was no doubt in anyone's mind that someone had called the office and I was pissed.

My favorite method of letting people know I knew was to get everyone together and talk to them. I would talk nicely to everyone *except* the person who had made the call, and I would all but ignore them completely. It didn't take them long to make the connection. I can't imagine they would be good poker players because they always gave themselves up with their expressions. The rest of the talent picked up on the message, too, and when they took over their workout, they would do what they needed to do. They would let the complainers know their attitudes weren't welcome and they would "out" them if they continued on the same course. On the flip side, those kids were good enough to also tell them they would work with them to help get them on track with the program. Some caught on, but there were a few who never did, and they were pretty much shunned by the others. When they weren't accepted by the others, they felt left out, which gave them more reason to blame me.

And while I was subtle when it came to sending a message, there was hell to pay whenever Joe got word about an e-mail or a phone call. He would call everyone together and cuss out the whole group. *"If you don't like it, or if you can't handle the pressure, get the fuck out because things aren't changing for anyone."* Even Johnny Ace came down a time or two and cussed them out. He told them he had my back and that what I said goes because I was following his directions. Like Joe, he would finish with, *"If you don't like it, you can get the fuck out because there are hundreds of people waiting to take your spot!"* (I still have some of Johnny's rants on tape)

Later, he would tell me privately, *"Don't let them walk all over you. I've got your back. If they can't cut it, weed them out and get rid of them."*

What a feeling that was, to have someone like Johnny come down to read the riot act and put me over ... until the following week, when I got another call from Johnny. *"What the hell are you doin' down there? I got another e-mail."*

One of the letters said I would get in the ring and stretch guys until they couldn't breathe, so the office banned me from getting in the ring and making physical contact. Johnny said, *"There's too much complaining. We need you to stay out of the ring."* By then, I was pretty much numb to the nonsense, so I didn't argue. I simply said, *"Sure."* I knew that, like everything else, it would only last until they had a "project" that needed to be done, or they planned to call someone up to the main roster and wanted them ready for the road. For some reason, during those times, it was okay for me to be in the ring with them. I was so proud of my kids, too, because they would speak up and tell Johnny and Tommy that things were beginning to suck.

I was more or less running the show and doing everything under the sun to make DSW successful, and in return, I constantly had negative feedback thrown at me. I was always made out to be the villain. They would have me fine the kids for things like being late, violating the dress code, or missing practice ... and then they would have me return their money. Nobody had the balls to stick to their guns. Agents would tell the kids to "grow a sack," to get the hell out of the building because they could be replaced, but then they would call them on the phone and tell them everything was okay. They would tell me *"Put so-and-so through the wringer. We need to know if he has a heart for the business."* The next day, I would get a call asking why I was working them so hard.

Even with all the drama, I never slowed down. I opened and closed the building every day and would spend extra time with anyone who asked. Nobody will ever know how much I really did for those kids ... not Johnny, not Tommy, not Joe, and certainly not the complainers. Even with all of that, I would do it all over again *the same way.*

Shortly after the first time I was banned from the ring, Johnny Ace told me to protect myself by taping every training session. I thought he was talking about protecting myself from false accusations from the students, but little did I know I would have to protect myself from WWE. I bought myself a recorder and I have hundreds of VHS tapes. I taped everything that went on in that building while I was there. Besides the training sessions, I recorded speeches by me, Dave, Johnny, the agents, and people from the creative team. I could easily have disputed 99 percent of the things said about me. As a matter of fact, every time an accusation, threat, or claim was made about my job, or how I was mistreating the talent, I offered them tapes (copies, of course) of the days in question ... and every time, the office told me they didn't need to see them. Looking back, I'm sure the company wished they had never given me the idea to tape things. If it was anyone else, they might have used the tapes to sue or bring forward what really went on behind the scenes of everyday training for WWE. I was so frustrated over being advised to tape the sessions, and then not being given the opportunity to present them to prove I was being railroaded. The tapes prove I was doing my job well.

I even have tapes of the famous Johnny Ace speeches telling the talent to *"stop being a bunch of pussies and act like you want to be here."* I couldn't come close to the number of times he called them pussies, losers, and liars. He didn't cut them any slack whatsoever, but they had to take it from Johnny because he was their boss. I have e-mails stating how he wanted certain talent "treated" and "trained," how he suggested I go about seeing who had "heart, and who he wanted to get "rid of."

The strange thing about it all was that everybody who wrote letters and e-mails trained with Dave Taylor. Not one percent of the people who trained with Bill De Mott ever complained. I have it all written down. Dave trained every one of the guys who quit, and yet, Johnny never called Dave to ream him out about something that happened. They never called Joe Hamilton, the owner-operator of Deep South, to ask him about anything that was going on. They never asked to see the tapes I made. They simply used me as their fall guy. The heat guy. Chris Benoit came to DSW and put those kids through cardio-hell, and yet, nobody called to complain about him. Why not? Could it be possible the kids knew they might have to work with (or shoot against) him some day?

At one time, I was responsible for 32 students. Yes, there were cliques ... two, to be exact. The first clique was made up of about ten lazy, no-talent individuals, while the rest of the students, the hard-working, dedicated kids, were in the second clique. The funny thing was, the kids I treated the worst, were the kids in the second clique ... which everyone called "Bill's clique." The people in my clique knew I expected more out of them, and I pushed them hard. And yet, as hard as I pushed them, they would drop by the gym in the afternoon for a second session, or on Saturday mornings.

That's the way it was everywhere in WWE developmental. Lance Storm, Al Snow, Danny Davis all had cliques when they were training. There were always a few students who wanted to skate and go unnoticed until they thought it counted, and then there were the kids who wanted to work and earn the opportunity to get a spot on the roster. It's human nature for people to think, *"How much can I not do and get away with it, while at the same time, looking like I want it as bad as I said I did when you hired me?"*

In the "real world," I can't imagine anyone in a corporation writing a letter to their boss to complain about how they're being mistreated. Their boss would tell them, *"If you don't like it, pack up your stuff and don't let the door hit you in the ass on your way out."* And what kind of career are they going to have when they begin "playing" with Shawn Michaels, Undertaker, and Triple H. Those guys wouldn't put up with attitudes like that, especially from a rookie who hasn't proven himself or drawn a dime for the company.

What I can't understand is, why would anyone in Titan Towers [WWE headquarters] care a whit about whether or not a developmental wrestler is unhappy? He's not someone who has drawn the company any money, and there's a good chance (based on the track record of guys who trained in DSW, OVW and FCW) he won't even make it to the main roster.

The kids who got called up from Deep South to the main roster got nothing but accolades. They knew what they were doing because they were prepared, both physically and mentally. They also looked good, they were in great shape, and they didn't blow up in the ring. The office would be so happy with the results.

A few days later, the office would get another letter from one of the complainers and the shit storm would begin again. I'd get another phone call from Johnny. *"What the fuck is goin' on down there?"*

My reports didn't seem to be enough, either. They always needed more information, so they'd send another agent down. Over time, we had visits from Steve Williams, Arn Anderson, Bruce Prichard, Michael Hayes, Dusty Rhodes, Dean Malenko, Steve Keirn, Tommy Dreamer, and Johnny Ace. They'd go back and tell everyone, *"They have that place rockin'. I love what they're doin'."*

When an agent came in, I gave them plenty of opportunities to talk and show things to the talent both in and out of the ring. In April 2006, they sent Greg Gagne down. The company was in the process of buying the tapes and TV rights from the American Wrestling Association, and they were inducting Greg's dad (Verne) into the Hall of Fame, so they gave Greg a job as an agent.

Greg's speech was okay the first time, but after that, he repeated the same things and didn't have a grasp about what was happening with Deep South, OVW, or even WWE. His ideas were throwbacks to the '70s and not believable, so while the students were listening closely to what he had to say,

WCW/NWO trading card

Bill De Mott, Bill Goldberg, and Stevie Richards at the 2004 WrestleMania XX in Madison Square Garden.

they were doing it to more or less mock him later. I felt badly because, after he left, the kids would be laughing about the way he wanted them to do things. I have to say it was very "humorous" to watch, although it was a bit sad because I had a lot of respect for Greg. He was a star in the business long before I got involved.

Over time, I lost that respect because of things he did. Greg would take the talent to dinner and tell them how he could move their careers along more easily if they would do things his way. I always got a report from the kids the day after those meetings took place, telling me about who he had met with. There were even a few who went to those meetings and called me late at night to tell me what he had said. He told them things like they'd be better suited at OVW, where he would be taking over. Greg prefaced every speech with, *"I'm not here to step on anyone's toes. I just want to watch and help where I can."* And yet, he would undercut me by painting bad pictures and telling the kids how much better things would be if they came to OVW. I'm a face-to-face guy. If you have a problem, tell me and we'll talk it through, but it's not good business to question my methods and tell stories to the kids I was training. He really had Kenny Omega and Chris Rombola on a different page and, in my opinion, gave them false hope. Both wrote letters to WWE complaining about Bill De Mott. The funny thing is, they were both training with Dave Taylor.

When Greg was there, a whole campaign of letter-writing began. I never had any arguments with Greg, but Joe didn't see eye to eye with him. He said Greg's ideas were hokey and unbelievable. Joe was very professional with Greg, but there were a few times when I had to talk Joe out of stabbing him in the heart.

Chapter 18

Crybabies and Complainers

One of the lead shit-disturbers was a guy named Jack Bull [Greg Groothius]. He could really talk the talk, but when push came to shove and it was time to prove his worth, he showed little value. He couldn't work a snow-cone machine. He became one of the biggest "Bill De Mott bashers" in Deep South and convinced a few others to join his little club. He didn't have what it took, so he blamed everything on everyone else. He only lasted three months before he was transferred to OVW, where he trained for a year. He finally got "the call" from WWE in January 2007 … and was told he was being released from his developmental contract (i.e. fired). Greg blamed the system for not being able to cut it and he dragged several others down with him.

Chris Rombola [Christopher Rombola], a student at Harley Race's Pro Wrestling Camp, got his contract after participating in a WWE training session in December 2005 in Buffalo, New York. One of the first things I learned about him (from a WWE printed interview) was that he was a manic depressive. I knew right then and there that he was going to be nothing but trouble. He told a WWE interviewer that he had mental issues … and they hired him. If someone has problems, do you think it's a good idea to move them from Buffalo (the north) to Atlanta (the south) and throw them into unfamiliar living conditions, just to see "if" they had anything to offer the company? The kid also was supposed to take meds every day (which he didn't). He was a fan and in good physical shape, but he knew nothing about the mechanics of wrestling, so when I wouldn't let him do what the other kids were doing, he began doing the "Dr. Jekyll and Mr. Hyde" routine. He eventually got hurt and blamed me when I told him he had to sit on the sidelines. He later wrote a long letter which blamed me for everything bad that had happened to him. He was sent to OVW in July 2006 and disappeared after WWE ended their relationship with OVW in February 2008. He never made it to the big leagues, but while he was at OVW, and long after I was gone from DSW, he sent me an e-mail thanking me for preparing him for the business. He said he finally understood the things I had tried to tell and show him.

Oleg Prudius [Olyeg Prudius] was the 2005 USA Open Heavyweight Sambo champion and United States Kick-Boxing Association grappling champion, and yet, when he came to DSW, he got in Johnny's ear and complained about it being "too hard." He couldn't understand what we were trying to teach him (or the reasons behind the lessons) and he was constantly getting hurt. He didn't know anything about professional wrestling, WWE, or the talent, either. That should tell you how much he knew about his career choice.

When Oleg finally realized he had to learn to do things like everyone else, he got on board and listened, and once he got over himself, I found him to be a really nice guy. WWE must have seen something in him because they had us working with him night and day to get him ready. When they finally called him up, we told them he wasn't ready. *"We're bringin' him up, Bill."*

"He's not ready."

"Well, we're bringin' him up."

"I'm tellin' ya. He's not ready!"

"We're bringin' him up, Billy."

"Listen to me. He's not ready!"

A week later, Johnny called and busted my balls because Oleg didn't seem to have learned anything. *"We're sendin' the mother fucker back down. He's not ready."*

"Really? Why would you do that?"

"We're gonna send him to OVW."

I put a lot of time and effort into evaluating the talent for the office. My evaluation reports were never biased due to my personal feelings for a particular talent. It was my job and I was willing to stand behind everything I wrote. Most of the time, when Creative had something in mind for one of the students, they would let me know so I could get them moving in that direction, but there were other times when they called up people who just weren't ready. When they asked me if I thought someone was ready, I would say "yes" or "no," but they made the ultimate decision. All I had to stand by were my evaluations and reports, and apparently, a lot of them were never looked at before decisions were made.

Whether Oleg improved a lot, or he just learned how to play WWE's politics, he deserves credit for making a name for himself in the business. He's been with WWE since 2008, and as Vladimir Kozlov, has been featured on *SmackDown*, *ECW*, and *RAW*. Personally, I still think he's the shits because he never learned his craft and what he does is little more than a comedy act.

Daniel Rodimer was a finalist in the *$1,000,000 Tough Enough* competition. When the company made him an offer to come to Atlanta to train, he turned them down because they weren't offering enough money. Two years later, they offered him more money, and he accepted. He had no heart for the business. It was all about money.

Dan had a lot of confidence in his ability. In fact, he made sure everyone knew he was Johnny Ace's boy, and that he could get away with anything: skipping practice, peeing "dirty," being late, taking time off for an injury, or murder (okay, Johnny drew the line at murder). I liked Daniel, and still do. I thought he had talent because he was smooth, so I went out of my way to help him. I wrote evaluation after evaluation on Daniel, and in every one of them, I stressed the fact that he had talent, but he wasn't ready. What did the company do? They rejected and ignored my evaluations, transferred him to OVW, and called him up to the WWE main roster. He didn't make any friends in the locker room while he was there, and he didn't make use of the lessons he had been taught in DSW. Someone from the office called to tell me, *"He isn't ready."* What a shock! During his short time in the WWE locker rooms, he made it his mission to tell everyone horror stories about Deep South and Bill De Mott. What he didn't mention was the fact that he didn't have the heart for it, and instead of concentrating on training and learning his craft, he was busy cheating on his fiancé with one of the girls.

Just five months with OVW, and wrestling on WWE television, Daniel was sent to train in the Florida Championship Wrestling [FCW] territory, only to be released two months later. Not only did Daniel not pursue wrestling with another company, but he chose to go back to his normal life. He really didn't want to wrestle. He just wanted to be a "wrestler."

Daniel's "valet," Brooke Adams, also jumped on the "I hate Bill De Mott" bandwagon. I don't have anything to say about her other than that.

Kenny Omega [Tyson Smith] had it all. He had the talent and he knew what he was doing. When they sent him to us, they said he would be "good to go" after we helped him "brush-up" on a few things. Kenny didn't take direction well from anyone. He became sour on DSW very quickly (thanks to help from Greg Gagne) and sent in his application and dues to join the "Bill De Mott Bashers Club." He was only with us for three months before he asked to be released from his contract (i.e. he quit). His close friends said he missed his girlfriend and wanted to be with her, but that's not a very manly thing to admit, so he chose to say Bill De Mott made him do it. Regardless of how he felt about me and the things he said after he left, I thought the kid was destined to be the next Chris Jericho. Kenny was really good and I thought it was a shame he didn't hang in there.

Kevin Matthews [Kevin McDonald] was another one of the guys who believed his own press. What a putz. He came to DSW with his girlfriend, Krissy Vaine [Kristin Eubanks], but lost her to Ryan O'Reilly, another trainee. Like Daniel Rodimer, he didn't get along with many of his peers and he got hurt a lot. I didn't care much for him from the first day he walked into the building because he bad-mouthed Johnny Rodz. Kevin was just another kid who had been "top dog" (or so he thought) in a small, independent promotion and believed he was better than he really was, and even though he was training with Dave Taylor, he blamed me for his shortcomings. He couldn't keep up with the true wrestlers there. He sat out a lot more than he trained. He spent a lot of time in the bleachers watching everyone else train and was released after being told to get into the ring and show some backbone. Mike Bucci, who had taken over as WWE's Head of Developmental, called Kevin into the office and told him, *"You are on the bubble,"* which meant he was close to losing his job. *"Step up and show us you want to be here and get called up."* When he was released, Kevin's response was simple and (I guess) honest: *"Well, at least I was a WWE superstar. I made it.* He truly believed that because he was under WWE contract, he was a superstar and had "made it to the dance."

"Big Time" Nick Mitchell [Nicholas Mitchell] was probably the most athletically-gifted guy we had at Deep South. He could do anything we asked. I could show him something and he would try it and get it right. Unfortunately, I believe Nick being immature was the same thing that kept him from winning the *$1,000,000 Tough Enough* contest. He was the class clown and didn't know when to turn that off and show us what he had. After a while, Nick developed the *"I'm hurt and can't work out today"* mindset and fell in with the group of complainers. Nick, who drove a Corvette and didn't make any bones about being in DSW and working for WWE, began seeing a high school girl. A high school girl! That was a problem. Shortly after that, he was in the ring with several other students while I was running a drill. Instead of listening and relaxing, he began to freak out and complained about being manhandled and abused. The next thing I know, he called the office and claimed I had beaten him up. He was eventually shipped off to OVW, where he became part of a group called the Spirit Squad. They were called up to *RAW* in January 2006, but he never took advantage of the opportunities of being on the main roster and was eventually released. That's too bad because I thought he was one of those guys who would have made a career in WWE. He just wasn't ready for what they wanted from him. He was a good kid and I pushed for him to get signed. I wanted him to succeed, but he just wasn't ready for what was ahead of him. It's too bad he didn't realize I was on his side.

What can I say about Trenesha Biggers other than that bitch was a huge thorn in my side. She had things outlined from the day of her tryout ... taking notes, telling stories, and engaging in adult activities with a few of the guys. She carried a notebook with her and wrote down things that happened. She also caused problems with her roommate, Kristal Marshall. Kristal told the office she wanted her to move out of their apartment because she didn't feel safe around her and some of her personal belongings were going "missing" whenever she was on the road. When Heath Miller got signed, Trenesha hitched her wagon to him and they were a couple for a while. More on Heath later.

From the very beginning, I told Dreamer, Johnny and Joe that she was trouble. I told them she wasn't there to wrestle, but to hitch a ride on the gravy train. At one point, she claimed she had head injuries and couldn't train, but miraculously recovered in time to work her way into TV storylines that required physical activity. The next day, she had another neck injury. They wasted money on her phony drama because she was no good for the business. She wanted the easy way in and didn't care how she got there. It didn't work though because she never did "get there." She was in Deep South less than six months when WWE rescinded her developmental contract. That was the last I heard about Trenesha until I read a newspaper report about her filing a "protection from abuse" order against Kurt Angle. I couldn't keep myself from giggling and thinking, *"I tried to tell everyone about this."*

Ken Thiessen, who was Vince McMahon's trainer, was both a liar and a crybaby. He caused a lot of problems before quitting (and blaming Joe and me, of course). He would throw around Vince McMahon's name in the hopes of intimidating Joe and me, but we didn't care. I told him on his first day there, *You have no background in wrestling, so there are certain things you won't be ready for or allowed to do."* He said, *"Okay,"* but then called Johnny and told him the opposite. After Ken and his wife were at my house with a bunch of others for a barbeque, he called Johnny and said I expected him to do what the others were doing without teaching him anything. When I confronted Ken, he began to cry in front of Joe and denied it, saying, *"I can't do this. It's just not for me."* When he called Johnny to tell him he was quitting, he claimed

I forced him out of DSW. Thiessen was a different cat. He just wasn't all there. It was almost like he had "caught" mental illness from Rombola. He didn't last long and I don't know what happened to him.

Just for the record, other than Oleg Prudius, all the complainers were either fired or cut from the main roster very quickly. I stand by my evaluations and judgment as a trainer and as a professional wrestler.

In January 2006, just four months after WWE began using DSW as a developmental territory, they thought Deep South could use another trainer. Dave Taylor, who had been wrestling since the late 1970s, lived in Atlanta and had been a fixture with WCW before WWE bought them out, so he was the obvious choice. Brad Armstrong and Tim Horner were also considered for the position. I actually think they brought Dave in to keep an eye on me, but I think he respected my work ethic and realized I was doing my job. We had worked with each other in WCW and I looked forward to his input. One of the first things I remember Dave saying was, *"I don't' know how you do it. Fuck all this stuff."* He saw the hours I put in, the problems I faced dealing with the talent, and the extra mile I went to help them. He said the drama gave him a headache and he didn't want any part of it.

I split the training into two sessions. Half of the students would work with Dave in the morning and the other half with me at noon. Every couple of weeks, we would mix it up so everyone was getting new and different training. It didn't take Dave long to pick out the students who were lazy and/or troublemakers. When he got tired of the attitudes and realized what he was up against, he quit putting the emphasis on the training. He just put them through a few drills and launched right into matches. When I asked him about it, he said he wasn't going to get mad and go out of his way to teach and train people who didn't listen. In time, though, he got so mad that he reversed course and began making them drill and train more.

Kevin Matthews was in Dave Taylor's class, but Kevin spent half his time blaming me for his short-comings and for things I had nothing to do with. He hurt his arm during one training session and went to the doctor's office. When he returned, his arm was in a sling. He sat around while everyone else trained. At the very least, he could have paid attention and tried to learn something through osmosis, but he didn't even do that. When Bob Holly visited the school, he spotted Kevin and asked me, *"What's that kid's story?"* After I filled him in on the details, Holly did what any veteran would have done to someone who was getting paid to train and join the main roster. He called him a pussy and said, *"Why don't you get off your lazy ass, get in the ring, and act like you want to be here."* Kevin didn't like being punked out in front of his peers, so he jumped into the ring to do one of the drills that involved the heavy bag. He immediately hurt himself again. And guess what? It wasn't long before he was telling everyone Bill De Mott hurt him!

Chapter 19

The Go-To Guys (and Girls)

As bad as the complainers were, I had several students step up and take leadership positions by helping demonstrate and train less-qualified students. They really knew their stuff. Angel Williams was my go-to girl for the ladies.

The Majors boys, Brett and Brian [Matthew Cardona and Brian Myers] were gold from the start and only got better. They were true wrestling fans who took advantage of all the things given and taught to them. I love those guys and am so proud of what they have done in WWE as Curt Hawkins and Zack Ryder. They were two of my all-time favorite kids. They were a true tag team. They hung out together, went to the movies together ... it was absurd! But they were the best team we had and they knew why they were there. No drama, no complaints, no trouble. They were ready to do what they signed up for.

Brett was on the tail end of one of my knife-throwing escapades. I'm good with a knife and I kept one in my briefcase in the office. On one promo day, Brett and Brian were acting obnoxious. I told them if they didn't leave, I would throw my knife at them. We jawed back and forth at each other (jokingly, of course) until I pulled out the knife. When they told me I wasn't going to throw it ... well, let's just say Bill De Mott isn't known to back down from a dare. I threw it. It stuck in the wall right next to the doorway ... the same doorway they ran through a second later. I never would have thrown that knife close enough to hit them and I knew exactly where I was throwing it, but to see the looks on their faces was priceless.

Brett and Brian were a good example of stand-up guys. The three of us knew it was all in fun. There were no complaints made and no reports submitted. It was just another good-time story for the gang at Deep South to tell each other. We had a lot of fun. We learned and trained together. I truly love those two boys.

Another good team at DSW was Derrick Neikirk [Derick Neikirk] and Mike Knox [Michael Hettinga]. Known as *Team Elite,* they came to Deep South from Les Thatcher's Heartland Wrestling Association and immediately set the pace for the rest of the crew.

An All-American in football and baseball during high school, Derick was drafted by the Detroit Tigers in the 1996 Major League Baseball Draft. When Derick decided to make pro wrestling his career, the thing he really had going for him was the fact he loved the sport and wanted it badly. He was a leader in the locker room and wasn't hesitant to speak his mind, which was one of the things I really loved about him. He was his own worst critic and it often hard to make him understand how to play "the game." Derick knew what he was supposed to do, and he knew what corporate was looking for, but he got pissed and emotional when he couldn't understand why he and others weren't called up or given a chance on the road when they were doing exactly what they were asked. Derick, who was labeled as one of my "headhunters" (someone I sent into the ring to hurt people on purpose) and stooges, almost got a break on WWE's *ECW* show, but it didn't work out. Derick later spent time with FCW before WWE released him from his contract for a violation of the Wellness Program. That was so far from the truth. Like many other good kids, he lost his way in the developmental system. He was just a talented kid who wanted to do what he was there to do. I believe Derick could still find his way in the business if he was willing to put up with the bullshit.

I found that if they kept the kids there too long, they stopped caring and developed attitudes. I couldn't help them because they were being fed bullshit from everyone in corporate. They keep trying, but after awhile, they would get bored, which led to them being sloppy and lazy, or worse, just giving up. Derick didn't do any of those things, but he did get frustrated a lot. It messes with your head when you do everything you're asked, but it's still not good enough to get you "called up."

Derick was so focused. He wasn't a drinker and wouldn't go out with us to party. When I did get him to loosen up one night and go to "D.D.'s," he got drunk and had a lot of fun. It was hilarious to watch. Derick was a consummate pro who had focus and wanted nothing more than to accomplish what he set out to do. What a great kid. I love Derick!

Mike Knox also had the heart for the business. He had the total package: he was big, was good-looking, and he moved really well for someone with such a big frame. He did everything the right way, but when they brought him up, they changed his look completely, from well-built and good-looking into an out-of-shape roughhouse character. It worked for him, though. Before his release in April 2010, he had a four-year run and appeared regularly on *ECW*, *RAW*, and *Smackdown*.

When it came to fun, Mike was the human highlight reel. He loves life, works and trains hard, and parties even harder. Mike was made for the wrestling business. He has a heart of gold.

The first time I laid eyes on Eric Perez [Eric Pérez], I knew he would be good. He languished in both DSW and FCW for a total of four years before getting his "break" with the main roster at WWE. Just four months after being called up, he was released from his contract. What the hell was that all about? Developmental isn't what it's cracked up to be. Guys like Eric do everything they're asked to do. They never get in trouble with the law or with the "wellness" bullshit, but they get cut while other douche bags get two and three chances. Eric was a talented kid who deserved more. I have nothing but love and admiration for him.

Eric was one of the most entertaining guys at the school. To prove he was one of the gang, on one "Make-A-Deal Friday," he put on one of the girls' bra and panties, stood in the middle of the ring, and let everyone hit him with a chop. It was hysterical ... and he did it with a smile. Again, just another kid I have so much love and respect for.

I don't really know where to begin with Freakin' Deacon [Drew Hankinson]. He had wrestled in the Northeast as Lorian Deville and came to me when he didn't make the cut in the *$1,000,000 Tough Enough*. When Drew first began training, he couldn't run the ropes and was kind of clumsy, but he picked things up quickly. He had such a great spirit during the time he was with us and I make it a point to watch him today whenever he appears on WWE programming. When he was with Deep South, he played as hard as he worked, but he never forgot the reason why he was there or let his personal life get in the way of his goals. I was in the shower one night when I thought of the name "Freakin' Deacon." When I pitched it to Drew and Joe, they loved it. Since then, he wrestled for the WWE as the Imposter Kane, Festus, and Luke Gallows, and currently wrestles on the independent circuit.

Freakin' Deacon, Steve Williams and Bill De Mott

One day, on a "Make-A-Deal Friday," Drew was coaxed into getting naked and hitting the turnbuckles, while swooshing jelly doughnuts with his ass into the face of the Bag Lady [Melissa Coates]. It was one of the funniest things I ever saw. The kids were all on the floor in hysterics. Regardless of what a few miserable assholes on the Internet say, that was a great group of kids.

I originally met Mike Taylor [Mike Sharrer] at OVW before he was given a developmental contract and was training on his own dime. I pushed hard to get him a developmental deal because he had a lot to offer. He worked all their TV and live events and really knew his stuff. When he came to Deep South, I relied a lot on Mike because he had an untouchable work ethic. He led by example. Whenever I wanted to demonstrate something to the group, Mike was the guy I used to get it done. At other times, when any of the kids lagged behind the others, Mike would help them while I worked with the more advanced students. Mike was at the top of the class when it came to conditioning, training, and work skills. He set the pace for everyone else and was the best all-around worker we had in DSW. On the other hand, he couldn't cut a promo and his people skills were lacking. Sadly, like so many other guys, Mike became miserable listening to all the hype and bullshit from the office. Mike can outwork half the talent in WWE today, but he never was given an honest shot.

Most of the time, when the talent went out at night, they would ask Lacey and me to join them. One night, Mike got so drunk that when we got to the car, he turned to me and said, *"Bill, I feel like shit."* With no warning whatsoever, he puked all over the place. Fortunately for him, he did it *outside* the car and he missed me. The funny thing is, no matter how much I drank, I didn't (and don't) puke, but that night in the parking lot, Mike Taylor made Bill De Mott puke all the way home. It's funny looking back on it, but it wasn't funny when Lacey was trying to get my big ass home.

MVP — that frickin' kid had the gift. His real name was Alvin Burke, Jr., but he first appeared as Antonio Banks, and later changed his to Montel Vontavious Porter, aka MVP. He knew why the company sent him to Atlanta and he went for it. He was a study of the business who constantly tried to improve on things and make them his own. He had a little bit of arrogance about him, but that was what set him apart from the crowd. He wanted to run with the ball and he let everyone know it. He cut a promo one time about a can of Campbell's Soup. Yeah, soup! One of my jobs was to record, copy, and send our promos to Talent Relations and Creative. That tape went along with the rest and I made sure they knew everything about him that they might need. He got called up and had a four-year run with the company. He now works for New Japan Wrestling. Banks was, and is, a hard worker, and I appreciated his way of doing things.

Brian Mailhot came to Deep South with probably the least expectations from any of us. During our workouts at Gold's Gym before the actual training began, he wasn't as agile as the others, but before my very eyes, he became one of the leaders of Deep South. Three months after he began training with us, an opportunity opened up for someone who might fit a certain character, so I threw his name to Stephanie McMahon. On the surface, Brian came across as a clean-cut, intellectual, office-type, which was exactly what Stephanie was looking for. I asked him to stop by the house and I gave him

Bill "congratulates" Palmer Canon after hearing about his call-up to the WWE main roster

my best pep talk. He took the script home, studied them, and we cut a promo the following day. Before I knew it, Brian was appearing on *Smackdown* as "Palmer Canon," a representative of the "Network," a backhanded shot at the UPN network for their attempted control of the content which appeared on the show.

During a tour of Italy, he returned home early to the States after citing harassment from John "Bradshaw" Layfield. There were a few WWE "superstars" in on the hazing and Brian felt it went beyond anything considered acceptable. When he called to tell me he was leaving Italy, I knew he was making the right decision. Brian is an intelligent man. He knew he was in a no-win situation and wasn't welcome there. When he arrived home, he asked for his release. The company begged him to reconsider, but Brian had made up his mind and wasn't going to back down. Afterwards, the company tried to paint a picture of Brian as a quitter and a pussy, but for those who knew him, Brian was far from being either of those. He was a standup guy. It was one of those few times I was really angry about the way someone had been treated.

I wish Brian hadn't quit, but he was convinced there would be more repercussions if he returned. Brian worked hard to make it to the main roster. I know for a fact he respected the talent he worked with and wanted to fit in and do his job. When the problems in Europe took place, he knew in his heart it wasn't the business he thought it was and made the best decision for himself.

The very first DSW diva was Angel Williams [Lauren Williams]. I think so much of Angel. We first met when she had her tryout at OVW. I knew immediately that she had the goods and made a quick recommendation for them to hire her. She trained with the guys and did everything they did without complaint. She was with Deep South for almost two years, which was much too long. Several times, corporate talked about bringing her up. Shortly before the one time when it was almost a certainty, she tore her ACL during a TV taping and was put on the sidelines. It was terrible timing and I felt badly for her. It took a long time for me to get her mentally back into it. When DSW shut down in April 2007, the company transferred her to OVW. One month later, she had her first match, only to be released from her developmental contract the following day. I don't know the whole story behind it, but some people said she had heat in the locker room. Others said she didn't mix well with the other girls. That was a shame because she could (and can) really work, but WWE's loss was Total Nonstop Action's gain as Angel has been working for them since September 2007. She has

Casey, Angelina Love and Keri

also appeared on several television shows and an independent movie called *Good Intentions*.

One story I remember about Angel was during a time when she was living in a "shady" apartment complex in McDonough. When her apartment was broken into one night (I believe she was home), she showed up on our doorstep looking spooked and nervous, as she should have. We told her she could stay with us as long as she wanted. That story is important only because there were many times when one or more of the students stayed at our house (for various reasons). Lacey always made them feel like family. We loved Deep South and were committed to doing everything we could for those kids. Lacey and I both love Angel and we stay in touch with her. She was a good girl and is one of my favorites.

Shantelle Taylor [Shantelle Malawski]. Wow! Shantelle had the goods. She could outwork most of the guys there. She needed help with her promos, but when it came to wrestling, she had it all. She was a very attractive girl, as well. Again, like so many other good talents, she never got the shot with WWE she deserved and was released from her contract in August 2007. They did bring her in a couple of times to appear on *SmackDown*. However, they weren't looking for a girl, so they dressed her up (hid her) in an "Ultimo Dragon" outfit and called her "Sans-Eye." The fans didn't know she was a girl because she was a good wrestler and worked like a Mexican or Japanese guy. Nothing came of it, but it was funny.

After she was let go, she had some photos taken by a photographer, who in turn was contacted by WWE, who asked about the girl (Shantelle) he was showcasing. Someone from WWE called and asked a few questions, which she answered, and ... BOOM! She was named "WWE Fan of the Month" in *WWE Magazine*. They didn't even know who she was! I mean, are you kidding? You would think someone who saw her photos would have recognized her. Then again, that's the problem with "non-wrestling people" running parts of a wrestling business. They don't know or follow the product.

Nine months after her release, while pursuing a college degree in psychology, she was contacted by Total Nonstop Action Wrestling [TNA] and given a contract. As with Angel, TNA benefitted from WWE's loss. Shantelle worked for them from May 2008 until December 2010.

Finally, there was Mike Mizanin, who now wrestles for WWE as "The Miz." I first met Mike at a charity event during the time when he was appearing on MTV's *Real World* Mike. We met again when he was a contestant on the *$1,000,000 Tough Enough*. What people don't know is that Mike was a diehard wrestling fan who wanted to be a professional wrestler long before he appeared on reality TV. I believe that was the edge he held over most of the other students. He wasn't just "camera struck." He really wanted it.

Mike was good. When he first came to Deep South, he wasn't the most talented, but man, did he ever work on his craft. He worked hard and proved himself every day. He could talk and he created his own "homegrown" character. He didn't play the "Miz" character. He *became* the "Miz" character. It was who he was (especially when drinking). The Deep South fans really took to Mike, and since the office was really high on him, we made him our first Deep South heavyweight champion.

Casey De Mott, The Miz and Keri De Mott

We brought in Matt Cappotelli to train with Mike in the hope that Matt's "babyface" appeal would help Mike. It wasn't a great fit. They were two good kids, but they just weren't on the same page. They were two different people with different personalities — Miz outgoing and Matt more reserved. Matt had just laid down roots in OVW (perhaps the girlfriend he later went on to marry) and he didn't want to relocate to Atlanta, a fact he let me know in no uncertain terms. He had no interest in training and did as little as possible. He even told me he wasn't going to stay too long to work out. All he wanted to do was get booked in matches on TV or with Miz on tag team stuff. As it turned out, Mike didn't really need help from Matt, anyway. Mike (as the Miz) became the standout, and judging by his career so far, I believe I'm correct.

We had a similar problem with Elijah Burke when he came to use from OVW. He walked into the building, watched some of the workout, and he was never seen again. He went back to Louisville, crying and telling stories about how hard we were on the students. Burke got his way and didn't have to report to us again. What a pussy. The kids at OVW had a different mindset and weren't willing to change what they did or didn't do.

When Miz was called up, there was something about him that rubbed some of the talent the wrong way. When he came in, they all thought he was going to steal their thunder because he was used to being noticed and the women were all over him. The only person I know who put Miz in his place was Lacey. One night, while were hanging out in a crowded bar, Mike was being "Mike," and Lacey just flat out told him he wasn't all he thought he was. They talked for a good while and they both walked away smiling. Lacey never hesitated to tell the kids what she thought when they asked (and at times when they didn't), and I believe there were times when they wished they hadn't asked.

Mike is currently at the top of his game with the company. I'm very proud of what he has accomplished and the way he carries himself.

Chapter 20

Falling Up the Wall

I worked with many other hopefuls and future stars. I was thrilled to get the opportunity to work with Afa Anoa'i, Jr., and help a member of the great Samoan family. Afa was a good kid who had a lot of talent.

Another one of the Samoans I had the opportunity to work with was Afa's tag team partner, Sonny Siaki. On the day I met him, I pegged him as one of the leaders. He was good and he had a real desire to advance, but I learned he wouldn't go the extra mile when it came to training or doing what it took to stand out. Sonny had worked for World Championship Wrestling [WCW] and TNA before coming to DSW, so he had already proven himself and deserved to be with the superstars. It didn't work out and he was released from his developmental contract in September 2007 after a short run at the FCW school. I wish he had done more for himself because Sonny had everything it took to make it in the business, although his personality and character alone should have found him a spot on the roster.

The best thing I remember about Sonny is what he did for his 35-year-old brother, Bernard, who was suffering from renal failure. Sonny donated one of his kidneys so Bernard could survive … but it also meant Sonny would no longer be able to wrestle. He worked hard for nine years to make it as a wrestler and sacrificed it all to save his brother. Sonny has a big heart. He has my utmost respect.

Big Vito [Vito LoGrasso] trained at OVW for just a few months before he was brought up to the WWE talent roster. After an 18-month run, he came to Deep South to train. Depending on who you ask, he chose to come to DSW, but WWE claims they sent him to us because they had nothing for him. We made good use of his talents, but shortly after we made him DSW heavyweight champion, he let his mouth get him into trouble. It wasn't so much what he said, but the way he said things and talked to people. I love Vito, but he was a walking campaign for putting himself over, especially after we made him Deep South champion. His peers told me he took being a "champion" way too seriously. For whatever reason, he was always throwing out his "wrestling resume" and accomplishments, and that turned off a lot of people. The funny thing is, he was a really good worker (in my opinion and others). If he had just let his actions "show" everyone how good he was, rather than "telling" everyone how good he was, people would have been impressed. He was released from his contract in May 2007 after a 20-month run with the company.

Big Vito, Lash Larue and Bill

From day one, Tony Santarelli [Anthony Salantri] had no self confidence. He was a train wreck. I mean, I always worried about walking into the gym to find him hanging from the rafters or something. He would go out and play tackle football with other students, get hurt, and then try to act like he got hurt during training so he could sit out. When I finally called him out on the football thing, he gave everyone else up, as well. They couldn't understand they were getting paid to train and wrestle, not get hurt playing tackle football. I had several conversations with him about toning things down so he didn't kill himself. Another time, when Lacey was cooking for the Deep South kids, he fell "up the wall" of my new house and left scrape marks on the wall. I can't explain what I mean by "fell up the wall," but his feet were above his head. It looked like he had jumped from the upstairs loft. I thought it was funny until he proceeded to fall over the sofa and break the candle holders Lacey had saved from our wedding. He was banned from our house for a good six months after that.

Tony was a good wrestler and made a very good tag team with Mike Taylor as "High Impact." They were our first tag team champions, but they just never caught on. That really bothered both of them, but Tony wouldn't get over himself and he began self destructing. Being released from his contract was the best thing for him. I liked him, but I worried about him even more.

Bradley Jay [Brad Bradley] was a big kid with no sense of humor and no people skills. He was always butting heads with other students. The first time we convinced Brad to go with us to D.D.'s with us, we tried to get him to drink. He wouldn't drink with anyone. He was too good for that. We tried to get him to flirt with the local girls. He was too good for that. He just wouldn't lighten up and become "one of the guys." It was kind of sad. Granted, he tried hard to fit in, but several people told me he would bury others to put himself over. I knew that because he would always tell me how the others didn't seem to take the training as seriously as he did, and he kept asking what he had to do to get out of Deep South. Of course, that's what people are supposed to be doing, but he had the attitude he shouldn't have to train with the others. He also was uncoordinated when he first came to us, not to mention dangerous to work with due to him doing things for himself. In time, he became pretty good and came out of his shell, but he just never hit his stride. His opinion of himself was much higher than his talent.

Claudio Castagnoli. What a talent! He came to spend a week with us and we immediately realized he had the goods. With just a little fine tuning, he would be "good to go." Sadly to say, after he took a physical, the company doctor called to tell me he wouldn't be coming back. Something about his blood work instantly threw up red flags. *"We can't touch this kid."* That was a shame because, in my opinion, he was one helluva talent.

One of the local kids we used and liked was Cru Jones. He was out of shape compared to the regular Deep South crew and he didn't want to go through what they had gone through. He was okay and I believe he could have been very good, but Cru was happy being a big fish in the little Georgia independent pond. He had an opportunity to get signed and blew it. In my opinion, it worked out best for everyone. He had a good job and, again in my opinion, was happy just "playing" pro wrestler.

Damian Steel [Damien Dothard] was another good, local kid. If I remember correctly, Eric Watts introduced him to us and I invited him to train to see what he had to offer. He came to the shows and did everything we asked him to do. When I introduced him to Johnny and Tommy and suggested he be given a chance, they signed him. While he was there, he really improved and he fit right in with the rest of the kids. However, like Castagnoli, something happened when he took his physical and I got a call telling me to send him home "right now!" Of course, his immediate dismissal sent up red flags among the talent, many of whom began to whisper about the possibilities of HIV or something. I didn't know that and didn't want people saying it was, but the office and students both freaked at the idea of him getting cut, accidentally or otherwise, and getting blood on another talent. When we were told to send him home, Joe and I were both asked if he had been cut or if he had been working with any open wounds. We never saw or heard from him again. He was only 34 years old when he died of a brain aneurism at his home in Smyrna, Georgia, on July 22, 2009.

Another local indy guy who came to every TV taping was Heath Miller. He would do whatever we asked and eventually began showing up to workout with my guys. He got signed to developmental and made his debut on the *WWE NXT* program as Heath Slater.

Danny Gimondo [Danny Gimondo], a fellow-Jersey kid who had been a great amateur wrestler in high school, had several tryouts with WWE before he began training in OVW. I had known Danny since he was a teenager in New Jersey trying to find a way to get involved in the business. He eventually began working the indies in Jersey and made the move on his own to Louisville. He paid his own way, worked hard, and was in the system for a couple of years before he actually got signed. Danny's biggest claim to fame was breaking CM Punk's nose on September 26, 2005 ... on the night Punk made his big OVW debut. Unfortunately, Danny became another casualty of the developmental program. He changed his look, his name (he had wrestled for almost a decade as the Inferno Kid and Danny Inferno), his ring gear, and did everything we asked of him ... and it wasn't good enough. It wasn't anything he did wrong. He just didn't have that "something" that made him stand out enough for someone to put their stamp of approval on him. He never got back on the WWE path after he was released from Deep South and moved back to New Jersey after some hardships and relationship issues. I have a lot of time for Danny.

David Heath, better known as Gangrel, worked with us during the latter part of 2006. Dave and I went back to my days in Puerto Rico, where he was the best roommate I ever had (not counting Lacey, of course). He would drive from Florida each and every week in the hopes of getting back on the WWE roster. He had a lot of experience and was always eager to share his knowledge with the Deep South talent. He had been in the wrestling business since 1988 and had worked a full-time schedule with WWE for the better part of three years [1998-2001], and yet, during his time with us, he acted like he was being trained. Even though Dave was a true veteran of the business, he never complained about lying down in the middle of the ring and doing a job for one of the students. Dave was good for DSW. He had a presence about him when he came through the curtain and got into the ring, and I enjoyed watching him change into Gangrel when his music began playing. The funny things was, he was always nervous before going out, just like when we first began wrestling in the old days. He was focused, worked snug, and was very believable. In fact, he scared the crap out of the kids — not just the kids in the audience, but the kids training with DSW.

Frankie Coverdale [Francisco Ciatso], who was buddies with the Shane twins, was another guy who drove from Florida for every TV taping. When the twins told him we would use him if he would come to Atlanta, he showed up with Ron Niemi, who we began using on our TV program as a commentator. Frankie worked hard, but we could never get him out of what I called the "independent mode." He was set in his ways and a throwback to the early '80s style of work. That's not a knock. He was good and knew his craft.

George Murdoch came into DSW with a great attitude and a glowing personality. In no time at all, he was accepted by everyone as a "Deep South guy." He would later turn out to be one of the biggest assholes I have ever met. He fell into the trap of being a stooge and refusing to be a part of the team. His attitude changed so suddenly — almost overnight — and the people he was closest to were the ones he treated the worst. Most of his relationships went bad during his last few months with Deep South. George was a no-talent phony who never amounted to anything,, although he was re-signed by WWE in December 2010 and now wrestles on the *NXT* program as Brodus Clay. The only interesting thing about him was his ring name — G-Rilla. I could really tear him down, but I won't. (or have I already?)

Jack Swagger [Jacob Hager], an NCAA All-American heavyweight wrestler at the University of Oklahoma, worked with us for a short time. In addition to being a "sponge" and soaking up everything there was to learn, he played a great game of dominoes. He was a great kid, a gifted athlete, and a lot of fun to be around. I wish they were all like him. He is now one of the biggest stars on WWE TV.

Mack Johnson, who had been training with OVW on his own, liked it there, but when WWE told him they would hire him if he moved to Atlanta, he took them up on their offer. They weren't real high on him, but they needed bodies in the new system. He was homesick from his first day there. During the next few months, he asked to be able to go back to Louisville to train, only to be told he would be fired if he left. He eventually quit, although he would have been released, anyway, because he didn't really make the grade and he fell short of peoples' expectations. He was another example of the wrestling business not being for everyone.

During training one day, Mack was jumping around, in, and out of the ring. One time, he jumped off the apron onto the bleachers and speared himself on the top of one of the rails. The rail went right up his ass and he actually split where he was already split, if you get my drift. We thought it was hilarious, but he didn't see anything funny about it, especially since he had to go to the hospital. I never did know whether or not he had to have stitches. There are just some things guys don't ask other guys.

Although they weren't under contract, Antonio Mestre, Lawrence Tyler [Lawrence Boyer], and Johnny Curtis [Jonathan Curtis] all came to Atlanta and paid Joe to train at Deep South. They all trained hard and acted like they were under contract. We had guys there who were making $500 to $1,500 a week who didn't put in as much effort as those guys. Not one of the three ever complained about anything and they deserved the opportunities that other less-talented individuals were getting. Antonio, who worked two part–time jobs to pay his way through Deep South, never made it to WWE, while Johnny was given a developmental contract and transferred to FCW when WWE cut ties with Deep South.

Johnny was a good kid who fit in instantly. He knew how to make friends and he proved himself every day. One time, Daniel Rodimer gave me a pair of cowboy boots. I have no idea why he did that. Anyone who knows me knows I don't wear that shit. One night, while we were drinking at my house, I gave Johnny the boots. They were meant for me, but Dan turned into such an asshole (after he gave me the boots) that I gave them to Curtis to wear in front of him.

Lawrence's original purpose for coming to Atlanta was to see Derrick Neikirk and Mike Knox. When he showed up, he had his hot wife with him, who I believed could have been signed right away. Lawrence actually had a shot to get signed, but on the day it was supposed to happen, he got cold feet and left the building. He was torn between wrestling and a very good business he ran in Arizona … a whorehouse! That's the truth! I was a bit miffed because it made me look a little stupid, but I respect him for getting out when he knew it wasn't going to be his cup of tea. He was a nice kid, but it just wasn't for him.

Johnny Parisi [Joseph Dorgan] had been in the business for 12 years and worked for WCW, TNA, and the original ECW as "Johnny Swinger" before he signed a developmental deal with WWE. After training with OVW for four months, he was transferred to DSW. He came in with the attitude that he didn't belong there, which both surprised and disappointed me because I was a fan of his work. I'm sure we can chalk up some of his attitude to Swinger being older and lazy. He was a friend of Dreamer and Tommy saved him a few times, which only added to Swinger's attitude of being untouchable. He got called up to wrestle on *Sunday Night Heat* almost a dozen times, but he never made the cut. Joe is a good guy, but as Johnny "Swinger," seems to think he's more than what he is. If he had remained a "good Joe," he could have been a leader of talent, rather than doing independents and getting occasional "rubs" in TNA (again, through Dreamer).

Matt Striker [Matthew Kaye] was the opposite of Joe. Having wrestled in extensively in the Northeast and in Japan, he was called up to WWE before ever appearing at the DSW building. Since he had so much publicity going in, he was hated by the guys on the main roster. They constantly kicked him out of the locker rooms on the road and at TVs because they looked at him as a greenie and didn't like the fact that he acted confident and was outspoken. When they sent him to us, I told him the past didn't matter. He would be getting a fresh start. One of the reasons I like Matt was that he was trained by the best trainer in the history of the business — Johnny Rodz. Have I already mentioned Johnny? Matt trained at Gleason's Gym, my old stomping grounds, and had his first professional match in 2000. Matt was so smart and such a student of the game that he had to dumb himself down and put up with a lot of crap when he was on the WWE roster, but not when he came to us. He fit right in. He was called up fairly quickly and became one of the "voices of WWE TV" hosting and commentating on *ECW*, *RAW*, *SmackDown*, and *WWE NXT*. From what I understand, he's now working in the office. I liked Matt a lot and miss our conversations. He has a real love for the business.

One of the classic stories from Deep South involving Matt had to do with Neil Pruitt. After Neil edited one particular show, he told Joe and I that he couldn't use a lot of the footage because Matt looked ridiculous, and called him out for "stuffing his trunks" to make his "package" look bigger. When Neil finished his rant, Matt politely told Neil, *"That's all me,"* to which Neil replied, *"Bullshit!"* I suggested Matt take Neil into my office and show him. When Neil walked back out a few seconds later, he said he had been wrong to think Matt was stuffing his trunks. I still think Matt was full of shit, but Neal shot Matt from all angles after that. He also talked to Matt more often (wink-wink).

Keith Walker, who wrestled as Keith Samson, and Robert Anthony both came to Deep South in November 2006, shortly before WWE pulled out and transferred everything to Florida Championship Wrestling.

Keith had some potential, but he just didn't catch on as fast as he should have. Originally trained at Harley Race's World League Wrestling, he had wrestled in Japan for Pro Wrestling Noah. He couldn't loosen up and was considered to be a "crowbar" who often hurt people, or put them in a position to get hurt. In part, it was simply clumsiness due to his size. He was an example of the guys who bring their indie habits with them and find it hard to change things up. It was a difficult transition, but as a whole, Keith was a hard worker and a great kid.

Robert also was a good kid who could really work. He had a few habits to break, but he trained hard and listened to what we told him. The only real problem he had was wanting to do high spot after high spot without slowing down to tell a story, or to give people time to take in what he was doing.

Both Keith and Robert were released from their contracts before they were called up.

Kid Kash [David Cash] had a good background as a professional fighter before being introduced to professional wrestling by Ricky Morton, one-half of the famous Rock 'n' Roll Express tag team. Like Johnny Swinger, the Kid had experience with ECW, WCW, and TNA before coming to Deep South. He had a veteran's attitude and wanted to be called up to the major leagues, and like Swinger, he thought having to train at DSW with kids who were just beginning their careers was beneath him. One day, Johnny Ace called and told me he was going to fire Kash, claiming he had an attitude (like most of the other guys didn't?). I told him he couldn't fire a Deep South guy without letting us tell him first. Joe and I went to bat for Kash and he was eventually called up. During his time on the roster, he won the Cruiserweight title, but he was released from his contract after nine months. I liked the Kid. He could really wrestle, but he refused to listen to the things that could have saved his job.

And then there was Kofi Kingston [Kofi Sarkodie-Mensah], who got a degree in communications from Boston College, but chose to put that aside to become professional wrestler. Wow! I repeat myself ... wow! What a great athlete. He did everything he came to do and was a great addition to the DSW roster. And look at him now. He is a WWE superstar!

The funniest thing about Kofi was the fact that he got hired to do the Jamaican gimmick ... and for the longest time, he never let anyone know he wasn't Jamaican. He worked his gimmick everywhere. I popped huge one night during *RAW* when he spoke perfect English and one of the stars asked, *"What happened to your accent?"* He just continued to speak perfect English, as if he had been doing it all along. It was an honor to know a guy like Kofi, who has so much respect for the business that he lived his gimmick 24/7.

One guy I was really high on was T.J. Wilson [Theodore Wilson]. I worked with TJ during his tryout week and I really liked him. I raved about him in the reviews I sent to Johnny Ace. By the time he reported, to DSW, I had been canned, so I didn't get to work with him. He was talented, though, and can be seen working as Tyson Kidd on WWE television.

I first met Ray Gordy [Terry Ray Gordy, Jr.] when he was brought to OVW with Joe Hennig. Ray had been wrestling in Japan for Pro Wrestling Noah and an independent promotion in Georgia. I liked Ray and pushed to get him signed to a developmental contract. He was signed in August 2005, but got frustrated fast when he was held to a higher standard than the others, especially by Michael Hayes. At times, he was a leader, but after a time, he would get disgusted and shut down. Ray could really work, but he just couldn't find the "character" they were looking for. As a person, Ray was one of the funniest guys I ever met, but when he got in front of the camera, he just couldn't get out a sentence. After awhile, he became the class clown. He was one hell of a worker, but he just couldn't talk. He was a great kid and it was an honor to work with him.

Roughhouse O'Reilly [Ryan Parmeter] started out a little rough (no pun intended) and was lacking in confidence, but he trained hard and learned quickly. He was one of the guys the complainers accused of being one of my "headhunters." Ryan made a couple of appearances on *RAW* in 2007, but asked to be released from his contract when his girlfriend, Krissy Vaine, asked for hers. I couldn't believe, after all he went through, he quit because he wanted to be with his girlfriend. Right or wrong, I have to give him credit for standing by his woman, but I was disappointed when it went down. I'm happy to say, however, that three years later, he was re-signed by WWE and spent

Michelle McCool (standing) clowns around with Roughhouse O'Reilly, Joe Hamilton and Bill Demott in the Deep South office

four months at the FCW training center wrestling as Conor O'Brian. He now wrestles on the *WWE NXT* show. I love Ryan and think he has a chance to make it big if he can stay focused. He's a good kid.

Tommy Suede [Thomas Farra] was one of the guys tied in with Matthews, Omega and Rombola. They knew each other from earlier days on the independent circuit. He had been taught one way and he wasn't going to change. He thought I was messing with him and just wanting him to do things my way. It was a struggle. And then one day, somebody who looked, sounded, and acted like Tommy walked into the gym ... but it couldn't have been Tommy. This guy listened intently to everything I said, did everything I asked, and became one of the leaders. He improved in every area of his training. Later, when I asked him about his change of attitude, he told me what I had been saying began to make sense. Unfortunately, he didn't catch anyone's eye at WWE, so he was released and he went back to wrestle and train in Pennsylvania. Tommy was a great guy. I wish I had been given more time with him. He was talented! Tommy went on to appear in the movie *The Wrestler*, helping train Randy "The Ram" [Mickey Rourke] for the part and wrestling Randy in the first match of the film.

My most lasting memory of Tommy is of what happened a few months after he was released. After going home to Pennsylvania, he sent me a message telling me he now trains his people the way I trained him. He closed by thanking me for "hanging in there" with him and the time we spent together.

Ryan Reeves [Ryan Reeves], who I first met at the *$1,000,000 Tough Enough*, was one of the kids who wrestled on our very first show. He was built like a brick shithouse. Ryan was a good kid who struggled with being in the mix of talent at DSW. Some of the kids were really good, while others, like Ryan, put a lot of pressure on themselves to keep up. Ryan was moved to OVW, but was later released for a year before being brought back. I liked Ryan a lot. He was one of my favorites both in and out of DSW.

Chapter 21

Deep South Divas

Oh, yes. The Deep South divas.

I've already written about Angel Williams and Shantelle Taylor.

I believe Daisy Mae [Jennifer Thomas] was Jack Bull's girlfriend. That was a shame because she was a nice girl and was good in the ring, but she inherited his heat. She didn't do anything to deserve it. It was just that Jack Bull was a dick, so she was guilty by association.

Kristal Marshall was a hard nut to crack in the beginning. She wasn't used to being physical, but she trained and tried everything we asked her to do. All of a sudden, it was as if a switch had been flipped and a light had been turned on. She was a different person. When she got the hang of things, she was good and she had a lot of enthusiasm. I grew to like her a lot and I was happy when she got called up to *Smackdown*. It was always funny and rewarding to me when kids like her came to the realization that I was on their side.

Luscious [LaQuanda Woodard] was a local girl from Roberta, Georgia, who paid Joe to be trained (by me), and since she was paying, Joe wanted to use her more on the shows. WWE always told us they wanted the contracted talent to be used before anyone, but it was Joe's show and Joe's call, and since she was paying him, he wanted her involved. "La La" was a nice girl, but didn't learn enough and quickly got full of herself. She felt like she had it all and was ready to move on ... which she did. She moved back to Roberta, Georgia ... population 727.

What can I say about Michelle McCool [Michelle McCool]. Like everyone else, I was in love with her. She had a never-say-die attitude and never quit, even though she battled several illnesses and personal issues. For a time, she was gone more than she was there, but she got called up and is the WWE Divas champion as I write this. Contrary to rumors among the DSW talent, I never spoke badly of Michele and was (and am) very proud of her. She is a good girl and I wish her well.

Rebecca DiPietro [Rebecca DiPietro] was Batista's girlfriend and she let everyone know it. When WWE found her, she was a model and beauty pageant contestant. In 2001, she did a photo shoot for *Playboy*, and me, being a subscriber (for the articles, of course), I asked her to sign my copy, which she did. She was a nice girl, but I really don't think she was cut out for what WWE signed her for. She was passable as an announcer for a while, but she definitely wasn't diva material.

Melissa Coates spent some time in OVW before coming to Deep South as "The Bag Lady," a great character for our TV. She trained hard and had a real desire to learn. Melissa was the female version of Shawn Stasiak. She was always trying to read into things and overanalyze what we were asking her to do. WWE had plans for her and was on the verge of signing her, but instead of just doing what they asked, she wanted to talk about it. *"Where is this leading?" "Can I do this?" "Wouldn't this be better? "Would the bag lady really do this?"* As the Bag Lady, she was a great character for TV, but every vignette took twice as long because of her ad libs. After a while, nobody wanted to work with her or help her. She made it harder than it should have been.

Mike Taylor's wife, Tracy [Tracy Castillio], moved to Atlanta when Mike was hired. After Angel Williams wrestled the guys for a few weeks, I asked Tracy if she wanted to train with her to keep her from getting so beaten up. Tracy was great. She trained with everyone in DSW and we got her signed to a developmental deal. I think Tracy on her own could have been brought up as a diva on the WWE roster, but she was linked to the High Impact [Mike Taylor and Tony Santarelli] angle and never broke away from it. Unfortunately, when Deep South parted ways with WWE, she left without getting a shot. Tracy didn't even got a phone call from Mike Bucci to tell her she was being released. Bucci simply told Mike to give her the news. It's a shame Bucci didn't even have the courtesy to "man up" and talk to her himself. I love Tracy. She's a really good girl and deserved better.

Krissy Vaine [Kristin Eubanks] was another girl who came in thinking she knew it all, and being the girlfriend of Kevin Matthews was another strike against her. She wasn't really comfortable at first, but like some of the others, I think she realized we were all there for the same reason. When Krissy finally came into her own, she owned everything she did. Her work and promos improved to a point where she became the "general manager" of the DSW TV shows and she got over great. I truly like Krissy and miss having her around. She had a great personality and a good spirit.

Earlier, I wrote about Kevin Matthews losing Krissy to Ryan O'Reilly. Kevin's world really fell apart after she left him, and before that happened, Greg Gagne was all over Krissy and Matthews did nothing about it. It was pathetic to watch. If he wasn't such an immature asshole, I might have felt sorry for him, but Krissy later told me Matthews had a problem with jealousy and had threatened her a few times.

The moral to the story is you shouldn't bring your wife or girlfriend around the business. There were a few times when I called certain talent into my office and told them how group relationships caused problems, but kids will be kids and there were some arguments after a few rolls in the hay. Things like that even happened when I was wrestling. The three examples that stand out most in my mind are Marc Mero and Sable, Kevin Sullivan and Nancy, and Matt Hardy and Lita, but there were guys who lost their "girls" to other guys all the time. I always told the guys, *"If your wife or girlfriend matters to you, keep them away from the boys. Shit happens and human nature takes over."*

Rule number one: Keep your girl away from the boys backstage, and *never* let them party with the guys, whether you're there or not.

Rule number two: Stay the hell away from another guy's girl ... whether they are still together or not! It just makes everybody uncomfortable.

During my years on the road, I saw a lot of guys struggling with their personal lives (me included). When people spend a lot of time together, they grow close, and they become the "shoulder" to lean on. It's hard on relationships, and being one of the boys didn't make it any easier. There are too many distractions and opportunities. I'm not saying everyone got distracted, but when you spend so much time on the road away from your significant other, problems develop. All the fame, money, and toys are no substitute for being solid with your relationships at home. It's a shame just how many couples ended due to a lack of communication or being apart.

One of the hardest things for me was to see guys with their "friends," and then seeing them with their girlfriend or wife at shows and events. It gets to a point where you forget which is which.

I think if anyone is going to be honest about this subject, the answer is simply, yes, there have always been and always will be problems with relationships when you are on the road ... but, it's the same in any professional sport or entertainment. It's just that we don't hear that about wrestling. We hear about death and drugs, but we very rarely hear about the human element and the toll separation takes on people, which, unfortunately, leads to problems.

Okay, back to the divas. Poor Natalie Neidhart signed a contract with WWE on January 5, 2007, exactly two weeks before I was released. Nattie and TJ Wilson came to the same tryout. After the tryout, someone from Talent Relations told them, *"We're gonna send you to Louisville."*

Nattie said, *"I'd like to go back to Atlanta to train with Bill. I like the way he does things."* Go figure! I had 10 to 12 guys complaining about how hard things were, and then there's a chick saying she'd rather go to Atlanta to train with Bill De Mott. Two days before Nattie got there, I was fired. She called me and asked, *"What do I do now?"*

Why doesn't anybody talk about that? About the kids like Nattie, who called WWE and asked to be assigned to me because they liked my method of training? They only talk about the one kid who was upset because he landed on his head every day and asked to be transferred.

I told Nattie that she got her job on her own merits and to do what they asked her to do. I absolutely *loved* Nattie's attitude and her passion for the business. She had the goods and I'm happy to know she's doing well today as one of the main divas on the WWE roster. I would have liked to have had the opportunity to work with her more. She was a great young lady.

Chapter 22

Attack of the Killer Squats

In January 2006, I was blessed with the opportunity to train a "movie star," the Great Khali [Dalip Singh Rana]. Most of you might know him as Turley, the giant in the movie *The Longest Yard* [2005]. That cat is 7-foot-4 and, at the time, weighed 400 pounds (or so). Tommy Dreamer carted him around for a month and then we had to "take turns" driving him to the gym and the grocery store, doing his laundry, taking his wife where she needed to go, setting up his computer, and taking care of his living arrangements. "Dali" had an agent who could do all that, but not in McDonough, Georgia. Nonetheless, all the talent and I had to babysit him. We were also told to train him separately from the rest of the talent and to appoint a few guys to be "bodies" for him. As always, it would be the guys who were there all the time (Palmer Canon, Mike Knox, Freakin' Deacon, Eric Perez). None of them ever complained. In fact, they volunteered to be Dali's punching bag and to help him with any and all aspects of his training. Those cats were there for every session *and* anything that would get them more ring time. He was treated very well and the guys took him under their wing.

Dali was the worst assignment I ever had because he had no business coming to Deep South. They didn't send him to us to teach him anything special. Johnny just wanted us to get some legs under him and teach him the basics because he was so clumsy and dangerous. *"He doesn't have any legs. He doesn't have any balance. But Vince says he's our next superstar, so get him some legs."*

It didn't take long before Dali began to complain about having to come in and train during the week. He told Vince, Johnny, and Undertaker that I made him run laps and do drills. I know I'm probably nit-picking here, but he never did run or do squats. He did stretches and things in the corner that resembled squats, but he never did anything too strenuous. The next thing you know, I get a call from Johnny telling me Vince and Taker were pissed because I was mistreating him. Well, how was I supposed to get legs under him if he didn't run or do squats? I didn't do anything for him after that. A lot of those guys trained extra hours to help me teach Dali things he needed to know and he crapped on us.

After getting a taste of traveling and working with Undertaker (whom I have the greatest respect for in and out of the ring and have had the privilege of training and working with), Dali decided he was traveling too much (a one-day-a-week trip to McDonough) and didn't need to come to the gym like he was told to do. I couldn't win. I even caught shit for that. I was told to "get him in the ring every day he isn't traveling and get his ass in shape."

That didn't sit well with Dali. He didn't like having to report in and worked the "language barrier" as an excuse for not showing up. The truth was, he understood everything we said, but he worked the "DUH" factor. I would call Johnny and say, *"Your high-priced giant wasn't here again today."* He was making a ridiculous amount of money just because he was big and he didn't want to do anything to get himself in shape!

When he did show up, he refused to do anything physical, so we decided to work on his "mannerisms" and teach him how to look more menacing in the ring. As tough as it was to get him to do what we asked, I had a good relationship with Dali from his first day there. When we were training, I was constantly saying, *"Quit smiling! You have to look angry!"* I finally decided that every time he smiled, I would hit him in the chin with my three middle knuckles. At first, the other guys couldn't believe I got away with it, but they later thought it was funny to see me swatting a life-sized giant. Every now and then, after I gave him a reminder, Dali would grab me and we would roll around the ring and wrestle. We had a lot of fun ... until Johnny told me I had to get serious about making him stop smiling. I told the group that every time he smiled or didn't follow through, he "and the rest of the crew" would have to run laps and/or do squats. It was a rib! "We" were trying to motivate the big son-of-a-bitch.

Well, Dali went to TV the following day and told Undertaker, Vince, and Johnny I "made him run laps around the training center and do squats. ("Bill made us do squats" was the thing everyone always said) All hell broke loose and I got another phone call from Johnny, who said Taker and Vince were pissed again and wanted to know why I was abusing "Vince's newest giant." People give me too much credit for "making a giant" do things he didn't want to do. I have to admit I broke him down in the ring a few times just for kicks and to show him that everyone is the same size when they're on their backs. Man, he was strong, and he would get pissed when I wrapped him up.

The truth of the matter was, the guy was a lazy mother fucker who listened to one of his "road chauffeurs" who complained about the training and Bill De Mott.

On Saturday morning, January 20, 2007, after I finished a morning training session, Johnny Ace called. It was the day after our January 19, 2007 live event in Jackson, Georgia. Some of the guys wanted to "bump" and hang out, so that's what we did. We were going to have breakfast for everyone that afternoon, so when I walked in the door, Lacey was already busy in the kitchen getting things ready. Before I could even give her a hello kiss, the phone rang. When I read Johnny's name on the Caller ID, I instinctively knew what it was about. You know, sometimes you just get that feeling.

Johnny told me I was being released due to the number of complaints I had received from talent about how they were being treated badly and not taught anything. I really don't think that was a legitimate or honest reason for my release, but that's the only one he gave. I always felt bad about that conversation with John because we were, and are, friends, and that part of his job must really suck. With all the drama and yelling between Joe and everyone in the office, you would have thought it would have been Joe ... but it was Bill.

Two days after my release, Joe "came clean" and told me he knew about it earlier in the week, but asked Johnny to wait until after his show in Jackson. He said WWE told him he had to fire me personally because I worked for him, and to cover their ass, he had to send me a notarized letter that stated he was releasing me. I had twenty years in the business and I was humiliated *twice* in one week. At the time (and probably still do), I thought waiting until I could get his event off successfully was a lousy thing to do. It was like, *"Yeah, you can get rid of Bill, but I need his help at my show in Jackson, so could you wait until Saturday?"* I know it must have been hard for Johnny to call and tell me I was being released, but that didn't bother me as much as finding out that Joe knew and didn't even have enough respect for me to give me the "heads up." I was always honest with the talent, even when I knew they were going to be released. I'd give them a heads-up so they weren't devastated when the office told them. I would have appreciated the same from Joe.

When I shared the news with the kids at our house, they fell apart, especially Brett and Brian Majors. Drew, Derrick, Mike, Ryan, Angel, Krissy, Shantelle ... they all hung around to be sure I was okay. Later that day, we all went to D.D.'s for one more round of drinks, and as the day wore on, others, like Keith, Robert, and Eric, showed up. Every time someone would show up, the tears would once again begin to flow. It was an amazing night for me. To see the kids make themselves vulnerable by showing their feelings (including the guys) made me understand how much they appreciated the 1½ years I had spent with them.

My release was immediate, and less than an hour after I got the call, it was all over the Internet. After getting permission to get my gear from the building, I called Joe, who played dumb about it. The funny thing is, Steve Keirn had been at DSW the week before my release. When Lacey and I pulled up to the back of the building, he called my cell and said he had "just heard the news" and wanted me to know him being there that week had nothing to do with it. Have I mentioned it just so happened that Steve was going to head up the new developmental territory in Tampa? I'm just wondering. I'm sure there was no connection.

Lacey was more upset than I was. She was "effing" mad. She couldn't believe the company put more stock into people who were trying to get *into* the business than from someone who had done everything they asked for nine years, and who had been in the business for more than twenty years. Even today, if you ask Lacey, be prepared for her to vent. She doesn't curse or use foul language, but she gets hot when asked about this. She cried while we were emptying my office, but she was awesome through it all and backed me in everything I did in the years that followed.

After I left, they brought in Tom Prichard to "turn things around" because "they weren't being taught anything." I was released on Saturday and he was there on Monday morning. I had some discussions with a few of the students during the three months Tom was there and they said the complainers were now "complaining about Tom Prichard's workouts." They also said that during the first month of training, all they did was bump and beat each other up. At one time, 15 people were sitting on the sidelines with injuries.

I'm not sure who made the call to put Tom in there, or to close the Deep South center and move everything to Florida, but I have no problems with either Tom or Steve. People, and especially wrestlers, are expendable, and when you work for a company like WWE, you should expect to be replaced sooner or later. In my case, I guess it was just my time. (This is my positive spin, but inside, I don't believe a word of that) If either Tom or Steve were fired, I would take my job back from them in a heartbeat and tell them both to stand by because they will be needed again when history repeats itself.

Oh, yeah. Unlike me, Tom didn't have to move to Atlanta. He drove back and forth and the company paid for his car and hotel. I also heard Tom would cut training sessions short so he could leave early. That kind of thing was never allowed when I was there.

The one thing I can look back on and smile about is that every one of those assholes who stirred the pot by writing letters and e-mails never amounted to anything and lost their job, as well. That, my friends, is poetic justice.

Before I was released, WWE sent me to arenas from time to time to put potential trainees through workouts to see if there was anyone we could bring into the system. At one tryout in Daytona Beach, they taped my training session ... and then used the tapes as their method to find future developmental students. The tapes included making them squat, run the bleachers, run the ropes, jump, bump, and everything else I used for the kids *who were getting paid to train!* If my methods were that bad, why would they duplicate my methods? I'll tell you why.

Because they work!

After I was gone, rumors began circulating that I was trying to undermine Tom and Joe. Someone must have believed it because Deep South talent was "banned" from associating with me. A highly-reliable source told me George Murdoch (G-Rilla) was telling people I was socializing with talent and filling their heads with negative garbage. I'm not saying I was and I'm not saying I wasn't, but the bottom line is ... so what if I was?

I don't know how much I want to say about Mike Bucci. I was very proud and happy for him with everything he accomplished in this business. He had a lot of success in OVW and later on the main roster. It was when he began running developmental that he forgot who he was and what it was all about. I believe he wanted to control OVW and Deep South, but instead, he was overwhelmed answering bullshit from Stephanie McMahon, Johnny Ace, Talent Relations, Creative, and even independent workers. Instead of manning up, he became the very thing he didn't like when he was breaking into the business: a pussy. On more than one occasion, when he would call or e-mail me for my opinion about something, he would say all he wanted to do was go back to Louisville and write OVW TV. That's a telling statement from someone who was the head of a major department.

I laid into Mike a bit during an interview I did after I left Deep South. At the time, I was really mad to think about how someone, who I had known for as long as I did, and who had gone through what those kids were going through, could turn into such an asshole. I guess I took it personally when I was released from the company. When my release from DSW came down, Mike was nowhere to be found. It was a full two days later before he left a message on my answering machine, saying, *"I knew nothing about it."* Man, oh, man. I never fail to be amazed by the bullshit that goes down in wrestling. I don't wish anything bad for Mike, but I lost of lot of respect for him. I hope that, someday, he and I can sit down and clear the air.

The most ironic thing of all? Mike was fired after his name was discovered on a client list taken during the raid of Signature Pharmacy, which had been investigated for illegally selling steroids and other drugs.

And just for the record: As the trainer and everything else I did for Deep South and WWE, I never once was accused of propositioning female talent, failed a drug test, or did anything publicly to embarrass myself or the company … and yet, my release was made a big deal. I was painted as a bad ass, a terror, and wanted people to fail. Yes, I was and did all those things, but not once did anyone go to bat for me … as they have for countless others in the company who were granted immunity due to their "status."

WWE severed their business ties to Deep South Wrestling in April 2007. Joe Hamilton was given no advance notice. Johnny Ace, Mike Bucci, and Bruce Prichard showed up on a Wednesday night and told him they wanted to have a meeting with the talent. After the meeting (to which Joe wasn't invited), they told Joe they were pulling out. They gave him no reasons for their decision.

There had been talk almost from the beginning that Johnny was unhappy with Deep South and thought dealing with Joe was too much trouble. Between Joe and Johnny, both of them made countless threats to shut down Deep South, but I knew the end was coming when I was released from my contract.

I guess what means the most to me from my time in Deep South is the fact that so many of my kids lived their dreams. Since my departure, one of the best things for me, both mentally and emotionally, has been the phone calls, text messages, and e-mails from the guys and girls, both those who are currently working and those who are no longer with the company. They always close them with "I miss you," or "I love you." They also make personal visits, showing up on our front porch with no advance notice, when they are in the area on tour. I value the relationships that came out of Deep South. Those young people will always be welcome in our home. Every Christmas card I receive, and every funny, drunken text sent from the road, makes me proud of what I did during my time with the company. To the people sending them, I wasn't the bad guy the company made me out to be. They realize that even though I might have been hard on them, I did it to get them ready for the road that lay ahead.

Nobody will ever know how much I went through with those kids: talking about their relationships with girlfriends, boyfriends, wives, husbands, fiancés; helping them find places to stay; keeping them out of trouble; getting calls in the wee hours of the morning to help them get home after an "all-nighter." There was more drama than anyone could imagine, both in the building during training hours, and in the world afterwards. It became very uncomfortable at times, but we got through it.

Surprisingly, I sit back and shake my head in wonder when I get text messages and e-mail from some of the people who "hated me" and blamed me for their downfall with WWE. The text I received from Chris Rombola was one such message. They tell me they finally understand why I worked them the way I did, and how I wasn't just preparing them for wrestling, but for their future lives in the world.

I hope each and every one of those kids knows how much I miss them. I can honestly say I even miss guys like Nick Mitchell, Daniel Rodimer, and Kenny Omega. They were a great crew of young people and their stories should probably be written in a book of their own.

When people ask who I stay in touch with, I tell them it's probably easier to ask who I don't speak with. I hear people say they can count the number of their true friends on one hand. Lacey and I would have to use all of our fingers and toes, and then some, to list those to whom we feel close. The wrestling business has blessed me with so many friendships, and even though we don't see each other all the time, when we do talk, it's like we never missed a beat. I'm amazed, and a little bit humbled, by the number of Christmas cards we receive each year.

I let people know that they are welcome to stop in whenever they're in our area, and if they're going to be here overnight, they have a place to stay and a home-cooked meal waiting for them. The greatest rush for me is when former Deep South guys drop by or we meet up at one of the local hangouts. We drink a few beers, tell stories about the things that happened at DSW, and laugh. It's funny, but for some reason, the stories seem to get bigger each time they are told. And, yes ... we still get drunken text messages and phone calls in the middle of the night. Many of them have made it to where they wanted to be, and yet, they still find time to stay in touch with the "coach."

I have been blessed to have people in my life who know me and my reputation ... and they still come back to see me. I would do anything for any of them.

Zack Ryder, Curt Hawkins, Mike Gallows, Bill De Mott, Mike Knox and Matt Stryker at the 3 Dollar Cafe in McDonough, Georgia

Chapter 23

A Real Job

When I first left Deep South, I was kind of lost. For more than eighteen years, all I had done was wrestle and coach, and now I had to sit back and figure out what I was going to do with the rest of my life.

My first thought was to get back out on the independent circuit and wrestle, but I hated dealing with dates being cancelled and changed, so that didn't last long. I didn't have to do much to get my name out to promoters who were looking for talent. Whenever a WWE talent is released from their contract, the information goes out over the Internet and word spreads quickly. Promoters begin calling and e-mailing the day the information gets out.

My first show was a double shot in the Carolinas. I spent more time talking and working with the young guys than I did working. They took care of me, but unfortunately, there are a lot of promoters who aren't very savvy when it comes to business. Many of them make promises they can't keep and go over budget. By the time the show rolls around, ticket sales aren't what they expected, so they are unable to pay their talent or run the show. Time and again, I would be booked, only to be cancelled out a few days before a show. In the meantime, I had passed up other opportunities to wrestle.

I soon became discouraged by the "indy" scene. My heart just wasn't into it. I accepted occasional bookings, but I wasn't going to put my life on hold for anyone. There just wasn't any security. To this day, I have trouble understanding why promoters pay so much to wrestlers who don't draw flies. They bring in "name" guys and pay them ridiculous amounts of money to appear on their shows, with no hope of bringing in enough people to break even. In January 2011, I worked a show for NCW Pro Wrestling in Greenville, South Carolina. There couldn't have been more than 50 people there, and that's including family members.

The upside is that, personally, I never had any problem getting paid what I had been promised. I never asked for money up front, either. We simply came to an agreement over the phone and my money was waiting for me when I got to the buildings. In fact, there were a few times (okay, very few, but there were a few) when I received more than the amount on which we had agreed.

The only time I didn't get paid was when Ronnie Gossett, the promoter of Universal Championship Wrestling, asked Lacey and me to help him straighten out his locker room and make his talent pay attention. He wanted to do more than just "put on" a show. He wanted someone to show him "how" to run a show. We said we would help with one of his shows and see how things went after that. Not only did he stiff us, but we later heard he screwed the people who ran the venue, his security, and half his talent. No wonder they disrespected him.

If a town was far enough away, I would ask for hotel and trans money, but normally I drove because I wanted to be home the same night. One guy tried to talk me down to $200 for two shots in the northeast and expected me to pay my own way there. It was ridiculous. He then had the nerve to send an e-mail to Lacey listing a number of hotels where we could "get a deal." I told him I wasn't interested and got on with my life. In the meantime, he continued to promote my appearance. When I didn't appear, people contacted me and asked why I "no-showed" the event. Some of those guys just don't get it. I mean, I've worked for a lot less. In fact, I've worked for free, but that was a long time ago when I was making my bones. None of these guys have the ability to do anything to boost my career. That might sound cocky, but it's an honest assessment.

Another problem was dealing with promoters who wanted me to put over their "champions," most of whom were as green as grass. Their standard line was always, *"It will be good for business."* Sure, it would be good for *their* business, but it wasn't going to do much for my reputation. Regardless, anyone who knows me will tell you I have no problem putting over the regulars. I never paid much attention to wins and losses. I know how to get over, even when I "lose." Besides, the promoters were paying me, so they were the boss.

One of the things I find funny is when the "regulars" know a "name" is coming in, they decide to bring their "A-game" to the dressing room. Not to the ring ... but to the dressing room. They tell their best stories and try to big-league the guys in the company that are "beneath" them. It's funny to sit and listen to the bullshit being thrown around. What they don't realize is that kind of stuff isn't talked in the "big leagues," but those kids think they invented the business and are the biggest thing out there.

Having said that, there are promotions that are managed well and boast good talent. During my time with the indies, I found myself spending a lot of time with the young wrestlers — helping them with their characters and giving them direction — and enjoying that more than actually wrestling. Don't get me wrong. I will still wrestle for anyone at any time, but I was (and still am) in training mode. I want to help prepare the young guys to get to the next level.

Lacey and I decided that if we moved to Georgia to train and work in wrestling, we might as well throw everything in the hat and open a training center, with the ultimate goal of building a promotion. We called the company *New Energy Wrestling* [NEW]. Whenever I appear with one of the independent promotions, I do whatever I can to help their boys move forward. I invite them to visit New Energy Wrestling and train with us. A few of them have taken us up on our invitation and, for the most part, the experiences have been positive.

I also decided to get a "real" job. My neighbors both worked for FedEx, so with their encouragement, I applied for a position with the company. I was more interested in the benefits than I was the job, but I wasn't doing much more than wrestling on independent shows, so I filled out an application. It's hard for people to take you seriously when you fill out a job application and the only entry under "Past Job Experience" is "Professional wrestler, 1988-2007." They thought I was making it up and asked, *"Why do you want 'this' job?"* I had to swallow my pride, but my past life was what it was.

When I got the call from FedEx and was told I would begin working on November 12, 2007, I had to take a three-day orientation course. It was probably the most "eye-opening" experience I have had in a long time because at least two people kept staring at me throughout the first two sessions. They knew who I was and they were looking at me like, *"What the hell is he doing here?"* On the final day, they just had to ask ... that's right! *"Didn't you used to be Bill De Mott?"*

I had to laugh and say, *"I still am."*

I don't think most people can wrap their heads around the fact that just because someone was a "celebrity," they shouldn't have to work a "regular job" ever again. There are always circumstances and things that make people do the things they do, and that's exactly what I did. I swallowed what was left of my pride and became a package handler at FedEx.

The funny thing about wrestling is that I thought it would prepare me for what was supposed to be the real world, but FedEx turned out to be more of a reality show than wrestling ever was. That's probably the reason why (at the time of this writing) I'm still with the company. It entertains me! The people who work there, the stories they tell, and the way in which they perceive things, are very entertaining to me! They tell me their "war stories" about women, sexual conquests, and things that happened when they partied too hard. It's like being in a different locker room. If I didn't know better, I would think I was in the dressing room of the FEWA ... FedEx Wrestling Alliance. The ladies do a lot of story-telling and gossiping, which makes me think of them as "wash women," the ladies who beat their clothes clean on rocks while talking about the new whore in town. We all know why we're there (to move packages and supply customers), but everyone acts like they're captives and thinks the company would go out of business without them. Just like wrestling, I guess.

The people I work for are an interesting band of gypsies. Led by "Ma Diva," who is the "promoter" (our boss and manager), the "main event talent" consists of Reggie, Pam, Monica, Kim, Drewskie, and "LB." The "mid-card guys" are Jackie, "Q," Tyler, and me, while the "enhancement talent" (everyone else, most of whom complain about those on the upper tier) makes up the remainder of the talent roster. And again, just like many people in the wresting business, the enhancement talent talks shit about each other and puts each other down. They feel like they do more than the guy (or girl) working in the truck next to them and that everyone else is a slacker. I love listening to them, and every so often, I "stir the pot" and help bring things to a boil.

Oh, yes. Did I mention we have our "groupies," as well?

I have been with the company for more than three years and, much like everything else I do in life, my job has become a part of my life. I load and unload trucks for four to six hours a day. When I finish work around ten o'clock in the morning, I have the rest of the day to train, hang with my son, and build our company, New Energy Wrestling.

The idea for the company came about one day when Lacey and I were sitting around brainstorming ideas. When I asked her what she thought it would take to form our own company, she began doing her homework and we came up with New Energy Wrestling [NEW]. I got in touch with my old friend Lash LeRoux and he created a logo for the company, while Lacey spent a few hundred dollars to get a promoter's license and set up the company as a limited liability company [LLC].

We looked everywhere for a building where we could train. It took us a year before we found a suitable facility. It was connected to a Gold's Gym. The owner had opened an mixed martial arts school there, so I thought our businesses would be tailor-made for each other. He knew who Lacey and I were (as did the entire county from our time with DSW) and invited us in. We quickly reached an agreement and shook hands on the deal.

Our first couple of students came from another wrestling school that had closed down. They saw our website and contacted us, which is the way most prospective students find us today. Our first student was a kid from Macon who didn't last long and didn't pay his dues. He thought he was better than what he was, or even could be, and never amounted to much in the ring.

I do the training, talking, and cleaning. Lacey takes care of the important stuff. When it comes down to it, NEW is Lacey's company and I work for her. I haven't made a cent and we were barely able to pay our monthly rent on the building. It cost us money every month, but it felt so-ooo good to be in the ring again — coaching and training — hoping that one day it would pay off and our students would make it to the place they want to be. As of this writing, we still haven't made any money, but we intend to make it work.

A few of the WWE guys stopped by now and then to get into the ring with our kids. I won't name names because they could get into trouble if it were known they had gotten injured during their days off. When we do have a visitor, it "pops" my guys when they see them.

The most students we have had at one time was six, so they get a lot of one-on-one time. Since we've been in business, only two have quit. One decided he didn't have to show up and train, while the other put the "heat" on his dad for not returning. No matter how you slice it or how they decide to explain themselves, they're quitters. I have to say I'm happy they quit when they did, rather than continue pursuing a business when they knew deep down they couldn't cut it.

None of my students have complained or asked for a refund of their money and we never enforced the "late fees" stipulation. We are very understanding about someone making late payments. We were stiffed by a few people when they failed to pay their fees, but we didn't go after them because we weren't interested in wasting time with people who really weren't cut out for it, anyway. Wrestling isn't for everyone, and we want to train and help the people who really want it.

We ran two live events in 2010, both in Locust Grove, Georgia. In my eyes, they were a great success. No, we didn't make any money, but the talent was paid well and everyone went home happy: the fans, the venue manager, and the talent.

One of our wrestlers, Chris Byson of Stockbridge, Georgia, has been with us the longest and finished his first year at the beginning of 2011. Chris is good and will only get better if he sticks with it. Chris and another of our students, Spiral, have good chemistry and have been very consistent with their matches. They both applied (without me telling them or suggesting to them) for the latest edition of *Tough Enough*. When they return (if they make the cut), it is my goal to get them ready to go to Tampa and tryout with Florida Championship Wrestling.

The Gold's Gym people were great to us, but we got caught up in the middle of court battles between the partners of the gym, which meant we couldn't grow our business and run the monthly shows we had planned until their litigation and legal problems were settled. At the beginning of 2011, we had to end operations at the Gold's Gym when they reached an impass. As of this writing (March 2011), we haven't trained in two months. That sucks because we had three potential talents waiting to join and we receive e-mails and calls regularly.

New Energy Wrestling is a vehicle for me to use to continue training the kids, as well as giving me an opportunity to be in the ring. I want to let my students know about the business and help them achieve all the things they want out of life, and that's not always just wrestling. I want to encourage them to be positive and stay focused. Forget the boozing, drugging, and womanizing. There is no need for more tragedy in our business.

In short, New Energy Wrestling is our outlet to maintain good, old-fashioned wrestling with a positive atmosphere, and to help the young guys move into life in a safe and productive way. Our logo is a fist holding a lightning bolt (because we are making lightning strike again) and "new energy" is for the way we go about training both in the ring and in our lives.

Old school training equals new energy!

I also have a personal reason for wanting to have interaction with these kids. I want them to know the "good news." I want them to know that Jesus Christ watches over us, both in and out of the ring, and just because we "act" a certain way on TV or at live events doesn't mean they can't be followers of Christ. I'm not a bible thumper, by any means, but I'm here to tell anyone who will listen that Jesus Christ "saved" me from myself and from the life I was living. We can be sports entertainers and Christians at the same time. I enjoy the conversations Lacey and I have with the members at our church. Many of them recognize me from television and I enjoy watching their reactions when they realize we're as normal as the next guy.

It began when I was working out at the World Gym in Merritt Island, Florida, with Mike Green, Mike Smith, Todd (can't remember his last name), and Cal

Dixon, who played football for the Miami Dolphins and the New York Jets. They knew I was lost and struggling with my career and marriage. Without me knowing what they were doing, they asked me questions that eventually led me back to the Lord. Not the church, but the Lord. In time, I began feeling good about myself again. By no means was I on the right path, and I hadn't made any life-altering changes, but I wasn't traveling down the road alone any more. Those men didn't know the extent of my problems, but they saved me from myself and helped me re-establish the lines of communication with God.

I know the Lord has always been with me. He let me walk a crazy, winding road, but he always made sure I didn't drift too far. One of the most favorite times for me when I was on the road was when the Misfits and others would bow and pray, thanking God for our jobs, our talents, and our lives.

I'm sure it will come as a shock to a lot of people that Bill de Mott is a very spiritual person. He continually asks for forgiveness and is very thankful for all he had, has, and has coming his way. While I know I'm no angel, I know I have salvation through Jesus Christ, my Lord and Savior.

Yes, the Laughing Man is a believer and follower of the Lord. That's something you didn't know, right?

Bill and Lacey talk to talent about an upcoming New Energy Wrestling show

Chapter 24

Billy De Mott, Celebrity

What a ride I've had!

I have had the pleasure and honor of meeting some of the biggest stars in sports, TV, and movies. The funny thing about that is, in most cases, those "stars" were coming to see the "wrestlers." For as long as I can remember, professional wrestling has been portrayed as "fake," "acting," "not real," and "phony," and yet, some of the biggest names in every industry stopped by to say hello. Our involvement in the wrestling business has also opened the doors for a lot of the wrestlers to get involved in their world, as well.

A few of the celebrities I've met include: professional football players Bruce Smith, Herschel Walker, Jim Kelly, Kevin Greene, and Reggie White; baseball players Kirby Puckett and Wade Boggs; basketball players Dennis Rodman, Karl Malone, and Tim Duncan. I've rubbed shoulders with movie and TV stars like Bruce Willis, Arnold Schwarzenegger, Chuck Norris, Adam Sandler, Henry Winkler, "Mr. Belding" (Saved by the Bell), Jay Leno, Indian Larry, Donald Trump, Michael Clarke Duncan, "Tiny" Lister, and Jean-Claude Van Damme.

I'm just Billy De Mott from Paramus, New Jersey, so it's weird to see, talk, and hang out with famous people I grew up watching or heard about, especially when they were there to see ME! I don't know what I was thinking, but I never had any photos of myself taken with any of them. I suppose I didn't want them to think I was a star-struck fan who was chasing them around for a photo op. I do, however, have fond memories of meeting them. I met several of them on more than one occasion and, more often than not, they remembered me. Those things never would have happened if it wasn't for the wrestling business.

On more than one occasion, the boys known as ZZ Top would be sitting front row at our shows (especially when I was with WCW). They always took time to come backstage to say hello and shoot the bull. They were totally awesome. I also was invited to play "celebrity softball" with the rock band Creed and the local radio deejays.

And then there was Kid Rock. While we [WCW] were on one of our "spring break" encounters, we wound up in Cancun, Mexico for four days. We only wrestled one day, but all the partying we did definitely counted as work. Anyway, we were going to wrestle on the beach and the live guest was to be Kid Rock. The event took place shortly before he became a household name. The man was so cool. We met up with him a couple of times and went out to a couple of bars.

Joe C [Joseph Calleja], Kid's sidekick and fellow rapper, also came to our shows. One night, Eddie Guerrero mistook Joe for a young wrestling fan and patted him on the head, until the boys told him who Joe was. It was hilarious to watch Eddie stammer out an apology, but Joe was so cool about it.

I also had opportunities to meet and talk with a lot of musicians from various bands: Ashanti, Limp Biscuit, Willie Nelson, Toby Keith, Motor Head, and Smashing Pumpkins. I also ran into Busta Rhymes at the Atlanta International Airport. I simply acknowledged him by saying, *"Hey, Busta!"* He gave me a look and mumbled something that didn't sound welcoming. I get the whole "I'm a celebrity and don't have time for you" thing, but what a dick.

But what has to be my all-time high was when we [WCW] were in Las Vegas for *Nitro* and KISS was going to perform at the event. I grew up listening to Kiss, so I was like a kid in a candy store. My brother and I had all their albums. We had Kiss posters and pictures from magazines covering our walls. And now, here I was in Las Vegas, about to be part of one of the biggest pay-per-views of the year, and Kiss was going to play music live! It was one of the greatest thrills I ever experienced. Everyone gathered around to watch Gene Simmons, Paul Stanley, Peter Criss, and Ace Frehley walk onto stage to set up. Exciting, right?

Wrong. My all-time favorite band lip synced to pre-recorded music. I, along with most of the other boys, was devastated.

Either way, it was a fantastic experience ... and for once, I wasn't the most unattractive person in the room.

Bill and Chavo Guerrero Jr. with basketball superstar Karl Malone

Chapter 25

The "Real" First Family

From Bill De Mott's personal journal

November 4, 2008

As I get closer to finishing this "diary," I have found myself needing to add some information about my life.

Early in 2008, Lacey got pregnant. I tell everyone it all came about because the New York Giants won Super Bowl XLII that year. When New York Giants fans celebrate a victory, they really celebrate!

Nine months later, almost to the day, a new member joined the "De Mott" clan. On November 2, 2008, at 2:32 p.m., William Charles De Mott III was born into this world!

Lacey and I were eating on that Saturday night when Lacey started to feel "not so good," as she puts it, so we knew that she was going into labor with the baby. We arrived at the hospital around 10:45 p.m. after speaking with the doctor on call. She was admitted right away and we were ushered to her room. At that time, Lacey was four centimeters (I hate all that girly/pregnant talk). To make a long story short, Lacey was in labor for just under 22 hours!!!

It was one of the most amazing things I have ever seen; not so much that she was having our baby ... it was the way in which he came into this world. Women are the most unbelievably strong people (pregnant women, that is). During the time she was in labor, her "epidural" had been "pinched" closed and she had no meds to ease her discomfort. Somehow, the line was not flowing and Lacey was in the most ridiculous pain I have ever been witness to. I felt so helpless. All I could do was hold her hands and try to talk to her, but it wasn't working. My wife was in labor with our son "naturally" without any meds or relief! I don't know how many of you who might read this understands the pain that these women go through, but they are completely overwhelmed with pain and grief, and all I wanted to do was find a way to get her to a better place "mentally and physically." But I couldn't. "Nature" was kicking her ass! Thank God ... and I mean "Thank God" for those wonderful nurses in the hospital who found the problem and got her to where she needed to be quickly (probably not quick enough for Lacey, but they did their best). So for the last forty minutes before she actually started the "push" of the baby, she was asleep and getting some rest and strength back.

And when the time had come to "push" and get my son out to meet the world, Lacey Michele de Mott sat up in her bed that she had been in for almost 22 hours and began to "push" that baby out into the world like she just got to the hospital and none of the "little things" that went wrong ever happened. I stood by my wife's head with my mom by her side as we watched the most amazing display of control and desire to do this the right way. I couldn't believe I was watching the same women who had been in so much distress for so long into the day. I was and am and will always be in awe of my wife as I watched my son through the same mirror as Lacey as he entered the world. And when he was finally with us and the doctor put him on her belly, as soon as he arrived, her face was in shock and couldn't believe that everything that she had been through the past nine months was this little baby sitting on her belly. Lacey was amazing, and when I saw my son for the first time, I was "calm" and ready for what was in front of me. So I checked on my son as he gave his first cry and then went back to the women who had just been through an incredible journey into "motherhood."

To say Lacey is a strong woman would be a gross understatement! I knew when we met that this girl was tough mentally and emotionally. She had to be to get involved with a guy like me, and when she took to Casey and Keri, and the three of them became so close and love each other so much, I knew she was a tough "nut." But when I lay witness to what she had just been through — and her and only her went through that — to watch her with her son (our son) for the first time ... it once again confirmed what many people have said to me time and time again ...

"Bill de Mott, you are truly blessed."

So just in case any of you "tough guys" out there think you can do anything, I am here to tell you; you couldn't be more wrong. It's my wife who can do anything, and it's my kids who benefit from her being the woman she is.

I have been through a lot and done a lot of things that most people will never experience. I have broken, bent, dislocated, and torn more shit than the average man will ever do, but on November 2, 2008, I tip my hat and bow down to the toughest chick I know — Lacey Michele de Mott!

It was a joy and honor to have my mom and dad there in the hospital and by Lacey's side (all 22 hours) the whole time.

They are extraordinary people and have been through a lot of shit with me, so I was glad this time it was a "positive" experience.

And now at the age of 45 years of age, my family is now complete.

When it came time to do something with (or for) the girls, Lacey was always enthusiastic and anxious to be a part of whatever it was we were going to do. When we were finally able to buy a new house and move out of our one-bedroom apartment in Titusville, she didn't whine when I told her we had to move to Georgia, a place where neither of us had ever lived. She left her job and the new friends she had made without protest.

I take that back. She wasn't happy in the least over having to leave Casey and Keri. They were together on an almost daily basis ... and being away from them was something she had a hard time accepting.

It's hard to believe there is an 11-year difference in our ages and that she would be willing to take on all the responsibilities that came with being a "wrestler's wife." She has done everything anyone has asked and more. She has been a mother to Casey and Keri since we met and is now raising our son, Billy.

Lacey has truly been a godsend to us. My ex once said, *"Why would anyone want you? You don't have two dimes to rub together."* That's the difference between my ex and Lacey. With Lacey, it was *never* about money, fame, fortune, or status in the community. Her focus is on family and she is the happiest when she is giving to others. Her attitude has made a big difference in my life. My family is as solid as they've ever been and I'm happier than I ever could have imagined I would be.

I think some people (like me) have to hit "rock bottom" before they figure out it's not what you have, but who you have that makes you who and what you are!

Lacey is my savior. She understands me when I don't deserve to be understood. She lets me vent and get mad and then helps calm me down. More importantly, Lacey loves me, Casey, Keri, and Billy unconditionally.

On the other hand, I love her with all my heart (the sound of violins playing in the background), and I can never truly explain how a little girl from Iowa saved the life of a 350-pound man.

For a time in the wrestling business, I was a part of Jimmy Hart's "First Family," but my family is the real First Family.

I was on the road (or out of the house) for most of my daughters' early childhoods. I was home from time to time, and during those times, I spent every minute I could with them. It's strange, but I really believe that when I left their mother and we got divorced, my girls and I grew closer. I hate the fact that they were caught up in the middle of a bad relationship, but Lacey and I worked hard to make their lives better. Again, the family hardships brought my daughters close to one another and, to this day, they love, protect, and communicate with each other very well.

Lacey made quite a few trips with me and she really enjoyed being on the road. Having her get a feeling for what I did, other than what she saw on TV, gave us something to talk about and helped her understand what I went through. Having her with me made the long trips much more bearable, as well.

My daughters never came on the road with me, but every time we worked in Florida, I would make plans to bring them to the arena where we were wrestling. I loved having them with me at work and the boys were all great to them. They grew up around their dad's co-workers and there were times when the boys would come to the house.

I was always so proud to show off my three girls to the boys. I can't tell you how many times I heard someone say, *"How is it a thug like you has such a beautiful family?"*

One of the things about the boys; whenever family was around, they were made to feel important. Everyone stopped by to say hello and talk for a bit. The boys really were a family ... a dysfunctional family, but a great, caring family, especially when kids were around. Casey and Keri loved the Misfits and Jimmy Hart because they all treated them with respect and made them feel welcome. My kids (and everyone else's kids, as well) were the center of attention. As they got older, the boys would wrestle with them, sit and talk to them, or tease them.

One night before the matches, Dustin Rhodes was talking to them. They were polite and seemed to be at ease around him. After talking for a bit, he excused himself and went to the back to get into his "Goldust" gear. When he came back out, he was "in character." They were scared stiff when he walked over to them. They didn't know it was Dustin. There weren't any people in the arena, so he invited them to get into the ring with him where he proceeded to horse around. At one point, he took a bump. He stayed down for a long, long time and didn't get up. The girls didn't think he would *ever* get up. It was the funniest thing ever.

When the girls were in elementary school, Lacey and I would join them at "lunchtime." They would get embarrassed because the kids would come up and say things like, *"Is that your dad?," Isn't he a wrestler?," "My dad knows who he is," and, "Can we eat lunch with you?"*

My daughters thought it was funny (once they got over their embarrassment) because they never looked at me as being anything other than "Dad." Hugh Morrus was a guy on TV and kind of famous, but Bill De Mott was the guy who went shopping with them, took them to restaurants, and fixed things around the house. He was just "Dad."

When we moved to Georgia with Deep South, the girls would come to Gold's Gym to train and stretch with the kids. I liked that for two reasons: it gave us something to do together and they were able to see what it was I did for a living.

One afternoon, I was really pushing the group. They were training hard. My girls, to their credit, stayed with them step for step ... stretching, flexing, and all the cardio the students did. I was in "push" mode (zoned out) and was making everyone go the extra mile. When I glanced out of the corner of my eyes, I saw a couple of the guys stop with a look on their faces of fear and disbelief. When I turned around, I saw my girls, still doing the exercises ... but they had tears in their eyes and were exhausted.

I was so focused that I never gave thought to the fact that they would keep going. I thought they would have taken a break. They never quit or made any noise. They just teared up and kept going. When I asked them why they didn't quit, they said, *"We knew the rules of the gym and we didn't want to drop out. We didn't want to let you down."*

Those two girls have their dad's mentality. They're not quitters. I don't know if it's a good thing, but if you ever meet my daughters, you'll know they're De Motts!

The funny thing about the whole situation was the reaction I got from the students. They couldn't believe those two little girls were pushing through the workout, but what bothered them most of all was thinking about what I was going to put *them* through when I wouldn't even give my daughters any quarter.

My best memories of my girls are from times when I got "hurt" or bloodied on TV. When I came home from the road, they would be waiting at the door to be sure I was okay and feeling better.

It takes a special person(s) to live with a wrestler and put up with his or her schedule. It takes a special person(s) to sit and listen, and not judge you for your past or for your mistakes. It takes a special "family" to get you through all you have been through when you've been on the road for 20 years. I have that in my family and I am a better person for it.

It would be very stupid to think life was going to be easy for any of us. I'm 45 years old and not the man I used to be (although, I'm not the boy, either, and that's a good thing), the girls are much older than their brother, and Lacey will be working through what every mother goes through. At the end of the day, though, I can honestly say *"we wouldn't want it any other way."* My only regret is that Pop wasn't here to experience the blessing of our newest family member.

During high school, Casey joined the Academic team and the Spanish Honors Society. Since she quit dancing, there wasn't much that has grabbed her attention. She has been very content just being at home, reading and making sure everyone is happy. She has grown into a beautiful, sensitive, caring, and strong young woman who I believe can save the world. Casey is always worried about her dad. Her caring and ability to help and calm people is amazing. She is a good soul and is very responsible. As this book goes to press, Lacey and I are proud and excited to say that Casey has begun receiving acceptance letters from the colleges to which she has applied. And, yes! They are all in Georgia. Casey is coming home!

Keri has come out of her shell (actually, she blew it up). She came full circle from the quiet "won't-talk-to-people" little girl who runs varsity track to participating in school activities and being the sophomore representative on the homecoming court. I had the honor of walking her onto the football field at halftime. The credit for Keri's transformation goes to Lacey. Keri is now a varsity track star and is involved in school projects and clubs. Unfortunately, she has a boyfriend (I hate this part), but I knew it was going to happen. I have tried to deny the fact that Keri and Casey will have boyfriends and relationships with boys, but the genii is out of the bottle. The sky is the limit for Keri, though, and I know she will accomplish whatever she sets her mind to do.

If you didn't know them from the beginning, you can't appreciate just how much growing and maturing the De Mott girls have done. I also know that somewhere, deep down, in those two girls, hides a little bit of the Laughing Man personality. They are their father's daughters. I have been blessed to have three loving, caring, and understanding (well, perhaps until they read this book) kids any man could dream of having.

A few years ago, Casey and Keri gave Lacey and me the best Christmas present I ever received. They gave us portraits of themselves! They dressed up, had their pictures taken, and had the photographs mounted in beautiful frames. It might sound ridiculous to think someone would get so excited about pictures, but you have to understand that after the divorce, my ex-wife refused to give me any of my daughters' pictures, and there were hundreds of them. When I opened the package, I broke down in tears and hugged them for a long time. They will never know how much that present meant to me.

This is the end of the "First Family" chapter, but it might not be the end of the De Mott family in wrestling. Wouldn't it be something to see "Billy de Mott" get into wrestling sixteen years from now with Casey and Keri at his side? If that's the case, I can truly say:

I had the last laugh.

Bill, Keri, Billy, Casey and Lacey, Christmas 2010

Addendum

Another Last Laugh

A few weeks before this manuscript was finished, I thought we were at the end of a long journey of writing, editing, and answering questions.

But then, at 6:45 in the evening on January 20, 2011, our phone rang. I was shocked when I heard the voice of my long-time friend (and WWE producer), John "Big" Gaburick, on the other end of the line. My heart began racing because I knew a phone call from Connecticut at night meant one of two things ... I was going to be hired or fired. Since I hadn't worked for the company in any official capacity for the past four years, I was pretty sure I wasn't going to be fired ... so that meant one thing. They had something in mind for me.

A few months before, I had heard (like most people in wrestling or those who follow wrestling) that WWE was joining forces with USA Network to bring back *Tough Enough*. Lacey and I had advised all New Energy Wrestling trainees to submit an application and try to get involved because *TE* would be a great opportunity for them. I had always taught them to do whatever it took to get noticed. To their credit, they had already done it without us having to ask or encourage them.

That led me to think one day, *"How can we tell our students to do whatever it takes to get their names out there ... and not do the same ourselves?"* That night, after I got home and talked with Lacey about it, I e-mailed both Johnny Ace and Kevin Dunn and told them I would love to have the opportunity to be involved in the filming of *Tough Enough* because I had things to offer the brand and the company. I left it at that and didn't bother them with a follow-up call. The worse that could happen was that I would get no response.

Much to my surprise, I got a response from WWE within two hours. I was told I was being considered for the show as a trainer and they would get back to me with their decision.

Whatever they decided, I was happy. Even if I wasn't asked to be a part of it, it was nice to know my name had been brought up and I had been considered for a spot. And, no, I'm not a dumbass. I know them telling me I was being "considered" could have been just a nice way of telling me, *"Okay, thanks for getting in touch."* Regardless, the comment meant the world to me and gave me "hope" that, someday, I would be back doing what I love most. I love training the kids in New Energy Wrestling and going to camps, but to be back with the biggest and the best was even better. And what a shot in the arm it would be for New Energy Wrestling to have their trainer involved again with WWE.

Back to my story about the phone call from Big — We had a great talk, and at the end of it, he told me that if I wanted to accept, I would be the trainer for *Tough Enough*!

In case you forgot what you have read up to this point, I live for this business and hold it in high regard. I would do anything for it, so let me say it again ...

I am the trainer for WWE and Tough Enough in 2011!!!!!

One of the weirdest things about the whole scenario is that the phone call came almost four years to the day — January 20, 2007 — from the time I was released from my obligations with Deep South Wrestling and WWE. It just goes to show that things are always up for grabs in wrestling and that it takes you on long, wild, and crazy journeys.

To know WWE wants the "De Mott guy" back makes me feel good as a man, and proves just how wrong all the Internet and dirtsheets were when they painted me as a failure. I still may be the best out there at what I do.

Lacey, Casey, Keri and I, and now Billy, have been walking down the long, hard road of surviving after wrestling. When I was released, things weren't easy for us. We struggled constantly with finances, to a point where we almost lost our home and were just getting by, but we never gave up and our faith became stronger than it had ever been. Perhaps I had to look everything to make me wake up and realize how quickly "things" could be taken away, and that my family was what was most important.

Bill at Universal Studios for *Tough Enough*, 2011

As we begin a new journey down a new road, we have a better understanding of ourselves, our lives, and what it takes to survive both the business and everyday events. My passion for the business and training hasn't changed, but other things will be different this time around. I am sober, happily married, and focused on my family. To list my priorities in order, they are faith, family, career — and bringing up the rear — self.

So, unlike the chapter where I admit I may not be tough enough, I'm here to tell you that I "am" tough enough, and I am blessed to be living and able to do it all over again.

And just so you don't have to wonder ... I still get "the last laugh." It's not a "ha-ha" laugh. It's a happy and relieved laugh combined with a smile and a chuckle.

Photos from Tough Enough

(from the top down)

Booker T, Trish Stratus and Bill ready for the obstacle course

Bill, Rey Mysterio Jr., Booker, Trish and Steve Austin on the set of *Tough Enough*

Trish, Bill and Booker address the contestants before the obstacle course begins

Trish, Booker and Bill after a trip to the "In and Out Burger" restaurant

— Photos courtesy of Bill De Mott

INDEX

$1,000,000 Tough Enough, 170, 195-196, 201, 204, 213
101 Reasons Not To Be a Pro Wrestler, 111
20/20 (TV show), 35, 44
Ace, Johnny (see Laurinaitis, John)
Acolytes, The, 120
Adams, Brian, 67
Adams, Brooke, 196
Albert (Matt Bloom), 127
All Japan Pro Wrestling, 53, 110
All Star Wrestling, 42
Alliance, The, 122
American Wrestling Association, 192
Anderson, Arn, 35, 43, 66, 71, 76-77, 80, 88, 102-104, 152, 159, 181, 192
Angle, Kurt, 115, 151, 160, 167, 197
Animal, Road Warrior, 36
Anoa'I Jr., Afa, 206
Anoa'I, Afa, 36
Anthony, Robert, 211, 219
Armstrong, Brad, 198
Atlas, Tony, 33
Aunt Carol, 15
Austin, Steve, 115, 159-160, 239
A-Wall, Sgt. (see Tuite, Jerry "The Wall")
Awesome, Mike, 104, 116, 119-120
Ayala, Hercules, 38-41, 45
Aykroyd, Dan, 60
Azzolino, Rose, 22
Bachia, Paul, 17, 22
Badd, Johnny B (Mark Mero), 69
Bag Lady, The (Melissa Coates), 201, 215
Bagwell, Buff, 119-122
Banks, Antonio, 185, 202
Barbarian, 69, 79, 81, 91
Barbed wire match, 61
Basham, Doug, 169
Batista, 214
Batts, Mikey, 184-185
Bauer, Charlie, 15
Beefcake, Brutus, 68, 73
Behrens, Bill, 175, 178-180
Bennett, Reggie, 62
Benoit, Chris, 80-81, 85, 89-90, 102, 118, 160, 162, 191
Benoit, Nancy, 54, 80-81, 162, 215
Bernard, Gigante (Matt Bloom), 127
Bialo the Giant (Allen Bialo), 27
Big Brother, 139
Big Bubba, 81
Big Show, 126, 128, 152
Bigelow, Bam Bam, 102, 114
Biggers, Trenesha, 197
Bischoff, Eric, 8, 63-64, 77-78, 92, 97-99, 101-102, 104, 107, 112
Blackman, Steve, 118
Blading, 35, 44-45
Blood (see blading)
Bloom, Matt, 127
Bonham, Bob, 24-25
Bonnie, Grandma, 169
Boogeyman, The (see Wright, Marty)
Boone, Johnny, 152
Boricuas, Los, 61
Bostonian, Ms., 15
Bradley, Steve, 130
Bradshaw (see Layfield, John)
Brady, "Diamond" Jim (Steve Cooper), 24
Brandi, Tom, 36, 42-43, 46
Brisco, Jerry, 115-116
Brock, Chad, 72
Bucci, Mike, 179, 181, 196, 215, 220-221
Buck, Tylene, 105-106, 111
Bull, Jack (Greg Groothius), 194, 214
Burke, Elijah, 205
Burnett, William, 9
Butcher, Abdullah the, 48
Butcher, Abdullah the, 61
Byrd, Adrian, 63-64
Byson, Chris, 227
C, Joe (Joseph Calleja), 230
Cade, Lance, 130
Cajun, Corporal (see LeRoux, Lash)
Cangimilia, Tommy, 17
Canon, Palmer, 185, 203, 217
Cappotelli, Matt, 137, 140, 144, 159, 205

Cash, Kid (David Cash), 211
Castagnoli, Claudio, 208
Castillo, Hurricane, 45
Century Wrestling Alliance, 33
Chase, Chevy, 60
Chicago Slaughter (football team), 89
Christian (William Reso), 119
Chubba Bubbas, 74, 76, 78, 81-82, 84-87, 89-90
Clark, Bob, 155-156, 158, 160, 163, 165
Clay, Brodus (see Murdoch, George)
Coates, Melissa, 201, 215
Collins, Steve, 54
Colon, Carlos, 38-39, 41-42, 44, 48
Comcast Sports South, 179
Cooley, Wendell, 42
Cornette, Jim, 99, 159
Coverdale, Frankie (Francisco Ciatso), 209
Crash the Eliminator, 36-37, 60
Crash the Terminator, 36, 39, 49, 51, 55, 64, 67
Crockett, David, 76, 78
Crockett, Jim, 62
Crowbar (see Ford, Chris)
Cruiserweight title, 110
Curtis, Johnny (Jonathan Curtis), 210
Cyberslam, 77
D'Acquisto, Joe, 81, 83, 85
Davis, Danny (Dan Briley), 159, 175, 177, 191
De Mott III, William Charles, 10, 17-18, 142, 231-233, 236, 238
De Mott Sr., William, 14
De Mott, Alice (see Galligan, Alice)
De Mott, Casey, 10, 17, 50, 55-56, 63, 142-143, 145, 147, 149-150, 153-155, 157, 169-170, 203, 205, 232-236, 238
De Mott, Darryl, 10, 15, 19-20, 125, 166, 169
De Mott, Debbie, 10, 16
De Mott, Keri, 10, 18, 56, 63, 142-143, 145, 147, 149-150, 153-155, 157, 169, 203, 205, 232-236, 238
De Mott, Lacey, 10, 17, 86, 140-151, 153-154, 157-158, 160-161, 165-171, 173-175, 183, 202, 204-205, 207, 209, 219, 222, 224, 226, 231-238
Deacon, Freakin' (Drew Hankinson), 172, 183, 185, 201, 217, 219
Dean, Simon (see Bucci, Mike)
Deep South Wrestling (DSW), 110, 168, 171, 174-223, 226, 234, 238
Delray, Jimmy, 54-55
Demento, Damien (see Kleen, Mondo)
Demon Jr., Blue, 60
Detroit Tigers, 199
Deville, Lorian (Freakin' Deacon), 201
Devon, Brother, 32, 172
Dillinger, Doug, 78
Dillon, J.J., 97, 99, 176
Dingman, Kathy, 87
Dink the Clown, 46
DiPietro, Rebecca, 214
Disqo (see Inferno, Disco)
Divas, Deep South, 214-216
Dixon, Cal, 227
Douglas, Shane, 110
Dr. Pain (movie character), 91
Dreamer 31-32, 124, 127, 130, 172, 175-177, 179-181, 185-190, 192, 197, 210-211, 217
Droese, Duke "The Dumpster", 114
Drug tests, 95
Drugs
— Advil, 97
— antidepressants, 155
— Clenbuterol, 94
— cocaine, 95, 98
— morphine, 95
— narcotics, 95
— OxyContin, 94-95, 98
— Percoset, 94
— Soma, 94-96, 155
— steroids, 93-94, 132
— Valium, 94-95, 97-98, 155
— Winstrol-V, 94
— Xanax, 155
Dudley Boyz, 172
Dudley, Bubba Ray, 32
Dudley, D-Von, 32
Dudley, Spike, 126
Duggan, Jim, 68, 84, 91, 102-103, 109, 113-114, 150, 167
Duncum Jr., Bobby, 71-72
Dungeon of Doom, 68-69, 72-73, 76, 79-80, 88, 91
Dungeon, The (Ramada Inn), 64, 66, 69, 83
Dunn, Kevin, 117, 135-136, 146, 163, 237
Durham, Mike (see Grunge, Johnny)
Earthquake (see Tenta, John)
Eastern Championship Wrestling, 61
Eastwood, Clint, 108
Eaton, Bobby, 71
Edge (Adam Copeland), 119, 151, 160
Entenmann's Bakery, 18

Bill De Mott, age 10

Estrada, Jose, 31
Express, Rock 'n' Roll, 211
Extreme Championship Wrestling (ECW), 32, 50, 61-62, 77, 122, 127, 132, 195, 200, 210-212
Fabiano, Louis, 162
Family Feud, 102
Fatu, Eddie, 130
Ferrara, Ed, 92, 104, 107
Fertig, Kevin, 172
Festus (Drew Hankinson), 201
Filthy Animals, The, 111, 156
Finkel, Howard, 128
First Family, The, 9, 91, 152, 154, 233
Flair, Ric, 66, 80, 101
Florida Championship Wrestling (FCW), 192, 196, 200, 206, 210-211, 213, 227
Flynn, Jerry, 91, 152
Foley, Mick, 126
Ford, Chris, 74-76, 114
Four Horsemen, The, 80
Frontier Martial-Arts Wrestling (FMW), 50
FUBAR, 108
Funaki, Shoichi, 164
G.I. Bro (see T, Booker)
Gaburick, John "Big", 135-138, 146, 237
Gagne, Greg, 177, 181, 192-193, 196, 215
Gagne, Verne, 192
Galamb, Dennis, 32-33
Galligan, Alice (Bill's mother) , 10-11, 14, 16, 18, 20, 23, 148, 152, 154, 169, 178
Galligan, John, 18-20
Gallows, Luke (Drew Hankinson), 172, 201
Gallows, Mike, 222
Ganette, Tommy, 32
Gang, One Man (George Gray), 70
Gangrel (see Heath, David)
Georgia Dome, 99
Giant, The (Paul Wight), 91
Gilbert, Doug, 51, 54, 61
Gilbert, Eddie, 44, 61, 162
Gill, Dwayne, 69
Gimondo, Danny, 172, 208
Gleason's Gym, 23-24, 27-28, 31-32, 35-36, 74, 211
Gloria (office manager), 40-41, 43
Gold Club, Atlanta, 83
Gold's Gym, 178, 186, 202, 226-227, 234
Goldberg, Bill, 102, 109
Goldust (Dustin Runnels), 234
Good Day, New York, 35
Good Intentions, 204
Gordman, Black, 38
Gordy, Ray, 212
Gossett, Ronnie, 223-224
Gowen, Zack, 123
Gray, George (see Gang, One Man)
Green, Mike, 227
Grignon, Shawn, 21
G-Rilla (see Murdoch, George)
Grunge, Johnny, 36, 74-76, 78, 83-85, 102
Guerrero, Chavo, 85-89, 105-108, 110-111, 116, 125-126, 132, 230
Guerrero, Eddie, 68, 85, 88-90, 118, 162, 230
Guidettie, Bobby, 17
Gunn, Billy, 124, 126, 164
Gunns, Major (see Buck, Tylene)
Haiti, Mr., 43
Halicion, 94
Halloween Havoc 2000, 109
Hamilton, Joe "Jody", 175-177, 179-180, 182, 190-191, 193, 197, 201, 210, 212, 214, 219-221
Hammer, Van, 104-106
Hankinson, Drew (see Deacon, Freakin')
Hardy, Matt, 215
Hart, Jimmy, 35, 69, 86, 88, 91-92, 99, 102-103, 152, 233-234
Hawk, Road Warrior, 68, 161-162
Hawkins, Curt, 199, 222
Hayes, Michael, 192, 212
Hayward, Jay, 14
Headhunters 54, 61-62, 65-66
Heartbreak Ridge, 108

Heartland Wrestling Association, 130, 133, 185, 199
Heath, David, 43, 209
Heck, Larry, 119, 155
Helms, Gregory, 126
Helms, Shane, 107, 119, 121
Hennig, Curt, 100, 105, 131-132
Hennig, Joe, 212
Hennigan, John, 159
Heyman, Paul, 24, 62, 122, 177, 179
High Impact, 207, 215
Hildebrand, Brian, 130
Hogan, Hulk, 8, 64, 69, 72-73, 80, 101, 108
Holly, Bob (Robert Howard), 124, 137, 152, 198
Holly, Crash (Mike Lockwood), 124, 127, 133, 155, 160-163, 165
Honky Tonk Man, 26
Horner, Tim, 198
Hornidge, Mike, 17, 25
Horsemen, The Four, 76
Houston, Barry, 65
Hughes, Devon, 32
Hurricane (Gregory Helms), 126
Iaukea, King Curtis, 68
Ibaragi, Kiyoshi "Mickey", 48-49, 54
IFBB, 24
Indoor Football League, 89
Inferno, Danny (see Gimondo, Danny)
Inferno, Disco (Glen Gilburdy), 70-71, 77
Invasion, The, 112-124
Ivory (see Moretti, Lisa)
IWA, 50
IWCCW, 81
IWF, Florida, 38
Jack, Cactus (Mick Foley), 68
Jackson, Tiger, 36, 46
Jakked, 125
Jamie (*Tough Enough* contestant), 139
Japan 50-52, 55-57, 64-65, 68, 70, 94
Jarrett, Jeff, 87, 114
Jay, Bradley (Brad Bradley), 207-208
Jay, Mickey, 85, 89
Jericho, Chris, 83, 85, 87, 89, 118, 196
Jho, Dr., 159, 162, 166-167
Jill (*Tough Enough* contestant), 139
Jindrak, Mark, 70, 116, 121, 164
Johnson, Mack, 209-210
Jonah (*Tough Enough* contestant), 139-140
Jones, Cru, 208
Jones, Nathan, 151-152
Jones, S.D., 43
Jovica, Victor, 48
Juster, Gary, 97, 99
Justin (*Tough Enough* contestant), 140, 144
Kalksma, Paul, 17
Kane (Glenn Jacobs), 119-120, 126
Kane, Imposter (Hankinson, Drew), 201
Kanyon, Chris, 119, 121
Keibler, Stacy, 116
Keirn, Steve, 181, 192, 219-220
Kelly (*Tough Enough* contestant), 140
Kenyon, J Michael, 9
Khali, The Great (Dalip Singh Rana), 217-218
Kid, Cheetah (Ted Petty), 36
Kid, Inferno (see Gimondo, Danny)
Kidd, Tyson (Theodore Wilson), 212
Kidman, Billy, 119, 128, 184
King, Rex, 41
Kingston, Kofi, 212
Kirchner, Corporal (see Kirchner, Mike)
Kirchner, Mike, 51, 54-55
KISS, 230
Kleen, Mondo, 30-31, 38-39
Knobbs, Brian, 91, 102-103, 152
Knox, Mike, 183, 185, 199-200, 210, 217, 222
Konnan [Charles Ashenoff], 81, 85, 89
Korakuen Hall, 54
Kozlov, Vladimir, 195
Kreuger, Freddie (see Gilbert, Doug)
Krush, Kid, 32
Kutztown University, 19
Ladd, Ernie, 117
Lancaster, Frankie "The Thumper", 42
Lane, Michael, 36
Lanza, Jack, 118
Laughing Man, The (Hugh Morrus), 69, 73
Laurinaitis, Joe, 36
Laurinaitis, Johnny, 115-118, 121, 123, 128-130, 130, 133, 159-161, 172, 174-176, 179, 181-183, 185, 189-192, 194-195, 197, 212, 217-221, 237
Lawler, Jerry, 119
Layfield, John "Bradshaw", 188, 203
Leatherface (see Kirchner, Mike)
Leave It To Beaver, 10
LeRoux, Kat, 36
LeRoux, Lash, 105, 107-108, 110, 127, 226
Leslie, Edward (see Beefcake, Brutus)
Lesnar, Brock, 128
Lisa (*Tough Enough* contestant), 137

Lita (Amy Dumas), 215
Loch Ness Monster, 72
Loco, Lieutenant (see Guerrero, Chavo)
Longest Yard, The, 217
Love, Angelina (see Williams, Angel)
Lozanski, Mike "Canadian Tiger", 51-52
Luger, Lex, 68-70, 80, 108, 114
Luscious (LaQuanda Woodard), 214
*M*A*S*H*, 137
Madden, Mark, 101
Madison Square Garden, 120-121
Mae, Daisy (Jennifer Thomas), 214
Mailhot, Brian, 202-203
Majors, Brett, 185, 199, 219
Majors, Brian, 185, 199, 219
Malenko, Dean, 83, 89, 118, 132, 181, 192
Malone, Karl, 230
Man of Question, The, 67
Mansfield, Eddie, 35-36, 38
Marshall, Kristal, 197, 214
Marvez, Alex, 111
Mascaras, Mil, 59-60
Mathews, Josh, 161, 164
Matsunaga, Mitsuhiro, 54
Matthews, Darren (see Regal, William)
Matthews, Kevin, 188, 196, 198, 213, 215
Maven (Maven Huffman), 140
MavTV, 182
McCool, Michelle, 214
McCullough, Russ, 124
McMahon, Shane, 115, 117-118, 122
McMahon, Stephanie, 122. 160, 163, 179, 202, 220
McMahon, Vince (Jr.), 32, 86, 97, 112, 115-117, 127, 136, 163, 197, 217-218
McMasters, Luke, 72
McMichael, Mongo (Steve McMichael), 85, 89
Meadowlands Arena, 62
Meng (Tonga Fifita), 68-69, 79, 81, 83, 89
Meow, Leia (Kristina Laum), 106
Mero, Mark, 69, 215
Mestre, Antonio, 210
Mexico, 13, 36, 46, 50-52, 57-58, 59-61, 67, 81
MGM Studios, 64, 88, 97
Miani, Tommy, 17, 23
Michaels, Shawn, 192
Midgets, 23
Millennium Germany, 70
Miller, Ernest, 161
Miller, Heath, 197, 208
Minus, Senor, 59
Misfits, The, 104-112, 128, 165, 234
Mitchell, Nick, 196-197, 222
Miyamoto, Koji, 9
Miz, The (Michael Mizanin), 140, 170, 188, 204
MMA, 170
Monday Night RAW, 132
Morales, Pedro, 23
Moretti, Lisa, 135-137
Morgan, Matt, 172
Morrison, John (John Hennigan), 140
Morrus, Hugh, 69
Morton, Ricky, 211
Mr. Perfect (see Hennig, Curt)
MTV, 134, 137-138, 146, 204
Murdoch, George, 209, 220
Mutoh, Keiji, 65
MVP (see Banks, Antonio)
Mysterio Jr., Rey, 85. 87, 239
Nash, Kevin, 91, 101
National Physique Committee, 24
Natural Born Thrillers, 111
NCW Pro Wrestling, 223
Neidhart, Natalie, 216
Neikirk, Derrick, 183, 185, 199-200, 210, 219
Network, The, 203
New Energy Wrestling (NEW), 224-226, 238
New Japan Pro Wrestling, 53, 70, 127, 202
Newton, Wayne, 64
Nick (*Tough Enough* contestant), 139
Niemi, Ron, 209
Noble, Jamie, 116, 155
Norton, Scott, 68, 79
Nubain, 95
NWA Anarchy, 180
O'Brian, Conor, 213
O'Haire, Sean, 70, 116, 119-120, 155
O'Reilly, Roughhouse, 183, 196, 212-213, 215, 219
O'Reilly, Ryan (see O'Reilly, Roughhouse)
Odd Couple, The, 180
Ohio Valley Wrestling (OVW), 130, 138, 158-160, 164, 171-175, 177, 181, 185, 192-194, 196-197, 201, 203, 205, 208-210, 212-213, 220
Okerlund, Mean Gene, 68, 109
Omega, Kenny (Tyson Smith), 193, 196, 213, 222
Ono, Sonny, 70

Onoa'I, Matt, 130
Orndorff, Paul, 26, 63, 68
page, 108
Page, Diamond Dallas, 69, 91, 102, 119-120
Palumbo, Chuck, 70, 116, 120, 164
Paramus, New Jersey, 13
Parisi, Johnny (Joseph Dorgan), 210
Patrick, Nick, 123
Patterson, Pat, 34, 115, 121
Penzer, David, 68, 83-84, 141, 162
Perez Jr., Miguel, 45, 48, 51, 58, 61, 65
Perez, Eric, 183, 185, 200, 217, 219
Perez, Melina (*Tough Enough* contestant), 139
Petty, Ted, 32, 36-37, 48, 74-76, 78, 83-85, 87, 98, 102
Pillman, Brian, 76-77, 79-80, 130
Playboy, 214
Pogo, Mr., 54, 65-66
Poling, Al, 62
Porter, Montel Vontavious (see Banks, Antonio)
Power Twins, The, 36, 38-40, 43
Presley, Elvis, 64
Prichard, Bruce, 115-116. 192, 221
Prichard, Tom, 159, 219-220
Pro Wrestling Noah, 211-212
Prudius, Oleg, 194-195, 198
Pruitt, Neal, 180, 211
Public Enemy, 74, 85
Puder, Daniel (*Tough Enough* contestant), 170
Puerto rico 13, 36, 38-49, 64-65, 67-68, 94, 129, 162
Punk, CM, 208
Putski, Ivan, 33, 107
Quiñones, Victor, 8, 45, 48-51, 57
Race, Harley, 194, 211
Ram, Randy the, 213
Raven (Scott Levy), 130
RAW is War, 125, 195, 197, 200, 211-212
Ray, Brother, 172
Ready to Rumble (movie), 102
Real World, 204
Rebekah (*Tough Enough* contestant), 138
Rection, Hugh G., 105
Reeves, Ryan, 172, 213
Regal, Steven (see Regal, William)
Regal, William (Darren Matthews), 71
Renegade, 67
Rhodes, Dustin, 234
Rhodes, Dusty, 181, 192
Rhymes, Busta, 230
Rhyno (Terry Gerin), 160
Richards, Ray, 57
Richards, Stevie, 130, 133, 161-162, 169
Riggs, Scotty, 102-103, 160
Rivera, Jose Luis, 31
Rivera, Juan, 61
Road Wild, 83
Roadblock, Rochester, 81
Robinson, Charles, 124
Robocop, 103
Rock, Kid, 229
Rock, Rocco (Ted Petty), 74
Rock, The (Dwayne Johnson), 115
Rodimer, Daniel, 195-196, 210, 222
Rodz, Johnny, 8, 23-31, 34-36, 38, 52, 94, 196, 211
Rogers, Bubba (Ray Traylor), 68, 79-80
Rombola, Chris (Christopher Rombola), 193-194, 213, 222
Romero, Steve, 164
Ross, J.R. (Jim Ross), 116, 119, 123, 134
Rotten, Axl, 61
Rotunda, Mike, 68-69
Rourke, Mickey, 213
Rumble, Tony, 33
Runnels, Terri, 118
Russo, Vince, 92, 101-102, 104-105, 107, 112, 156
Ryder, Zack, 199, 222
Sable (Rena Mero), 215
Sammartino, Bruno, 23
Samoans, The, 26

General Rection with Casey and Keri

Samson, Keith (see Walker, Keith)
Sanders, Mike, 110, 116
Sandler, Adam, 91
Santana, Ricky, 45, 48, 51, 65
Santana, Tito, 33-34
Santarelli, Tony, 183, 207, 215
Saturn, Perry, 118, 131-132
Savage, Randy, 67-69, 72, 80, 102
Savinovich, Hugo, 41
Savoldi, Joe, 32-33, 35, 81
Savoldi, Tommy, 34
Sawyer, Bart, 152
Schiavone, Tony, 101
Scott (*Tough Enough* contestant), 140
Serving Sara, 142
Shark (John Tenta), 68-69
Sharp, Alan, 113
Sherrod, Nigel, 181
Siaki, Sonny, 206
Silverman, Billy, 122-123
Simmes, Misty Blue, 36
Sincere, Salvatore, 42
Six Flags Over Georgia, 181
Skiba, Eddie, 34
Skiba, Joey, 34
Skipper, Ellix, 70
Skynyrd, Lynyrd, 83
Slamboree, 104
Slater, Dick, 70
Slater, Heath (see Heath Miller)
Slaughter, Sgt., 26
Smackdown, 125, 133, 146, 149, 151, 156, 163, 195, 200, 203-204
Smith, Mike, 227
Smoky Mountain Wrestling (SMW), 43
Smothers, Tracy, 51
Snow, Al, 127, 135-140, 145, 169-170, 172-174, 177, 191
Snuka, Jimmy, 26, 33
Sontag, David, 36, 38, 40
Sontag, Larry, 36, 38, 40
Spangler, David, 15
Spies Like Us, 60
Spirit Squad, The, 197
Starr, Chicky, 38-41, 43-45
Starrcade 2000, 124
Stash, Private (see Hammer, Van)
Stasiak, Shawn, 70, 105, 116-117, 124, 130-132, 215
Steamboat, Vic, 33
Steel, Damian (Damien Dothard), 208
Steiner, Rick, 105, 110
Steiner, Scott, 104
Sting, 67, 69, 80, 102., 108
Storey, Lacey (see De Mott, Lacey)
Storm, Devon (Chris Ford), 74
Storm, Lance, 70, 109-111, 114, 116, 118, 156, 171
Stratus, Trish, 118, 239
Striker, Matt (Matthew Kaye), 211, 222
Striker, MVP (see Banks, Antonio)
Strong, Steve, 41-42
Strongbow, Chief Jay, 30-31
Suede, Tommy (Thomas Farra), 213
Sullivan, Kevin, 8, 43, 54-55, 63-68, 72-74, 76-81, 87-88, 92, 99, 215
Sunday Night Heat, 128, 210
Survivor, 135
Swagger, Jack (Jacob Hager), 209
Swinger, Johnny, 178-179, 210-211
T, Booker (Booker Huffman), 104, 107, 119, 121, 239
Taskmaster (Kevin Sullivan), 68
Tatanka, 114
Taylor, Dave, 186-187, 191, 196, 198
Taylor, Mike (Mike Sharrer), 183, 185, 201-202, 207, 215, 219
Taylor, Shantelle, 185, 204, 214, 219
Taylor, Terry, 67-69
Teal, Scott, 8-9, 156
Team Canada, 111
Team Elite, 199
Tenta, John, 68, 79, 118
Thatcher, Les, 130, 199
The Millionaire's Club, 101, 104
The New Blood, 101, 104
The Texas Chainsaw Massacre, 51
The Waterboy, 91
Thiessen, Ken, 197-198
Three-Minute Warning, 130
Thunder, 99
Titan Towers, 120, 175, 192
Toi, Masaru, 49
Total Nonstop Action (TNA), 32, 204, 206, 210, 212, 203
Tough Enough 3, 134-135, 137-138, 140, 142-146, 154, 159,
Tough Enough 4, 170-173, 182
Tough Enough 5, 237-238
Tough Enough, 12
Tracy (Tracy Castillio), 215
Triple H (Paul Levesque), 71, 115, 188, 192

Tuite, Jerry "The Wall", 107, 110, 124, 162, 165
Turner Broadcasting, 115
Twilight Zone, The, 100
Tyler, Lawrence (Lawrence Boyer), 210
U.S. heavyweight title, 110
U.S. Kick-Boxing Association, 194
UltraClash, 61
Undertaker, The (Mark Calloway), 115, 120, 126, 152, 192, 217-218
Universal Championship Wrestling, 223
Universal Studios, 74, 78, 91, 238
USA Network, 237
Vachon, Luna, 43
Vader (Leon White), 63-64
Vaine, Krissy (Kristin Eubanks), 196, 212, 215, 219
Valentine, Greg, 26
Vampiro, 58-59
Vaughn, Taylor, 87
Velocity, 146, 160, 163, 170, 172, 181
Ventura, Jesse, 23
Viewer's Choice, 113
Vito, Big (Vito LoGrasso), 32, 206
Volkoff, Nikolai, 26
W*ING 45, 48-50, 54, 57, 62, 65-66, 70
Walker, Keith, 211, 219
Wallstreet, V.K., 69
Ware, Koko B., 26, 33
WCW Monday Nitro, 70, 76, 99, 104-105, 230
WCW Nitro Grill, 103
WCW Saturday Night, 68-69
WCW Superbrawl IX, 141
Weller, Peter, 103
Western Wrestling Alliance, 107
Whipwreck, Mikey, 62
Wight, Paul (see Big Show)
Wildside, 180
Williams, Angel (Lauren Williams), 178, 185, 199, 203-204, 214, 219
Williams, Big Sweet, 27-28, 32, 35, 39, 43
Williams, Luke (Brian Wickens), 27
Williams, Steve, 192, 201
Wilson, David (aka Pop), 11, 16, 18-20, 23, 25, 27-28, 36, 43, 94, 148, 166, 169, 178, 235
Wilson, T.J. (Theodore Wilson), 212, 216
Wilson, Torrie, 119, 122
Winkler, Henry, 91
Winters, Brendon, 17
Winters, Debbie, 17
Winters, Jesse, 22
Woman (see Benoit, Nancy)
World Championship Wrestling (WCW) 8,32, 35, 43, 46, 61-116, 206
World Gym, 227
World League Wrestling, 211
World Wrestling Council, 38
World Wrestling Entertainment (WWE), 8, 30, 32, 34, 41, 61, 67, 71
World Wrestling Entertainment, Inc. [WWE], 133
World Wrestling Federation (WWF), 80, 87, 112, 114-115
World-Wide Wrestling Federation (WWWF), 23, 32
WrestleMania XVII, 116
Wrestler, The, 213
Wright, Alex, 68, 70, 107
Wright, Marty, 171-172
WWC 41, 48
WWE Magazine, 204
WWE NXT, 208-209, 211, 213
WWE Velocity, 161
WWF draft, 132
WWF Entertainment, Inc., 110
Xtreme Pro Wrestling, 111
Young, Danny, 100
Youngblood, Dr., 160, 163
Zayak, Elaine, 35
Zodiac (Ed Leslie), 68-69, 79
ZZ Top, 229

Bill and Lacey

— Also from Crowbar Press —

Most books ordered directly from Crowbar Press come autographed or with a photo signed by the author(s).

Order by mail from:
106 Tattnall Court
Gallatin TN 37066
or on the Web at:
crowbarpress.com